Larissa Fleischmann
Contested Solidarity

Culture and Social Practice

Larissa Fleischmann, born in 1989, works as a Postdoctoral Researcher in Human Geography at the Martin Luther University Halle-Wittenberg. She received her PhD from the University of Konstanz, where she was a member of the Centre of Excellence »Cultural Foundations of Social Integration« and the Social and Cultural Anthropology Research Group from 2014 to 2018.

Larissa Fleischmann
Contested Solidarity
Practices of Refugee Support between Humanitarian Help
and Political Activism

Dissertation of the University of Konstanz
Date of the oral examination: February 15, 2019
1st reviewer: Prof. Dr. Thomas G. Kirsch
2nd reviewer: PD Dr. Eva Youkhana
3rd reviewer: Prof. Dr. Judith Beyer

This publication was funded by the Deutsche Forschungsgemeinschaft (DFG, German Research Foundation) - Project number 448887013.

The author acknowledges the financial support of the Open Access Publication Fund of the Martin Luther University Halle-Wittenberg.

The field research for this publication was funded by the Centre of Excellence "Cultural Foundations of Social Integration", University of Konstanz.

Bibliographic information published by the Deutsche Nationalbibliothek
The Deutsche Nationalbibliothek lists this publication in the Deutsche Nationalbibliografie; detailed bibliographic data are available in the Internet at http://dnb.d-nb.de

This work is licensed under the Creative Commons Attribution-Non Commercial 4.0 (BY-NC) license, which means that the text may be remixed, build upon and be distributed, provided credit is given to the author, but may not be used for commercial purposes.
For details go to: http://creativecommons.org/licenses/by-nc/4.0/
Permission to use the text for commercial purposes can be obtained by contacting rights@transcript-publishing.com
Creative Commons license terms for re-use do not apply to any content (such as graphs, figures, photos, excerpts, etc.) not original to the Open Access publication and further permission may be required from the rights holder. The obligation to research and clear permission lies solely with the party re-using the material.

© 2020 transcript Verlag, Bielefeld

Cover layout: Maria Arndt, Bielefeld
Cover illustration: fsHH / pixabay.com
Printed by Majuskel Medienproduktion GmbH, Wetzlar
Print-ISBN 978-3-8376-5437-0
PDF-ISBN 978-3-8394-5437-4
https://doi.org/10.14361/9783839454374

Printed on permanent acid-free text paper.

Contents

1. **INTRODUCTION: The Contested Solidarities of the German 'Welcome Culture'** . 9
   1.1. The Spirit of Summer 2015: "We Want to Help Refugees!" 9
   1.2. The Political Ambivalences of Refugee Support 16
      1.2.1. Refugee Support as Political Action 16
      1.2.2. Refugee Support as Antipolitical Action 21
   1.3. Conceptualizing Solidarity in Migration Societies 23
      1.3.1. Solidarity as a Contested Imaginary 25
      1.3.2. Solidarity as Utopian Ideal 26
      1.3.3. Solidarity as a Transformative Relationship 27
      1.3.4. Solidarity as Power Asymmetry 28
      1.3.5. Solidarity as Social Glue 29
   1.4. The Political Possibilities of Grassroots Humanitarianism 30
      1.4.1. The Mobilizing Effects of Emergency Situations 31
      1.4.2. Reflecting on the Causes of Suffering 32
      1.4.3. 'Humanity' as a Political Identity 33
      1.4.4. The Political Power of an 'Apolitical' Positioning 34
      1.4.5. Humanitarian Dissent 35
   1.5. Rethinking Political Action in Migration Societies 36
   1.6. Researching Solidarity in the German 'Summer of Welcome': Field, Access, Methods, Ethics 40
   1.7. An Outline of *Contested Solidarity* 46

2. **MOBILIZING SOLIDARITY: Building Local 'Welcome Culture' through a Moral Imperative to Act** 51
   2.1. The Notion of a 'Welcome Culture' and its Mobilizing Effects 51
   2.2. Humanitarian Dissent: The Solidarity March 'Ellwangen Shows its Colours' 55
      2.2.1. Mobilizing a Moral Imperative to Act 56
      2.2.2. Behind the Scenes of 'Apolitical' Action 61

	2.2.3. The Political Messages of the Solidarity March	66
2.3.	Humanitarian Governance: Volunteering with Refugees in Ellwangen	71
	2.3.1. Mobilizing a Need to Help	72
	2.3.2. Volunteering as a Symbiotic Relationship	76
	2.3.3. The Role of Social Welfare Organizations	79
2.4.	Concluding Remarks: Practices of Solidarity between Dissent and Co-Optation	83

3.	GOVERNING SOLIDARITY: Volunteering with Refugees as a Field of Governmental Intervention	85
3.1.	Governmental Interventions in the Conduct of Volunteering with Refugees	85
3.2.	(Re)Ordering Responsibilities in the Reception of Asylum Seekers	88
	3.2.1. The Birth of 'Civil Society' as a Responsible Actor	89
	3.2.2. "Civil Society is the Music between the Notes": The Impetus for Meaningful Cooperation	92
	3.2.3. Negotiating the Boundary between 'State' and 'Civil Society'	96
3.3.	(Re)Shaping the Self-Conduct of Committed Citizens	100
	3.3.1. "Volunteering Makes You Happy": Promoting the Personal Benefits of Volunteering	100
	3.3.2. Shaping 'Socialized Selves'	104
	3.3.3. Coordinating Volunteers through Professionals	108
3.4.	Depoliticizing "Uncomfortable" Practices of Refugee Support	112
	3.4.1. The Dark Side of 'Civil Society'	112
	3.4.2. Deportations and the Contested Space of Disagreement	115
3.5.	Concluding Remarks: The Government of Refugee Solidarity	119

4.	POLITICIZING SOLIDARITY: The Contested Political Meanings and Effects of Refugee Support	121
4.1.	"We are also Political Volunteers!"	121
4.2.	Politics of Presence: Enacting Alternative Visions of Society	125
	4.2.1. The Deficiencies of National Citizenship	125
	4.2.2. Presence as an Alternative Mode of Belonging	127
4.3.	Contestations around Equal Rights	131
	4.3.1. Solidarity Cities: Universal Demands for Equal Rights	132
	4.3.2. Ambivalent Positions and Conditional Hospitality	135
4.4.	Contestations around a Right to Stay	139
	4.4.1. Taking, or not Taking a Stand against Deportations	139
	4.4.2. Counteracting the European Union	145
4.5.	Contestations around a Right to Migrate	147

4.6. Concluding Remarks: Emerging Meanings of Political Action
in Migration Societies 152

5. **RECASTING SOLIDARITY: The Political Agency of Asylum Seekers in Relationships of Solidarity** 155
5.1. Insubordinate Recipients: Asylum Seekers' Interventions in Relationships of Solidarity 155
5.2. The Intermediated Agency of Asylum Seekers 158
5.3. (De)politicizing the Meanings of Food: The Intermediation of Migrant Protest in Bad Waldsee 161
    5.3.1. The Unheard Requests of the Protesting Asylum Seekers 162
    5.3.2. Depoliticizing Responses to the Protests 165
    5.3.3. Recasting Relationships of Solidarity 171
5.4. Deterring 'Economic Migrants': The Intermediation of Migrant Protest in Offenburg 176
    5.4.1. Depoliticizing Responses to the Protests 176
    5.4.2. Food Provision as a "Strategy of Deterrence" 180
    5.4.3. Politicizing Responses to the Protests 184
5.5. Concluding Remarks: The Agency of Asylum Seekers in the Contestation of Solidarity 189

6. **BREAKING SOLIDARITY: Refugee Activism as a Conflicting Imaginary of Solidarity and Community** 193
6.1. At the Frontlines of Solidarity and Community 193
6.2. A Short History of Refugee Activism in Schwäbisch Gmünd 197
6.3. The Breaking of Relationships of Solidarity 201
    6.3.1. Breaking with "Deceptive Solidarity" 202
    6.3.2. Refusing to Help 204
    6.3.3. Forging Solidarity beyond the Local 209
6.4. The Conflicting Imaginaries of Community 214
    6.4.1. Local Community as an Antidote to the World 'Out There' 214
    6.4.2. The Spatial Contingencies of Local Community: A Landscape of Unequal Rights 219
    6.4.3. The Temporal Contingencies of Local Community: A Landscape of (Post)Colonial Injustice 223
6.5. Concluding Remarks: The Intimate Relationship between *Community* and *Solidarity* 226

7. **WORDS IN CONCLUSION: Lines of Contestation in Contemporary Migration Societies** 229
7.1. The Contested Line between Insiders and Outsiders 230
7.2. The Contested Line between 'the State' and 'Civil Society' 233
7.3. The Contested Relationship between 'the Local' and 'the World Out There' 236

References 241

Acknowledgements 271

1. INTRODUCTION: The Contested Solidarities of the German 'Welcome Culture'

1.1. The Spirit of Summer 2015: "We Want to Help Refugees!"

In the summer of 2015, an extraordinary number of German residents felt an urge to provide "help" to refugees. This unprecedented outburst of compassion for newly arrived migrants made history as a German "welcome culture" or a "summer of welcome" (cf. Hamann & Karakayali 2016; Karakayali 2017, 2019; Sutter 2019). My interlocutor Maria Papadopoulos[1], a volunteer supporting refugees, described in vivid terms the spirit of this exceptional moment:

> "Oh, you should have seen it! Yes, it was September last summer. I had just got back from my holidays and I came here and was confronted by loads of enquiries and I didn't know why. I'd been abroad for one and a half months and, when I returned, suddenly the whole of Germany was all stirred up, with people saying 'We want to help refugees!' And in the meantime, via Facebook [...] groups like 'We help refugees in Ludwigsburg' were set up. And then it all started happening – because most people think that if they clear out their closets and clear out their apartments and then dump their rubbish here, they're helping. And so that's what started happening here ... oh my God, I can still remember it so well – we had ten to twelve cars per day, people driving up to the accommodation centre and unloading bags. We needed one huge container per week to get rid of all the rubbish. [...] And then I thought, 'My God, we need to do something' and, of course, I didn't have a clue how to use Facebook [...] Out of desperation, because it was so bad, I published my contact details in the group ... and from that point on, my

---

[1] In order to preserve the anonymity of my interlocutors, their names have been changed throughout this book.

phone didn't stop ringing and I was getting phone calls like: 'I'm here with a three-and-a-half-tonne truck full of stuff, I'll bring it round now' and I'm thinking 'Nooooo!'. The scale of it, it was beyond normal. And then, one day, refugees started fighting over stuff and people were just throwing stuff out of their cars ... It was insane, just insane!"[2] (Interview with Maria Papadopoulos, 18/2/2016)

In our conversation, Maria Papadopoulos recalled the extraordinary scale of donations to the refugee accommodation centre in her neighbourhood. Her telling account, though, indicates that practices of refugee support are situated, relative and contested. Different individuals judge and evaluate such practices based on their conceptions of the 'right' way to support refugees. Whether something is considered help or not is thus contingent on interpretation and classification. In Maria Papadopoulos's neighbourhood, some sought to help through dispensing with a share of their belongings for the benefit of 'needy' others. However, my interlocutor did not consider these donations to be a help at all. Quite the opposite, in fact she was deeply stressed by the arrival of what she perceived to be piles of old "rubbish" that was no longer of use to anybody. As a volunteer supporting refugees[3] in the neighbourhood, her idea of the 'right' way to help consisted of a willingness to build personal relationships with refugees and to give large amounts of spare time for their benefit. My interlocutor's account also illustrates that refugee support has unintended consequences and adverse effects. She remarked that she had "to get rid of all the rubbish" dumped at the refugee accommodation centre, while refugees started fighting each other over their share of the donations.

This insight into the spirit of summer 2015 sheds light on the contested nature of refugee support that lies at the heart of this book. 'Doing good' for refugees, in other words, is not as simple and straightforward as it might appear. Practices of support and help are embedded in differing and at times contrasting interpretations, with various actors[4] and individuals competing

---

2   Translation from German by LF.
3   In this book, I use the terms 'refugees' and 'asylum seekers' interchangeably. This mirrors how people throughout my field of investigation used the terms. Most of the time, they did not distinguish between those whose asylum case was pending and those who represented legally recognized refugees.
4   In this book, I employ the term 'actors' in order to distinguish analytically between different groups of people who intervened in practices of refugee support from a partic-

over the 'proper' conduct of support. There are diverse interests and motivations at stake, which might not primarily be those of their ostensible beneficiaries. Refugee support is thus deeply intertwined with questions of power and comes with ambivalent political meanings. What are the visions, motivations and imaginaries that guide such differing practices for the benefit of newly arrived migrants? How do actors and individuals with various positionalities and interests influence, appropriate and shape the 'proper' conduct of refugee support? When and how do such practices and discourses turn political? This book sheds light on these questions. It investigates the contested practices of refugee support that emerged around the German 'summer of welcome' in 2015, while providing empirical insights into the imaginaries, interests, politics and conflicts at stake.

Unlike those who supported refugees through a single act of donating second-hand items, my interlocutor Maria Papadopoulos spent most of her spare time volunteering with asylum seekers in her neighbourhood. She was the head of a local citizens' initiative supporting refugees in a medium-sized town in southern Germany, the area where most of the research for this book took place. The initiative consisted of around thirty volunteers who together aimed to support refugees in the neighbourhood, for instance by organizing joint leisure activities such as a weekly handicraft group for women, providing German language classes or advising asylum seekers on administrative matters. Such loosely constituted citizens' initiatives in support of refugees formed in almost every corner of Germany in the course of 2014 and 2015, when the number of people willing to volunteer rose sharply (cf. Turinsky & Nowicka 2019). Similar tendencies occurred in other European countries, such as in Italy (Sinatti 2019), Sweden (Kleres 2018; Povrzanović Frykman & Mäkelä 2020), Belgium (Vandevoordt 2019), France (Sandri 2018; Doidge & Sandri 2019) and Greece (Parsanoglou 2020). Around this time, there was extraordinary coverage in the national and international media of the growing numbers of migrants heading to Europe, migrants who were crossing the

---

ular subjective and situated point of view. These include governmental actors, volunteers, church representatives, self-declared political activists and others. As such classifications might give the false impression that those in question constitute seemingly homogenous types of actors, I should emphasize that an actor itself is always marked by internal differences, conflicts or heterogeneities and comprised of further actors nested within. When speaking about 'actors', it is thus important to keep in mind that the term always entails a certain necessary simplification of a more complex reality.

external borders of the European Union irregularly in their search for asylum. Numerous media accounts presented this situation as an unprecedented and historical moment of intensified global migration (cf. Pries 2019). For instance, the New York Times wrote of a "mass migration crisis" and proclaimed that "there are more displaced people and refugees now than at any other time in recorded history – 60 million in all – and they are on the march in numbers not seen since World War II" (New York Times: 31/10/2015)[5]. The article also depicted the migrants heading to Europe as "heralds of a new age" and claimed that they were arriving in an "unceasing stream, 10,000 a day at the height, as many as a million migrants heading for Europe this year" (ibid.).

From at least 2014 on, the number of asylum seekers arriving in Germany also began to rise sharply, reaching its climax in late summer 2015. When existing schemes of accommodation eventually proved to be insufficient and overcrowded, local authorities established new makeshift accommodation centres in residential neighbourhoods or rural villages that had never previously hosted asylum seekers (cf. Hinger 2016; Hinger, Schäfer & Pott 2016). In consequence, the local reception of asylum seekers moved to the centre stage of public and media debate in many places across Germany. This notion of an extraordinary emergency situation mobilized many established residents 'to help' by volunteering in their neighbourhood, village or town – among them was my interlocutor Maria Papadopoulos.

Not only did the immediate practices of Maria Papadopoulos differ from those of residents donating belongings to asylum seekers, her intentions and interpretations of supporting refugees did too. For her, volunteering with refugees served as a means to take a stand *against* nationalistic and xenophobic attitudes and to signal support *for* a multicultural society, as she told me during my interview. She decided to get involved as a volunteer in response to the hostile attitudes that emerged among established residents in her neighbourhood when local authorities announced the decision to accommodate 200 asylum seekers in an untenanted building in the area. In many places across Germany, reactions towards the arrival of asylum seekers were equally divided, entailing both hostile and migrant-friendly attitudes and actions (cf. Fontanari & Borri 2018; Hinger, Daphi & Stern 2019). Through her volunteering activities, my interlocutor sought to enact an alternative to the

---

5   See: https://www.nytimes.com/2015/11/01/world/europe/a-mass-migration-crisis-and-it-may-yet-get-worse.html (last accessed 1/8/2020).

hostile and right-wing attitudes that were on the rise around that time[6] – an alternative based on togetherness and mutual support despite cultural differences. For many of my interlocutors, volunteering with refugees represented a similar means to bring about positive transformations and to enact a vision of what society should look like in an age of migration.

What follows from these insights is that practices of refugee support are embedded in social imaginaries that quite often go far beyond an urge for altruistic giving to those 'in need'. As Maria Papadopoulos' intention to counteract hostile right-wing attitudes in her neighbourhood illustrates, volunteering with refugees can also come with *political* meanings and effects. Interestingly, though, my interlocutor did not consider her practices to be political at all. Instead, she framed her commitment as an "apolitical sign of humanity", as many of my interlocutors did. Let me be clear here, I believe that the idea of 'apolitical' and 'neutral' forms of refugee support is a powerful and persistent myth (cf. Fleischmann & Steinhilper 2017). 'Doing good' for refugees does not take place in an 'apolitical' vacuum. Those who set out 'to help' are entangled with governmental actors in different and ambivalent ways and embedded in a context marked by discriminating migration and border policies. Unknowingly or unwillingly, even those who describe their actions as purely 'apolitical' might end up reproducing structural exclusions and discriminations, or, to the contrary, might challenge and alter them. The contested imaginaries at play thus elaborate on current parameters of living-together and speak out on contemporary voids, deficiencies and challenges in migration societies. Like Maria Papadopoulos, volunteers might aim to bring about changes for a 'better society' and create new ways of relating among different groups and individuals who might formerly have been isolated from one another. Practices of refugee support can therefore offer revealing insights into how an individual imagines and makes sense of the world around her or him. At the

---

6   From late 2014 on, a new movement going by the acronym "Pegida" (its full name translates as 'Patriotic Europeans against the Islamization of the Occident') brought thousands of German citizens out onto the streets of Dresden as well as of other major cities across Germany. Through its weekly Monday demonstrations, the alarming extent of xenophobic, nationalistic and Islamophobic attitudes within German society became increasingly visible. At around the same time, the newly founded right-wing populist party, the AfD (short for "Alternative für Deutschland") was gaining in support and attracting a growing number of voters. After its success at the 2017 federal elections, it became the first right-wing party to enter the German parliament in the history of the Federal Republic of Germany.

same time, these practices can also be world-building in that they enact alternative ways of living-together – an aspect of refugee support that I consider to be deeply political.

Thus, practices of refugee support do not fit neatly into such clear-cut boxes as 'humanitarian volunteering' and 'political activism', which are quite often thought of as contrasting types of action. Instead, the uncertain, oscillating and ambivalent entanglements with questions of power constituted a defining feature of the practices and discourses that I observed around the summer of 2015. Rather than distinguishing between 'apolitical' and 'political' forms of acting from the outset, I therefore suggest to focus on the notion of *contested solidarity*. Throughout this book, I employ the term *solidarity* as an analytical bracket for exploring the diverse practices of refugee support as well as their ambivalent political meanings and effects. This perspective interrogates the social imaginaries of those who offered help and support and argues that they are central to understanding the manifold practices of refugee support and their diverse effects. I regard *solidarity* as a transformative relationship that is forged between established residents and newcomers in migration societies, one that creates collectivity across or in spite of differences. Such relationships of solidarity hold the potential to invent new ways of relating that challenge the divide between citizens and non-citizens, a divide scholars have identified as a central source of sovereign power and a locus of the modern nation-state (Agamben 1998; Minca 2017).

In social anthropology, a long line of thought has investigated acts of gift-giving. Dating back to Marcel Mauss (1990 [1925]), these investigations highlight how acts of giving foster social bonds and mutual obligations and thus produce sociality (see for instance Mallard 2011; Komter & Leer 2012; Paragi 2017; Heins & Unrau 2018). In her foreword to a reissue of Mauss's famous *The Gift*, Mary Douglas suggests that "the theory of the gift is a theory of human solidarity" (Douglas 2002: xiii) but, while 'the gift' became the focus of numerous empirical studies and conceptualizations, 'solidarity' received considerable less attention from anthropologists. With this book, I aim to contribute to the empirically grounded understanding of solidarity and its practices in migration societies.

The book at hand also sheds light on current conceptions of, hopes and challenges for the way people live together in an increasingly diverse society. Perhaps better than any moment before, the developments in the summer of 2015 illustrated that the idea of culturally homogenous and sealed-off nation-states is a persistent yet ever more untenable illusion. The increasing numbers of asylum seekers entering the country provided a striking demonstration of how intensified global migration flows are profoundly altering and redefining existing ways of living-together in society. In western European countries, societies are becoming ever more heterogeneous and diverse in response to growing influxes of migrants, turning into what I refer to as 'migration societies' throughout this book (cf. Matejskova & Antonsich 2015; Hamann & Yurdakul 2018). The extraordinary willingness to support refugees in the German 'summer of welcome' thus revealed a desire to build new forms of collectivity and togetherness amidst intensified migration flows. These solidarities put forward social and political alternatives that included whoever was present on the ground, whatever their national origin or cultural belonging.

This book is therefore very much in the spirit of what Cresswell (2006: 53) calls "nomadic metaphysics", in that it regards human mobility and flux as a defining criterion of our times. We live in an age of intensified migration, in times when the 'imagined community' (Anderson 1983) of the modern nation-state is undergoing significant changes (cf. Castles & Miller 1994). Based on such a perspective, this study sheds light on how social orders and social identities are constituted through movement. It focuses on mobility and becoming rather than on embeddedness and stasis (see also Malkki 1992; Castles & Miller 1994; Urry 2007; Feldman 2015).

Throughout the book, I refer to the developments in the second half of 2015 as the "long summer of migration", a term frequently used in academic accounts (Kasparek & Speer 2015; Mezzadra 2018; Yurdakul et al. 2018). This expression was coined by Hess et al. (2017) in order to describe the increased numbers of asylum seekers crossing the European Union's external borders around this time. These movements, they argue, constituted a destabilizing force that brought the fault lines of the European migration and border regime to the fore – a migration regime that had been increasingly built on control, exclusion and selectivity (see also Kasparek 2016). The phrase 'the long summer of migration' is, to my mind, preferable to the term 'refugee crisis' since the latter expresses a problematic and alarmist take on the developments in the second half of 2015 (cf. Collyer & King 2016; De Genova & Tazzioli 2016; Agustín & Jørgensen 2019).

While this book is published, the spirit of summer 2015 has long since faded. European migration and border policies have become ever more draconian and restrictive, as other commentators have previously outlined (cf. Heller & Pezzani 2017; Hess & Kasparek 2017a; Kasparek & Schmidt-Sembdner 2019). Right-wing attitudes in Germany and other European countries are enjoying new levels of popularity (cf. Jäckle & König 2017; Castelli Gattinara 2018). Nonetheless, this book is based on the premise that the spirit of summer 2015 produced lasting effects. My empirical investigation in the five subsequent chapters explores how the long summer of migration served as a laboratory of alternative socialities, how it shaped visions of a more egalitarian and inclusive social order, and how it created new ways of relating among different actors in migration societies.

1.2. The Political Ambivalences of Refugee Support

Building on the premise that refugee support can never be located 'outside' or 'above' politics, this book traces solidarity's complex and ambivalent entanglements with questions of power. Practices and discourses of refugee support are always embedded in a wider social and political context. Even if they are framed as purely 'apolitical' humanitarian or altruistic helping, they nonetheless come with ambivalent and contested *political* meanings and effects. This book investigates how the contested solidarities of the migration summer constantly *oscillated* between political possibilities to bring about alternative ways of living-together in an age of intensified migration, the fulfilment of personal needs and a complicity in the governance of migration. Before we look in more detail at these political ambivalences of refugee support, however, it is important to come to terms with what I understand as the 'political' and respectively, its antidote, the 'antipolitical'.

1.2.1. Refugee Support as Political Action

My reading of 'the political' throughout this book is inspired by the works of French philosopher Jacques Rancière (1998, 2001, 2009). For Rancière, political change occurs when the established order is interrupted and those who are not represented make claims to be counted. In his reading, "dissensus" or "disagreement" forms the essence of the political (Battista 2017). "Dis-agreement" goes beyond the mere confrontation between opinions and occurs whenever a "wrong" is voiced that challenges the partitioning of the dominant order. Rancière (1998: 11) puts this as follows: "Politics exists when the natural order of domination is interrupted by the institution of a part of those who have no part". In critical migration studies, asylum seekers or irregular migrants are often thought of as 'a part of those who have no part', since they are excluded from the dominant order of the nation-state. As non-citizens, their rights are substantially limited and they are rendered vulnerable to the arbitrary operations of government (see for instance Vandevoordt 2020: 4f). Rancière also argues that what is conventionally understood as party politics usually constitutes the very opposite of the political, namely the consolidation of inequalities pertaining to the dominant order and the relegation of those 'who have no part' to a non-political place – something he describes as 'police' (not to be confused with 'police forces').

Building on Rancière's writings, I refer to *the political* as those moments when conditions of exclusion, domination and discrimination in migration societies are challenged, contested, interrupted, altered or reformed in favour of a different alternative (see also Fleischmann & Steinhilper 2017: 6; Sinatti 2019). What follows from this is that practices of refugee support turn political when they – intentionally or unintentionally – challenge the exclusions and discriminations of refugees and asylum seekers and aim to foster change towards what those engaging in relationships of solidarity consider a 'better' alternative. During my fieldwork in southern Germany, I witnessed numerous instances when practices of refugee support came with such political meanings and effects. Many of those who sought to help around the long summer of migration were striving to instigate change, to transform the status quo and build a 'better society' (see also Schmid, Evers & Mildenberger 2019; Togral Koca 2019). Many also regarded their practices of refugee support as a means to counteract the rise of hostile and xenophobic attitudes in society. Others voiced a will to participate directly in political decision-making processes in order to bring about the positive change they were striving for.

The *political* meanings and effects of refugee support thus come in manifold shapes and in varying forms. Sometimes they crystallize more visibly and openly around disagreements and criticisms directed at governmental actors, asylum policies or laws. At other instances, they are hidden and implicit, taking the shape of practices that *enact* different alternatives on the ground, without directly making claims towards 'the state'.

On the one hand, thus, practices of refugee support can turn political when they directly contest the status quo, voice dissent and subvert dominant exclusions and discriminations of asylum seekers in migration societies. For instance, many of the volunteers I talked to perceived their actions as a means to take a stand against flawed European migration and border policies and the perceived lack of coherence among European member states (see Chapter 4). Shortly before the events of the summer 2015, a major focus of such criticisms was the Dublin III Regulation[7] (for more information on the regulation see Kasparek & Matheis 2016). Volunteers often openly criticized the law and participated in nationwide campaigns calling for its abolishment. Some even deliberately blocked Dublin III deportations and, in doing so, openly counteracted governmental decisions in the handling of asylum seekers. The subversive potential among those seeking to help refugees also crystallized in the context of governmental distinctions between 'genuine' and 'bogus' asylum seekers. Most strikingly, volunteers in the area of my field research openly took a stand against governmental attempts to classify further countries of origin as 'safe countries'[8] that have asylum recognition rates of almost zero, such as Gambia or Afghanistan.

On the other hand, practices of refugee support can turn political when they strive to instigate change by *enacting* alternative modes of togetherness and belonging on the ground. In this case, changes are brought about not through acts of claims-making but through immediate hands-on interventions. Around the long summer of migration, many volunteers regarded their practices of refugee support also as a means to build a 'better' alternative in their village or neighbourhood, an alternative characterized by mutual support, togetherness and hospitality towards strangers (cf. Turinsky & Nowicka 2019). They often emphasized the act of being 'here', of an imagined personal connection among all those present on the ground, regardless of national origin or cultural belonging. Such imaginaries painted a romanticized picture of 'the local' as an antidote to the world 'out there' (see Chapter 6). However, they also represented an implicit challenge 'from below' to the nation-state's discrimination between aliens and those deemed legitimate citizens – and thus turned political in the sense outlined above (see also Chapter 4).

Seen in this light, volunteering – conventionally thought of as an 'apolitical' practice in the name of the public good – can function as a "politics by other means", as Thomas G. Kirsch (2016) puts it. In his case study on the

---

7   This EU law states that the country through which an asylum seeker first entered the European Union is responsible for processing the asylum case.

8   The German constitution defines a set of "safe countries of origin", "in which, on the basis of their laws, enforcement practices and general political conditions, it can be safely concluded that neither political persecution nor inhuman or degrading punishment or treatment exists" (Article 16a(3) Basic Law). Recognition rates for asylum seekers originating from these countries are approximately zero. For more information, see: http://www.asylumineurope.org/reports/country/germany/asylum-procedure/safe-country-concepts/safe-country-origin (last accessed 1/8/2020).

role of volunteers in crime prevention in South Africa, Kirsch outlines how temporal aspects determined the social imaginaries at play as well as their political consequences: "the volunteers' (re)interpretations of the past have a bearing on their present-day attempts to become 'moral citizens' and to create a better society" (ibid.: 203). Such temporal aspects also proved central for the volunteers acting in support of refugees in the area of my field research. Their imaginaries, however, were inspired less by the past than they were by an ideal vision of future society (cf. Vandevoordt & Fleischmann 2020). Practices of refugee support thus often go beyond the focus on the here and now that is associated with an urge to alleviate immediate suffering (Brun 2016).

Around the long summer of migration, 'the local' became an important locus for both openly contesting exclusions, injustices and discriminations and enacting alternative visions of future society in migration societies. Quite often, volunteers formulated their criticisms towards local politicians and local authorities. For instance, they wrote letters of complaint, called for mediating meetings or collaborated with the local press in order to voice dissent with the immediate governmental handling of asylum seekers. Many also asserted that they aimed to build a local alternative to the 'inhumane' European migration and border policies. Hinger, Schäfer and Pott (2016) point to the central importance of the local level for the reception, accommodation and governance of asylum seekers around the long summer of migration (see also Mayer 2017). In a similar vein, 'the local' also played an important role for those supporting refugees. It was often their neighbourhood, town or village that appeared most likely to be shaped or transformed through their immediate practices and criticisms (cf. Turinsky & Nowicka 2019).

Despite these meanings and effects of refugee support, which I would consider deeply political in a Rancièrian sense, many of my interlocutors claimed that they did 'not want anything to do with politics' and considered their actions 'neutral' or 'apolitical' (cf. Karakayali 2019; Parsanoglou 2020: 8). Most of those who set out to help openly distanced themselves from what they depicted as left-wing political activism. Such forms of overtly 'political action'[9] in support of refugees were often deemed 'destructive' and condemned for their empty criticisms and unrealistic demands. In contrast, many of my interlocutors regarded their practices as constructive 'hands-on'

---

9   In order to distinguish what my research subjects termed 'political' or 'apolitical' from what I analytically depict as political action throughout this book, I use single inverted commas to highlight the self- and other-attributions that I encountered in the field.

interventions that sought to build a 'better society' by practical means. Those who described their actions as 'political activism', on the other hand, often deliberately refrained from labelling their support as 'help' since they claimed that such a wording perpetuated dominant forms of marginalization and paternalism. As one of my interlocutors, a self-described 'political activist', told me, what all those who seek 'to help' are doing is 'having coffee' with asylum seekers.

In the course of my field research, however, this declared distinction between forms of 'helping' and 'political activism' was often not as clear to me or to my interlocutors. The boundary between these ostensibly contrasting types of acing in support of refugees often appeared rather blurred (cf. Feischmidt & Zakariás 2019). There were instances when 'volunteers' or 'helpers' combined with 'political activists' to form influential alliances (see Chapters 2 and 3) and moments when the political positions of volunteers or helpers did closely resemble those of 'left-wing activists' (see Chapters 4 and 5). At times, volunteers themselves were also well aware of the contradictions that arose between their claims to remain 'outside' or 'above' politics and their immediate practices in support of refugees. Some of my interlocutors openly reflected on these inconsistencies or acknowledged the difficulty of implementing an 'apolitical' stance in practice. Some asserted that they were somewhat 'political' or framed their practices of refugee support both as a means to alleviate suffering *and* as a political statement (cf. Schmid, Evers & Mildenberger 2019). Others started their commitment with an 'apolitical' impulse to alleviate suffering and, over time, developed openly critical and dissenting political positions towards the governmental handling of asylum seekers (cf. Kukovetz & Sprung 2019). Some also deliberately made use of an 'apolitical' positioning in order to conceal their political intentions and make them more effective (see Chapter 2).

Around the long summer of migration, thus, an ostensibly 'apolitical' positionality served as quite a powerful political position from which to explicitly or implicitly challenge, contest or interrupt dominant exclusions and discriminations in migration societies and to instigate change towards a different alternative. However, as I will scrutinize in the following section, there is another side of refugee support.

1.2.2. Refugee Support as Antipolitical Action

Refugee support is not simply about positive intentions and outcomes for those deemed its beneficiaries, nor does it always empower asylum seekers to take up a more egalitarian position in the dominant social and political order. Rather, as with many other ostensibly good things, there is also a 'dark side' to practices and discourses of refugee support. They can sometimes help first and foremost those who are 'doing good', and thus primarily serve the interests of those who are, as legitimate citizens, already in a privileged and more powerful position. At other moments, practices of refugee support (re)produce dominant exclusions or introduce new modes of discrimination, while relegating asylum seekers to a non-political place - something Rancière would describe as 'police' rather than as political.

In order to grasp these adverse effects of refugee support, I introduce the concept of *the antipolitical* as a necessary antidote to the political. My reading of the antipolitical is inspired by Ticktin's (2011) seminal work on *Casualties of Care*. In her study on the adverse effects of care and compassion in the context of immigration politics in France, Ticktin found that:

> "brutal measures may accompany actions in the name of care and rescue – measures that ultimately work to reinforce an oppressive order. As such, these regimes of care end up reproducing inequalities and racial, gendered, and geopolitical hierarchies: I suggest that this politics of care is a form of *antipolitics*" (Ticktin 2011: 5; emphasis in original)

Building on Ticktin's work, I consider practices of refugee support as antipolitical when they silence, intensify, consolidate or aggravate conditions of exclusion and discrimination in contemporary migration societies – and ultimately relegate asylum seekers to a marginalized and deprived position. This reading also connects with Ferguson's (1994) seminal work on discourses and practices of development aid in Lesotho. The resulting 'development apparatus', he argues, functions as an "anti-politics machine" that *depoliticizes* the reasons and effects of poverty. Rather than rendering their structural roots open for political discussion, disagreement and contestation, development aid reduces them to "a technical problem" and proposes "technical solutions to the sufferings of powerless and oppressed people" (ibid.: 256). This "anti-politics machine", Ferguson shows, comes with the side-effect of extending the power of the state, albeit in a hidden way. Similarly, I would suggest that practices of refugee support can also turn into an 'anti-politics machine' in

Ferguson's sense. They become a *depoliticizing* force when they silence the exclusion and discrimination of asylum seekers, while coming with a similar side-effect of extending state power over domains conventionally considered non-governmental (see Chapter 3).

In the course of my field research, I came across various intriguing moments that illustrated these antipolitical meanings and effects of refugee support. For instance, I soon realized that practices of refugee support responded to diverse interests and were not always and not only driven by a will to contribute to the 'public good' or to empower marginalized others. Instead, they often also served the helpers' own agendas, responding to self-interested motivations and personal ends. At times, refugee support functioned as a means for volunteers to establish new contacts to other residents in the neighbourhood or to counteract personal crises or feelings of isolation. In her monograph *The Need to Help*, Malkki (2015) suggests that helping is actually a primarily self-interested activity. She argues that acts of helping respond to the needs and desires of the helpers rather than to those of their ostensible beneficiaries. Similarly, for many volunteers in the area of my field research, refugee support also – but not only – functioned as a site of self-improvement and self-fulfilment.

In other instances, volunteering with refugees served the purposes and intentions of governmental actors rather than those of marginalized newcomers. I came across numerous instances when refugee support became a site of governance – and thus came with antipolitical meanings and effects (see Chapter 3). Similar to Ferguson's 'anti-politics machine' it extended state power over committed citizens and made them complicit in acts of governing. My reading of government and governance throughout this book is deeply inspired by a Foucauldian perspective. Drawing on his thoughts on the "conduct of conduct" (Foucault 1982, 1991), I interpret *government* as being "constituted by all those ways of reflecting and acting that have aimed to shape, guide, manage or regulate the conduct of persons – not only other persons but also oneself – in the light of certain principles or goals" (Rose 1996: 41). Through various instruments and programmes, governmental actors in the area of my field research influenced, shaped or intervened in practices of refugee support in order to ensure the 'right' kind of conduct (see also Fleischmann 2019). Refugee support thus also functioned as a new possibility to govern citizen-subjects through "technologies of the self" (Foucault 1988) and to extend governmental control to the ostensibly non-governmental sphere of 'civil society'. In consequence, those who sought to help were made complicit in the governance of migration, while practices of refugee support were stripped of subversive and dissonant and hence political potentials.

I employ the term *governance* in order to depict the very principles and objectives that guide acts of governing. With the terminology *governance of migration*, I refer to the particular techniques with which migrants are governed in contemporary European migration societies. One is the ordering of migrants into neat categories of victims and villains of migration. Such modes of governing draw a neat demarcation line between those who become the 'rightful' subjects of protection and those who are excluded, marginalized and rendered deportable (Papadopoulos, Stephenson & Tsianos 2008; Squire 2009; De Genova 2010; Scheel & Ratfisch 2014). Around the long summer of migration, this demarcation crystallized most strikingly in the discrimination between 'genuine refugees', who fled war and persecution, and 'bogus asylum seekers' or 'economic migrants' who ostensibly claimed asylum for false pretences. At times, volunteers in the area of my field research appeared to act as "street-level bureaucrats" (Lipsky 2010 [1980]) who uncritically accepted and implemented such categorizations in the governance of migration. For instance, some of my interlocutors had quite clear preconceptions of who was deserving of their support and who was not, based on the asylum seekers' legal "perspective of staying" ("Bleibeperspektive"). As Agamben (1998: 78) aptly puts it, those who care for the marginalized can "maintain a secret solidarity with the very powers they ought to fight".

An 'apolitical' positionality can thus not only serve as a political position from which to explicitly or implicitly challenge, contest or interrupt dominant exclusions and discriminations. At the same time, ostensibly 'apolitical' forms of refugee support might also end up reproducing or aggravating exclusions and discriminations in migration societies. The five empirical chapters of this book shed light on these ambivalent and contested (anti)political meanings and effects of refugee support around the long summer of migration.

1.3. Conceptualizing Solidarity in Migration Societies

This book revolves around the concept of *solidarity*. I use this analytical term to describe the social dimensions of 'doing good' – the manifold social imaginaries pertaining to practices of refugee support. In social anthropology, 'solidarity' has long been neglected as a field of interest. As Komter (2005: 1) states, the term has traditionally been used in a highly descriptive and abstract way, while there has been a notable lack of empirically grounded studies investigating concrete instances of solidarity behaviour. In 2016, however, the journal *Social Anthropology* published a special issue on the "Anthropology of Solidarity" focussing on the practices of solidarity that developed around the fiscal crisis in Greece (Cabot 2016; Green & Laviolette 2016; Rakopoulos 2016; Rozakou 2016; Theodossopoulos 2016). In one, Rakopoulos (2016: 142) argues that "solidarity has not received the attention it deserves from ethnographers".

In the field of critical migration studies, the term solidarity is frequently mentioned (see for example Ataç, Rygiel & Stierl 2016). Until recently, however, it was often more or less taken for granted, with little conceptual reflection (cf. Zuparic-Iljic & Valenta 2019: 134; Schwiertz & Schwenken 2020: 408). Many works employ it vaguely in reference to political lobbying for marginalized others, or they use it as a synonym for activist stances on the topic of migration. In the past years, however, the term began to attract more thorough attention from scholars working on migrant or refugee solidarity (Zamponi 2017; della Porta 2018; Squire 2018; Agustín & Jørgensen 2019; Bauder 2019; Hansen 2019; Siapera 2019; Bauder & Juffs 2020; Parsanoglou 2020). For instance, Agustín and Jørgensen (2019: 2) analyse the meanings of solidarity around the so-called 'refugee crisis' in 2015, arguing that "solidarities, in their different forms and practices, afford a lens for understanding how the crisis also presents a moment for rupture and for creating new imaginaries and for testing new alternatives for more inclusive societies". In their introduction to a special issue on "inclusive solidarity and citizenship along migratory routes in Europe and the Americas", Schwiertz and Schwenken (2020: 406) propose a non-essentialist understanding of solidarity, one that focusses on 'doing solidarity'. Such a perspective, they argue, "sheds light on how practices and acts of solidarity adopt, transform, or produce discourses, spaces, subjectivities, and networks" (ibid.: 418). Thus, scholars have begun to take into account the transformative potentials of practices of solidarity in migration societies.

This book adds to these discussions by (a) contributing to the conceptual understanding of the term solidarity in social anthropology and (b) providing an empirically grounded understanding of solidarity and its practices in migration societies. On the one hand, solidarity is the analytical prism that guides my empirical investigation into practices of refugee support. On the other hand, I sketch out instances in the subsequent chapters of this book when people used the term solidarity as an emic expression. As Parsanoglou (2020: 4) notes, in the wake of the migration summer, solidarity became a "self-defining label" that is frequently used as a signifier for different forms of collective action (see also Oikonomakis 2018).

My conceptual take on migrant solidarity considers the diverse interests, motivations, effects and imaginaries pertaining to practices of refugee support and argues that they are subject to contestation. Such a perspective allows consideration of the ambivalent (anti)political effects and meanings of refugee support outlined in the previous section. Existing works on refugee support often tend to overlook such ambiguities and ambivalences, distinguishing between forms of 'political activism' and ostensibly 'apolitical humanitarian assistance' from the outset of their analysis then focussing on one or the other. With the analytical bracket of *contested solidarity*, this book demonstrates that it is fruitful to think about both aspects together and to take into account how the political and the humanitarian intermingle in complex and ambivalent ways.

The concept of *contested solidarity* is underpinned by five key elements. Firstly, solidarity is shaped by social imaginaries that are contested among different actors. Secondly, solidarity entails ideals of a 'better society'. Thirdly, solidarity brings into being transformative relationships. Fourthly, solidarity is intertwined with power asymmetries in migration societies. Fifthly, solidarity forges collectivity across differences in migration societies. In the remainder of this section, I introduce these five elements on which my analytical consideration of *contested solidarity* rests in more detail, while connecting my arguments to works that have so far conceptualized the term across the social sciences.

1.3.1. Solidarity as a Contested Imaginary

Migrant solidarity is embedded into social imaginaries that are contested among different actors. These social imaginaries are shaped by personal needs and interests as well as by claims made in the name of the greater public good. What is central here is that these social imaginaries vary among actors and individuals and thus inspire various ideas of solidarity and of the 'right' way to 'do good'. I refer to these differing ideas as *solidarities*, in the plural form. Solidarities come with contrasting meanings and effects and are the subject of constant negotiation between different actors. They give rise to various claims made in the name of solidarity and open up a struggle over the interpretive power to define its parameters. As Agustín and Jørgensen (2019: 28) put it strikingly: "solidarity is itself a battlefield, concerning which type of solidarity should prevail and how". Bähre (2007: 52), in a similar vein, argues that "solidarity is the conflict about the parameters of inclusion". In my reading, thus, conflict and rivalry are part and parcel of solidarity practices. It is these moments of claims-making among different actors, of negotiating the social imaginaries at play, of highlighting certain interests over others that I aim to capture with the notion of *contested solidarity*.

Solidarity is thus a highly ambiguous word that opens up differing interpretations and imaginations (see Fillieule 2001). This ambiguity could even be seen as a central aspect of the term, as Karakayali (2014) argues. Like concepts such as 'democracy' or 'freedom', he asserts, solidarity represents an "empty signifier" (Laclau 1996) that can be filled with a variety of particular messages (Karakayali 2014: 111; see also Agustín & Jørgensen 2019: 25). Lagroye (1996) points to the socially constructed and elusive nature of the term and exhorts us to search for the essence of solidarity, writing: "the expression does not always have the same meaning, being itself the object of controversy between those involved in its promotion" (cited and translated in Fillieule 2001: 54).

In her book *The Ironic Spectator*, Chouliaraki (2012) analyses how the meaning of solidarity has been subject to historic shifts and transformations. She identifies chronologically successive understandings of solidarity that went from an understanding of 'solidarity as revolution' to 'solidarity as salvation' to the recently dominant notion of 'feel-good altruism' (ibid.: 3). The book at hand argues that there is not only a chronology of successive or neatly distinguishable 'types' of solidarity. Migrant solidarities, in my reading, always exist in the plural form. A typification of different forms of solidarity thus risks overlooking how contestation and interpretation always form a constitutive factor in the different understandings ascribed to the term.

1.3.2. Solidarity as Utopian Ideal

Migrant solidarity is driven by ideals of what society should look like in an age of intensified migration and how people should relate to one another in migration societies. In the course of my field research, such ideals of social togetherness were revealed to be a central mobilizing factor in the emerging solidarities around the long summer of migration (cf. Rozakou 2016). Practices of refugee support often sought to enact certain visions of future society and thus related as much to the present as they did to the future (cf. Vandevoordt & Fleischmann 2020). As Alexander (2006: 3) suggests, there is an important transcendental aspect to solidarity: "Solidarity is possible because people are oriented not only to the here and now but to the ideal, to the transcended, to what they hope will be the everlasting". Scherr (2013) argues that a utopian moment is central to the meanings of solidarity in that they contribute to the creation of a society based less on competition and inequality and more on cooperation and mutual help.

Migrant solidarity is thus "inventive" of new social relations and political possibilities (see Featherstone 2012: 6; Agustín & Jørgensen 2019: 34). It gives rise to new ideas of belonging beyond the parameters of the nation-state (Rakopoulos 2016: 144). As I outlined in the previous section, however, there is also a 'dark side' to solidarity (see also Komter 2005). Solidarity does not necessarily make for a more egalitarian society; it can have unintended consequences and adverse effects. For instance, it can serve the interests of those who are already 'better off', or it (re)produces dominant categorizations and discriminations, further excluding those who are already marginalized. In the empirical analysis of this book, I thus examine how solidarities foster alternative ideals of social togetherness in migration societies while also considering their contradictions and adverse effects.

1.3.3. Solidarity as a Transformative Relationship

Migrant solidarity brings into being transformative relationships between established residents and newcomers. It creates new ways of relating across social groups and places that were formerly isolated from one another (see Featherstone 2012: 4). Put differently, solidarity constitutes a "bridge concept" (Rakopoulos 2016) that directs our attention to the relationships that are forged between 'insiders' and 'outsiders' in a society. As Reshaur (1992: 724) argues, solidarity is "world-building" in that it establishes a relationship between those who are marginalized and those who are 'better off'. In a similar vein, Hansen (2019: 8) regards solidarity "as a relationship forged between actors in unequal power relations that aims towards a more equal order".

Migrant solidarity is also generative of collective identities and forms a central part of political subject formation (cf. Bauder 2019). For instance, Agustín and Jørgensen (2019: 30f) outline how solidarity is "central to the formation of transformative political subjectivities", while "alliance building is a crucial aspect of solidarity". Quite connectedly, my empirical investigation revealed how practices of refugee support produce transformative networks that involve various actors and individuals and that go far beyond the linear relationship between benefactors and beneficiaries. Practices of solidarity can also forge new relationships between and among volunteers, established residents, local and national governmental actors, political activists, church representatives, social welfare organizations and other actors involved in the reception of asylum seekers. Migrant solidarity situates these different actors in relation to each other, assigns functions and responsibilities among them and (re)produces hierarchies. These relationships are not primarily established through the rule of law or via formalized regulations, but might be better described as a "sphere of non-contractual relationships" within the nation-state (Karakayali 2014: 115). However, they nonetheless become subject to governmental control and influence: in the third chapter, I illustrate how governmental actors increasingly sought to govern such ostensibly non-contractual relationships through interventions in the self-conduct of committed citizens.

These relationships of solidarity in migration societies are far from static. As I will illustrate in the following chapters, they are highly volatile and elusive. Bauder (2019: 3) puts this as follows: "solidarity is a never-finished practice that prevents political closure and preserves plurality, while acknowledging the complex, fragmented and multifaceted relations between people and groups in different circumstances". This book takes into account how relationships of solidarity are forged and mobilized (see Chapter 2) but also how they dissolve again and can ultimately even be deliberately broken (see Chapter 6).

1.3.4. Solidarity as Power Asymmetry

Migrant solidarity is intertwined with power asymmetries. It is thus central to consider the power dynamics at play when investigating relationships of solidarity. Those depicted as the ostensible beneficiaries of support, the asylum seekers, do not hold the same citizenship rights as their benefactors. As non-citizens they are in a disadvantaged position, with their rights, possibilities and resources limited in comparison to those recognized as citizens. I would therefore echo the interpretation of Hannah Arendt (1966 [1963]: 84), who calls solidarity a principle that establishes a "community of interest with the oppressed and exploited". Put differently, solidarity produces relationships between groups and individuals with unequal rights and resources.

On the one hand, migrant solidarity can come with possibilities to bridge such inequalities between non-citizens and citizens. Giugni (2001: 236) points to the positive effects of such relationships for their ostensible beneficiaries in that they "put the needs of those populations higher in the political and public agendas". Solidarity can thus contribute to the social integration and empowerment of asylum seekers in spite of their limited rights. Seen in this light, solidarity functions as "a powerful force for reshaping the world in more equal terms" (Featherstone 2012: 4).

On the other hand, relationships of solidarity can themselves contribute to the creation or aggravation of power asymmetries (see also Paragi 2017: 317). The practices of refugee support explored during my field research produced ambivalent effects that ranged from a levelling of inequalities and an empowering of individuals to the cementing of existing power asymmetries and the production of new discriminations (see also Theodossopoulos 2016; Kirchhoff 2020). Either way, the book at hand aims to contribute to our understanding of solidarity's ambivalent and complex entanglements with power asymmetries in migration societies.

1.3.5. Solidarity as Social Glue

Migrant solidarity forges collectivity across differences. It serves as a social cement or glue that produces an 'imagined community' centring on the mutual dependency of diverse groups of individuals for the fulfilment of their needs and interests. With this conceptual approach, I highlight how migrant solidarity is driven by both individual *and* collective interests, with the fulfilment of each being dependent on the other. It is a notion that has parallels with the writings of Durkheim (1965 [1893]), a pioneer in the conceptualization of solidarity. He argued that there had been a shift from 'mechanical solidarity' to 'organic solidarity' in light of an increasing division of labour in industrialized societies. In consequence, social cohesion was no longer based on the homogeneity of individuals but on the mutual interdependence of different societal components. From his perspective, "collective consciousness", a unifying force in increasingly heterogeneous societies, emerged from the interdependence of different parts for the fulfilment of individual needs (ibid.).

Building on Durkheim's concept, I would argue that the solidarities that emerged around the long summer of migration responded to individual needs as much as they contributed to a greater public good. In other words, in migration societies, one's own place within a harmonious collectivity necessarily depends on the ability to integrate 'others'. Zoll (2000: 200) sums this up well, arguing that solidarity in migration societies is based both on notions of "concrete difference" and "abstract sameness". Mecheril (2003: 241) even asserts that solidarity actions are only possible on the premise that the actual living situations of those involved differ from each other. Similarly, I would suggest that rather than erasing differences, the solidarities of the long summer of migration needed those very differences in order to effect meaningful action. Thus, this book also sheds light on the 'imagined communities' that were produced by practices of migrant solidarity.

1.4. The Political Possibilities of Grassroots Humanitarianism

The practices and discourses of migrant solidarity that emerged around the long summer of migration often resembled what academic studies identify as key features of a humanitarian imaginary (cf. Vandevoordt & Verschraegen 2019: 103). Barnett (2005: 724) describes this as the idea of an ostensibly "impartial, independent, and neutral provision of relief to those in immediate danger of harm", often thought of as being located 'outside' or 'above' politics. Traditionally, academic works on humanitarianism have focused on professionalised international relief operations by large non-governmental organizations, such as *Médecins Sans Frontières* (see for instance Fassin 2007; Scott-Smith 2016). Recently, however, scholars have also directed their attention to what has been termed "grassroots humanitarianism" (McGee & Pelham 2018; Sandri 2018; Vandevoordt & Fleischmann 2020) or "citizen aid" (Fechter & Schwittay 2019). These works account for the increasing engagement of 'ordinary citizens' and less formalized non-professional groups in practices that are driven by a similar humanitarian logic. This book contributes to these debates by investigating the contested meanings and effects of grassroots humanitarian action around the German 'summer of welcome'.

Works in the field of the *anthropology of humanitarianism* have intensively discussed how actions based on a humanitarian imaginary, in fact, end up reproducing the unequal power relations at play (cf. Bornstein & Redfield 2011b). They illustrate that humanitarian action is deeply contradictive, entangled with governmental actors and complicit in the discrimination of marginalized subjects – and hence comes with antipolitical effects (cf. Ticktin 2011). My field research, however, revealed that there is more to such actions: an exclusive focus on the adverse antipolitical effects of humanitarianism risks overlooking how such an imaginary simultaneously opens up transformative political possibilities in the Rancièrian sense. I would thus echo the observation by Ticktin (2014: 283) that overly pessimistic interpretations lead conceptual works on humanitarian action into a "cul-de-sac of critique". In order to move beyond this dead end, she calls for research that explores "new and emergent meanings of the political in and around humanitarian spaces" (ibid.). It is these emergent meanings of the political from within a humanitarian imaginary to which I devote particular attention. In the following paragraphs, I outline in more detail how this book contributes to an understanding of the political possibilities of grassroots humanitarianism.

1.4.1. The Mobilizing Effects of Emergency Situations

Humanitarian action is often discussed as being intrinsically connected to the notion of a 'crisis' or a 'state of emergency' (Nyers 2006a; Calhoun 2010). Due to this emphasis on 'emergency', Ticktin (2016: 262) argues, humanitarian action is viewed from a narrow temporal perspective that focusses on the immediate events and leaves no room for embedding them in a historical context or for considerations of the future. Such an imaginary would neglect the (wo)man-made causes of events (cf. Calhoun 2010). It thus resembles discourses pertaining to natural catastrophes, thought of as 'acts of God' or 'bad luck' (cf. Agier 2010). Such perceptions of 'crises', however, are said to discourage the assignment of blame and "rarely lead to protest movements" (Jasper 1998: 410). Others have argued that the spatial movement of refugees is generally depicted through the use of crisis metaphors, which in turn inspires humanitarian action (cf. Soguk 1999; Mountz & Hiemstra 2013). In consequence of such an imaginary, the reception of asylum seekers is said to become a non-political phenomenon while the power relations at play are ignored (Nyers 2006a).

Indeed, in the course of my field research, I realized that the image of the 'crisis' played an important role for those who engaged in practices of refugee support. From September 2015 on, crisis metaphors circulated widely in public and political discussions. Almost on a daily basis, new developments surrounding Europe's 'refugee crisis' hit the front pages of national and international newspapers, for instance with stories about the movement of asylum seekers via the 'Balkan route'; deteriorating conditions of reception in Germany and other western European countries; and the reintroduction of national border controls in the Schengen area (for a more detailed account on the political developments see Kasparek & Speer 2015; Kasparek 2016; Heller & Pezzani 2017; Hess & Kasparek 2017b; Hess et al. 2017). This image of the 'crisis' in late summer of 2015 mobilized thousands of citizens to get involved and help 'those in need'. Many of these helpers stepped in where governmental actors failed to provide even the most basic services to the newcomers.

And yet, in spite of their emphasis on 'crisis' and emergency, those who sought to help did not necessarily ignore the structural political causes of events or hold a narrow temporal perspective. Often, their actions were guided as much by a focus on the immediate event as they were by future visions of society (cf. Vandevoordt & Fleischmann 2020). Quite connectedly, in his telling analysis of the search and rescue operations of NGOs in the Mediterranean Sea, Cuttitta (2018: 632) outlines how these organizations draw attention to the structural causes of humanitarian emergencies and, in the course of their actions, turn the Mediterranean in a "political stage". In a similar vein, humanitarian volunteers in the area of my field research sometimes also turned the local reception of asylum seekers into a "political stage". Many openly reflected on the contradictions of their practices and acknowledged that they might be helping to sustain flawed asylum policies. The notion of an acute emergency situation can thus also function as a powerful mobilizing force that draws people into actions that come with possibilities to bring about change towards a different alternative.

1.4.2. Reflecting on the Causes of Suffering

Scholars have argued that humanitarian action is frequently guided by an emphasis on human suffering (see Ticktin 2006; Agier 2010; Bornstein & Redfield 2011b). The ultimate aim of humanitarians is the alleviation of immediate suffering through the temporary provision of food, shelter or medical care (see Ticktin 2014: 274). Various authors have problematized how actions guided by such an impulse to alleviate suffering (re)produce unequal power relations (Barnett 2016). They argue that humanitarian action reduces asylum seekers to their suffering while perpetuating inequalities between passive recipients of aid and active, benevolent citizens (see Fassin 2007). In consequence of such actions, asylum seekers would become "mute victims" (Rajaram 2002) or "speechless emissaries" (Malkki 1996). With reference to the writings of Agamben (1998), others have discussed how an emphasis on suffering paints asylum seekers as "bare life", i.e. beings stripped of political rights and reduced to their bare biological existence (Ticktin 2006; Schindel 2016; Vandevoordt 2020). In his often-cited book *Distant Suffering*, Boltanski (1999) outlines how the media periodically serve up "spectacles of suffering" that inspire a "politics of pity" among those who are better off. According to Boltanski (ibid.: 13), such expressions of pity depend crucially on physical distance and end when the unfortunates "invade the space of those more fortunate".

The humanitarian imaginary at play during the summer of 2015 clearly did not end at the helpers' own doorsteps. Instead, the arrival of asylum seekers triggered an unprecedented level of compassion despite or because of spatial proximity. I came across many instances when those supporting refugees claimed that they felt morally obligated to step up in order to alleviate immediate human suffering. Indeed, many provided for the basic needs of the newcomers, such as food, clothing and medical care. However, this emphasis on immediate human suffering often went hand in hand with a reflection on unequal power relations and the structural conditions that lead to the marginalization of asylum seekers. Quite connectedly, Sinatti (2019: 143) found that volunteers and aid workers supporting refugees in Milan did not only respond to migrants' basic needs in terms of 'bare life' but also "empower[ed] migrants and facilitate[d] their autonomous agency", what she calls "enabling humanitarianism". Feischmidt and Zakariás (2019: 89) also point to the entangled nature of humanitarian charity and political action in practices of refugee support around the long summer of migration, arguing that "the consideration of the suffering and neediness of others may increase awareness of political responsibilities, and thus stimulate the birth of political critique". This book contributes to an understanding of how a grassroots humanitarian impulse to alleviate suffering can be coupled with a desire to bring about change towards a 'better society' and the articulation of dissent towards governmental decisions and policies.

1.4.3. 'Humanity' as a Political Identity

Scholars have outlined that humanitarian action is often inspired by the notion of a shared "humanity" (Agier 2010; Feldman & Ticktin 2010; Barnett 2011). Such an imagined category of 'humanity' unifies all human beings under a common identity, transcending distinctions established between groups of people by means of national citizenship (Nyers 2006a: 32). Many works have foregrounded the essentializing effects of the notion of a shared 'humanity' (Fassin & Pandolfi 2010; Ticktin 2016). For instance, Edkins (2003: 256) outlines how "such an approach depersonalizes and depoliticizes, and operates in symbiosis with the state". Asad (2003) argues that the ostensibly unifying category of humanity is always an illusion since divisions resulting from unequal power relations persist. Fassin (2007: 518) illustrates how humanitarianism itself establishes "two forms of humanity and two sorts of life in the public space", namely those who become the passive recipients of aid and those who are active for the sake of others.

In the course of my field research, I came across many instances when those supporting refugees framed their practices as 'acts of humanity'. They told me that they felt morally obligated towards 'humanity', thus establishing a shared identity with asylum seekers. On closer examination, however, it transpired that many had quite clear preconceptions of who deserved their help and support and who did not, preconceptions that reproduced governmental discriminations between 'genuine' and 'bogus' asylum seekers. For instance, many volunteers regarded Syrians as 'suffering victims' and hence rightful recipients of their help and support. Asylum seekers originating from African countries or Eastern Europe, in contrast, were frequently depicted as bogus 'economic migrants' who should be deported. However, there were also many instances, when the notion of a 'shared humanity' inspired political actions that transcended and challenged dominant distinctions between 'genuine refugees' and 'bogus economic migrants'. At times, volunteers employed the idea of 'humanity' as a political identity from which to contest deportation orders or the classification of further 'safe countries of origin'. Furthermore, a feeling of being obligated towards 'humanity' mobilized a moral imperative to act that not only led thousands to get involved but also facilitated the formation of powerful alliances (see Chapter 2). Thus, the imagined category of 'humanity' also opens up important political possibilities in the context of grassroots humanitarian action. This book explores the notion of a 'shared humanity' as quite a powerful political identity from which to voice dissent and advocate for a 'better society'.

1.4.4. The Political Power of an 'Apolitical' Positioning

Scholars have problematized how humanitarian action is commonly understood as an 'impartial', 'neutral' or 'apolitical' practice (see Barnett 2011; Fassin 2012). Practices inspired by an impulse to alleviate suffering are often depicted as being 'outside' or 'above' politics (Bornstein & Redfield 2011b; Ticktin 2011; Fassin 2012). As Nyers (2006a: 32) puts it: "Humanitarian action and political action are cast as two distinct and separate modes of acting and being-in-the-world". While the realm of politics is often associated with negative attributes (cynical, self-interested, amoral), humanitarianism is commonly seen as a positive counterweight or remedy (compassionate, principled, impartial) (ibid.).

During my field research, many of my interlocutors also asserted that they 'only' wanted to help but did not want anything to do with politics. Elsewhere, I problematized such an understanding of ostensibly 'apolitical' humanitarian action as a persistent and powerful myth (see also Redfield 2011; Fleischmann & Steinhilper 2017). A claim to act 'beyond' or 'outside' of politics masks the fact that such action is always embedded in a specific political and social context marked by unequal power relations. Nonetheless, supposedly 'apolitical' practices of refugee support were also frequently imbued with transformative political meanings and effects in the Rancièrian sense: they came with possibilities to challenge, contest or reform conditions of exclusion and discrimination in migration societies. Many did not hesitate to take a stand in public, others voiced dissent at governmental actors and migration policies or demonstrated a clear will to influence political decision-making processes. I also came across instances when an 'apolitical' position was strategically employed in order to make political aims more effective (see Chapter 2). At times, thus, claims of 'apolitical' action present a powerful political position from which to instigate change towards a different alternative.

1.4.5. Humanitarian Dissent

Scholars have also outlined how humanitarian actions are often deeply entangled with governmental actors and policies. Most strikingly, Fassin outlines how humanitarianism and government have increasingly tended to merge and argues that they have developed into forms of "humanitarian government" in which human beings are managed and regulated in morally charged ways (Fassin 2007, 2012). In her study on the role of compassion in French immigration politics, Ticktin (2011) likewise illustrates how "regimes of care", spanning both civil society and state actors, govern migrants through an emphasis on care and compassion. In consequence, Ticktin argues, asylum seekers need to highlight their physical suffering in order to obtain entitlements and rights. In his book on international paternalism, Barnett (2016: 10) points out how Marxian analyses have long blamed humanitarians and philanthropists for helping to maintain a system of exploitation. Humanitarian action thus seems to form part of the very 'cynical', 'self-interested' and 'amoral' world of politics that it claims to remedy.

Despite their claim to remain 'outside' of politics, grassroots humanitarians in the area of my field research also became the object of governmental intervention and control and complicit in the governance of migration (see Chapter 3). However, at the same time, many volunteers criticized such governmental interventions in their role and conduct, voicing a strong will to remain independent. They embedded their actions in a humanitarian imaginary that simultaneously expressed criticisms of governmental actors, openly counteracted their decisions and voiced dissent at existing policies (see also Fleischmann 2017). In a similar vein, Stierl (2017: 709) found that dissent and criticism might also be articulated "from within humanitarian reason". He analyses the subversive potentials of humanitarian action and argues that there is a "wide spectrum of humanitarian imaginary" that comes with differing possibilities for subversive acts (ibid.). Walters (2011: 48) contends that the relationship between humanitarianism and government is complex and ranges from co-optation to provocation. Vandevoordt and Verschraegen (2019) suggest that practices of refugee support around the long summer of migration might be approached as a form of "subversive humanitarianism", which they define as "a morally motivated set of actions which acquires a political character not through the form in which these actions manifest themselves, but through their implicit opposition to the ruling socio-political elite" (ibid.: 105). Thus, I would argue that not only humanitarianism and government are tending to merge, as Fassin (2012) previously outlined, but also humanitarianism and grassroots political action.

1.5. Rethinking Political Action in Migration Societies

The contested solidarities that emerged around the long summer of migration developed in response to a politically tense environment. EU member states were deeply split over how to distribute the growing numbers of asylum seekers fairly, some reintroduced national border controls, while more and more migrants drowned on their perilous journey across the Mediterranean Sea (for a more detailed account on the political developments see Kasparek & Speer 2015; Heller & Pezzani 2017; Hess et al. 2017; Agustín & Jørgensen 2019; Rea et al. 2019). In addition, the German public appeared increasingly divided in relation to the topic of migration (cf. Hinger 2016; Hinger, Daphi & Stern 2019). From late 2014 on, many German cities became sites of weekly protest marches organized by the Pegida movement and its regional offsprings, marches that openly displayed hostile attitudes towards asylum seekers and stirred up anti-immigration sentiments (see De Genova 2015; Virchow 2016; Vorländer, Herold & Schäller 2016; Jäckle & König 2017). Many of those who supported refugees around that time depicted their actions as a means to influence these tendencies in specific ways and bring about changes towards a 'better society'. At times, thus, refugee support turned into political action in the Rancièrian sense outlined above. Although works in the field of critical migration studies have engaged with political action in migration societies for years, the transformative potentials stemming from practices that are not openly depicted as "left-wing political activism" have gone little noticed. In the following paragraphs, I sketch out how this book contributes to ongoing discussions in the field. I argue that the contested practices of refugee support and migrant solidarity invite us to rethink political action in migration societies in more relational terms.

Works in the field of critical migration studies have often turned the notion of asylum seekers as mute and passive victims on its head, while drawing attention to their expressions of political agency (Bojadžijev & Karakayali 2010). Thus, scholars have dealt intensively with instances of refugee and migrant activism (see for example Johnson 2012; Nyers & Rygiel 2012; Tyler & Marciniak 2013; Ataç, Rygiel & Stierl 2016; Steinhilper 2017). They argue that it is only through the subjectivization of non-citizens who are structurally excluded and stripped of political rights that the unequal power relations at play can be challenged (Topak 2016). Such works draw on the concept of the *autonomy of migration* (see for instance Papadopoulos & Tsianos 2013; Scheel 2013; De Genova 2017). This line of thought regards the irregular border crossings of migrants as subversive acts that challenge sovereign power and contest the parameters of the modern nation-state. From this perspective, the spatial movement of irregular migrants is always also a social movement that crucially alters the way people live together in the arrival countries (cf. Karakayali & Tsianos 2005).

Around the long summer of migration, the growing influx of asylum seekers did indeed set in motion profound transformation processes that affected the basic parameters of living-together in migration societies. However, my findings suggest that the migrants' capacity to bring about change and transformation depended largely on the *responses* of established citizens and their contested social imaginaries and practices. In other words, the parameters of change were subject to contestation and negotiation between different actors and individuals in the arrival society.

Scholars also often take their cue from Isin's works on "acts of citizenship" (Isin 2008; Isin & Nielsen 2008; Isin, Nyers & Turner 2008; Isin 2012). Isin regards instances when migrants claim an own voice as disruptive moments that challenge the distinction between legitimate citizens and non-citizens, the central premise of sovereign power (see for instance Walters 2008; McNevin 2011; Nyers & Rygiel 2012; Ilcan 2014). In his seminal book *Being Political – Genealogies of Citizenship* (Isin 2002), he outlines how the category of citizenship had historically become ever more inclusive in response to such disruptive acts, gradually integrating groups that were formerly excluded, such as slaves or women. Through such "acts of citizenship", asylum seekers and irregular migrants become claims-making subjects within the nation-state in which they reside (Johnson 2014).

In the course of my field research, I came across numerous moments when asylum seekers claimed an own voice and made themselves visible as claims-making subjects contesting the conditions of their reception. In the fifth chapter, I investigate the spontaneous protests of asylum seekers in so-called 'emergency reception centres', interim forms of accommodation that came with increasingly intolerable living conditions for its inhabitants in the wake of the long summer of migration. In the sixth chapter, I investigate more organized and long-term instances of migrant activism that occurred in a small town in the area of my field research. In both cases, however, the asylum seekers' scope to demonstrate political agency and to influence their conditions of reception proved highly contingent on the (de)politicizing responses of various actors on the ground, including those who engaged in practices of refugee support. The migrants' acts of citizenship were thus *intermediated* through their relationships with established residents. This chimes with the thoughts of Johnson (2012: 118) who, writing on migrant activism, argues that "the citizen becomes a necessary partner [...] for change to be effective". Political action in migration societies, I would argue, is thus always relational, unfolding in practices and relationships of solidarity.

Works in the field of critical migration studies have also engaged intensively with activist networks that advocate for the rights of migrants and asylum seekers and act from a decidedly 'leftist' political position. Scholars point out how such groups openly denounce injustices related to the modern nation-state and its territorial borders (see Millner 2011; Rygiel 2011; King 2016; Monforte 2020). For instance, there has been great interest in *no border activism*, a loosely connected network of activists who call for the abolishment of territorial borders, advocate for a right to free movement, and take a stand against the nation-state (Walters 2006; Rigby & Schlembach 2013; Burridge 2014; Gauditz 2017). These works shed light on the transformative and subversive potentials that emanate from practices of refugee support. However, they often focus solely on groups and individuals who describe their practices as 'leftist' and deliberately 'political'.

Many of those who supported refugees around the long summer of migration, by contrast, openly set themselves apart from 'leftist political activism' and were much more hesitant to depict their actions as a means to counteract the nation-state. Often, their practices were embedded into an 'apolitical' humanitarian imaginary that, nonetheless, offered manifold political possibilities to bring about change and transformation. There were also instances when those who engaged in practices of refugee support in their village, town or neighbourhood simultaneously held local political offices. For example, a volunteer turned out to be the deputy mayor of her village, while others asserted that they were long-term party members of the SPD, the German Social Democratic Party. These encounters made me realize that the ostensibly separate entities of 'state' and 'civil society' are in fact much more entangled and elusive (cf. Abrams 1988 [1977]; Mitchell 1991; Ferguson & Gupta 2002). I would therefore argue that political action in migration societies does not necessarily need to be formulated in opposition to 'the state', as is the case with *no border activism*, while political transformation does not always happen in a linear fashion, proceeding upwards from an entity imagined as 'civil society' openly counteracting 'the state'.

With this in mind, this book analyses how relationships of solidarity in migration societies inspire more indirect, hidden or everyday forms of political action. My aim is to investigate how political transformation can also be *enacted* on the ground through the immediate practices of committed citizens, without them necessarily making direct claims towards an entity imagined as 'the state'. This chimes in with Youkhana's (2015: 11) writings, in which she emphasizes the value of everyday practices as a means to transgress existing modes of belonging centring on the nation-state. In a similar vein, Martin, Hanson and Fontaine (2007) emphasize "the role of individuals in creating change" and argue that activism also "entails an individual making particular kinds of new connections between people that alter power relations within existing social networks" (ibid.: 80). They thus propose opening up the category of political activism to include not only actions that are conventionally considered 'political' but also everyday actions with a more limited geographic reach. Based on his case study on practices of refugee support in

Milan, Artero (2019: 158) also suggests that volunteering with refugees can become a "micropolitical practice". Stock (2019: 136) points to the transformative potentials of relationships forged through refugee support, relationships that enable both volunteers and refugees "to engage in acts of citizenship through care practices that are conducive to more inclusive migration politics". Bosi and Zamponi (2015) also stress the political significance of actions that seek to transform certain aspects of society without making direct claims towards governmental actors (see also Zamponi 2017).

Such conceptions of political action chime strikingly with what I witnessed around the long summer of migration. Many of those who engaged in practices of refugee support aimed to change the status quo through 'hands-on' interventions in their local communities. In order to take into account such more hidden, subtle or indirect forms of political action, I approach solidarity as a transformative relationship that inspires actions with contested political meanings and effects. In this way, this book aims to provide a more nuanced understanding of political action in migration societies by stressing its *relationality*, a relationality that unfolds in relationships of solidarity between established residents and newcomers.

1.6. Researching Solidarity in the German 'Summer of Welcome': Field, Access, Methods, Ethics

This book is underpinned by qualitative and ethnographic field research conducted between late 2014 and mid-2016 in various localities across Germany, particularly across the southern state of Baden-Württemberg. In the course of my 20 months of fieldwork, I held more than 30 semi-structured interviews ranging in duration from half an hour to four hours. The majority of these interviews were recorded, transcribed and analysed. They allowed me to gain insights into the motivations, interests and social imaginaries of a diverse range of actors involved in the contestation of solidarities. This spanned volunteers who sought to help refugees; self-declared political activists; governmental representatives at municipal and federal state level; people professionally employed in the field of the reception of asylum seekers, for instance in social welfare organizations; and, last but not least, asylum seekers themselves. In order to gain insights into the discussions that evolved among and between these different actors, I conducted participant observation in numerous meetings, conferences, trainings and other events related to practices of refugee support. For instance, I regularly attended conferences organized by the Refugee Council of Baden-Württemberg, which brought together volunteers from across different localities in the state. Moreover, I participated in several conferences organized by the state government of Baden-Württemberg, such as the regular "Forum for Refugee Help" events, which aimed to facilitate volunteering for refugees. I also participated in workshops that brought together self-declared 'political activists' acting in support of refugees across the country, for instance in cities such as Berlin and Hannover. This empirical fieldwork was backed up by an analysis of relevant written materials, such as newspaper articles, online sources and position papers.

Over the course of those 20 months of empirical research, I was confronted with a highly dynamic, fluctuating and constantly changing field of investigation. In November 2014, at the start of my fieldwork, nobody would have predicted the extraordinary explosion of refugee support that took place some months later. My impulse to start investigating practices of refugee support stemmed, however, from a sense that a profound change had already begun to take shape that year. At this early stage of my field research, the reception of refugees began to attract growing public attention, while the numbers of citizens seeking to support refugees was also on the rise. In addition, more and more actors began intervening in the conduct of committed citizens. For instance, governmental actors implemented programmes that targeted the increasing citizen engagement around refugees. By the summer months of 2015, the reception of asylum seekers and the notion of a German 'welcome culture' had taken centre stage both in the media and in public debate. The extraordinary spirit of that long summer of migration mobilized an unprecedented number of established residents to engage in practices of refugee support. Only in 2016 did the public focus on the reception of asylum seekers slowly begin to diminish. Despite the decreasing media attention in the first half of 2016, however, various actors intensified their efforts to influence and gain authority over the contested solidarities that had developed over the previous months. What I witnessed over the course of my field research was thus a gradually growing diversification of actors and an expanding and increasingly complex field of investigation.

This growing complexity in my field of investigation also led me to narrow the spatial focus of my fieldwork. As I was based in Konstanz, a town on the southernmost edge of Germany, I conducted the majority of my field research across the southern state of Baden-Württemberg. I complemented my data collection with occasional field trips to relevant events in other parts of Germany, such as Berlin, Leipzig and Hannover. This enabled me to consider how events in the area of my field research did not occur in a vacuum and to take into account the area's spatial connections to and relationships with other regions in Germany and beyond (Allen, Massey & Cochrane 1998). I should, however, acknowledge that this narrowing of the spatial focus of my field research necessarily involved selection processes that limit my findings. With the state having the only Green-Social Democrats (SPD) led government[10] in Germany, my field research in Baden-Württemberg took place within a specific political climate (see Chapter 3). It was contingent on the particular historical, regional and socioeconomic context of this part of Germany. In the following empirical chapters, I provide information on the local and regional context of my investigation where it appears pertinent to an understanding of my findings, although I am unable to provide a complete picture of all the relevant contextual factors.

Since I moved back and forth between various localities across the area of my field research, my investigation might be labelled a "multi-sited ethnography" (Marcus 1998; Falzon 2009). However, as Hannerz (2003) remarks, this terminology is misleading in several regards as it might suggest a comparative study of different and isolated 'cases'. It is therefore important to stress that the purpose of my investigation was not simply to study practices of refugee support in different localities and compare my findings afterwards, but rather to analyse relationships and connections across and between these sites. Moreover, I should mention that my multi-sited ethnography necessarily entailed selecting certain locations from the many potential candidates (ibid.: 207). Some localities were chosen because they became the site of specific problems or events of interest, such as protests by asylum seekers (Chapter 5 and Chapter 6); other choices were shaped by governmental decision-making processes and policies, such as the decision to inaugurate a new initial reception centre in Ellwangen (Chapter 2); while some also responded to particularities of my field or may have been guided by mere coincidence.

Starting ethnographic research on one's own doorstep might appear to be a rather unusual approach for an anthropological study. Historically, studies in social anthropology were almost exclusively based overseas, in regions

---

10   At the time of my field research, the Greens and the Social Democrats (SPD) were in a coalition that had governed the state of Baden-Württemberg since 2011. See Chapter 3 for a more detailed discussion on the implications of this specific political context for the findings of my field research.

that appeared different and unfamiliar to the ethnographers themselves (see for instance Mauss 1990 [1925]; Douglas 1991 [1966]; Malinowski 2014 [1922]). In contrast, Baden-Württemberg is the region that I am most familiar with, having been born and raised in a town close to Stuttgart, the state's capital. While research in regions further away from the ethnographer's 'home' continues to be a major focus of research in social anthropology, more and more scholars are conducting research in regions familiar to the anthropologist, Europe for instance (cf. Koutsouba 1999; Alvesson 2009). In his monograph *Reversed Gaze*, Ntarangwi (2010: 78) highlights the value of "using anthropology not only to study others but also to reflect upon one's own culture". Indeed, doing fieldwork on 'home turf' offered several advantages for the purpose of this investigation. For instance, it allowed a greater degree of flexibility in that it substantially shortened the distances to travel and thus enabled me to react spontaneously to developments over a relatively long period of time. This proved particularly useful since, as I outlined above, my field of investigation was highly dynamic and constantly changing. My tacit knowledge of the region and light Swabian accent often made it easy to gain access to those supporting refugees on the ground and to build trustful relationships with them. However, the spatial overlap of research area and 'home', coupled with the high visibility of my research topic in public debate, led to a situation where it became increasingly challenging to 'step back' and retain a critical distance to my topic of investigation. Scholars, however, have outlined the importance of both 'immersion' *and* 'distance' for the research process (see Hammersley & Atkinson 1995: 115; Ybema & Kamsteeg 2009). Distancing became easier for me when the visibility of and euphoria around refugee support begun to fade in early 2016.

Gaining access to those who engaged in volunteering with refugees generally proved to be a smooth endeavour. Most of the volunteers or citizens' initiatives I contacted in the course of my field research were available for interviews and conversations; many willingly opened their doors to me or invited me to take part in their sessions and activities. Such interviews frequently lasted several hours or spanned multiple sessions. Volunteers – especially those who were retired – often enjoyed talking about their personal histories and motivations, and expounding on the achievements or challenges of volunteering with refugees. All in all, volunteers often seemed quite enthusiastic about my research project and asked me for findings and insights into the research process. Participating in my research seemed to present a welcome opportunity to share experiences and thereby to contribute to the greater public good. Thus, the participation in my field research, at times, appeared to form part of their very commitment to refugees. Many times, people also felt 'honoured' to be included in a scientific research project since it appeared to give them a feeling of doing the 'right' thing. This easy access to volunteers contrasted sharply with my experiences with deliberate "political activists" supporting refugees. Such groups and individuals often appeared to be largely unavailable for interviews and generally suspicious of my research project; at one time, an activist even suspected me of being a government spy. This might in part be explained by the fact that left-wing activism in Germany has long been subject to severe government crackdowns and infiltrations, as typified by the harsh treatment of anti-G20 protesters in Hamburg in 2017 (see Haunss et al. 2017). Governmental actors and those professionally employed in the field of the reception of asylum seekers also proved open towards my research and were happy to talk about the extraordinary scope of refugee support in their sphere of influence. Nonetheless, I often had the impression that what I was being offered by such actors was an incomplete or sugar-coated account of reality. With a few exceptions, it was often quite difficult to talk about problems, disagreements or other controversial topics with these professionals or governmental representatives. A prime example came when I investigated asylum seeker protests at emergency reception centres and had numerous interview requests bluntly rejected, with the explanation that this was a 'confidential area' or a 'sensitive topic'.

The familiarity with my field of investigation also meant that I struggled less with the unequal power relations that affect research encounters in the Global South (see for instance Sidaway 1992; Scheper-Hughes 1995; Comaroff & Comaroff 2003; Monteith 2017). Nader (1972), for instance, problematizes how most anthropologists have "studied down", investigating people less prosperous and powerful than themselves. Ethnographic research focussing on marginalized 'others' has therefore often been accompanied by issues of paternalism, exploitation or postcolonial continuities (see also Madison 2008). My field research, in contrast, mostly centred on German citizens with a broadly similar social, political and economic status to myself. Added to this, in early 2015, I myself got involved with supporting refugees in a small initiative committed to building bridges between asylum seekers and local residents in Konstanz. In consequence, the boundary between my research subjects and myself often appeared rather blurred. Ethnographic research concerned with peers or groups of people who cannot be treated as 'others' and themselves participate in othering has been discussed as "studying sideways" (Hannerz 1998: 11). However, having talked to a variety of different actors in the course of my field research, including not only volunteers but also governmental actors and asylum seekers, I would suggest that my approach might be better described as *"studying through"* (Wright & Reinhold 2011). Such an approach seeks to trace "ways in which power creates webs and relations between actors, institutions and discourses across time and space" (Shore & Wright 1997: 14). In the case of my own field research, this translated to a close examination of the webs and relations that emerged among different actors in the area of investigation and a multi-perspective approach to the practices of refugee support.

That said, the process of data collection and analysis was clearly neither entirely objective nor free from power dynamics. While it was difficult to remain in a critical distance to some of the opinions and positions I encountered, I also came across others with which I did not personally agree. As a result, I may myself have unintentionally participated in the contestation of the solidarities I was investigating. Various scholars have pointed out that the researcher is a socially embodied and far from value-free human being who substantially shapes the research and writing process (see Rose 1997; Nencel 2014). England (1994: 82) thus argues that "reflexivity is critical to the conduct of fieldwork; it induces self-discovery and can lead to insights and new hypotheses about the research questions". In order to avoid the "God-trick" (Haraway 1988) and its "view from nowhere", I will, in the course of the following empirical chapters, reflect on my own positionality and on personal challenges faced at specific moments in my field research.

Before turning to my empirical investigation, I should also acknowledge that this book is written from a politically and morally engaged perspective. Starting from a point of view that is sympathetic to those who support refugees, this investigation is informed by a desire to uncover contemporary forms of exclusion and oppression; by a critical stance towards the idea of culturally homogenous national identities; and by a sensitivity towards postcolonial continuities (see also Thobani 2015). It is a search for more egalitarian alternatives of togetherness in an age of migration. I therefore also consider it the researcher's obligation to name and speak out against injustices witnessed during the research process (cf. Scheper-Hughes 1995). Nevertheless, I want to stress that I view my study as being separate from works focussing on what has been described as *action research* (Reason & Bradbury 2008), *participatory research* (Pain & Francis 2003) or *activist ethnography* (Juris & Khasnabish 2013; Montesinos Coleman 2015). Despite writing from a politically and morally informed perspective, I take a critical view of the deliberate blurring of the distinction between scientific research and political activism, something evident, for example, in works by scholars associated with *Krit-net*, the German network of critical migration and border research (see for instance Kasparek & Speer 2013). Publications in this research network often speak from explicitly left political perspectives, calling for the unrestricted free global movement of people. Moreover, the network tends to regard itself as a mouthpiece for refugee activists and, in turn, contributes ideologically to activist networks (see Carstensen et al. 2014). This book, by contrast, is guided by the notion that it is a key responsibility of social researchers to consider the multiple perspectives pertaining to a field of investigation; to remain as independent as possible from the subjects of investigation; and to keep a certain critical distance to the topic of investigation. As Czarniawska (1992: 73) aptly puts it: an empathetic stance towards the research subjects should go hand in hand with "a constant urge to problematize, to turn what seems familiar and understandable upside down and inside out".

1.7. An Outline of *Contested Solidarity*

The following empirical investigation into the contested solidarities that developed around the German 'summer of welcome' consists of five chapters. These distinct but interrelated parts analyse differing forms of *contesting*, that is, of making claims and intervening in the conduct of refugee support. The outline of this book thus attests to the elusive character of solidarity. Practices and discourse of migrant solidarity continually adapt to new circumstances; are subject to constant intervention and manifold negotiation processes; and respond to the needs of various actors involved in their contestation. Each of the five subsequent chapters deals with another form of intervention that I encountered in the course of my field research: the *mobilizing, governing, politicizing, recasting* and *breaking of* solidarity with refugees. In the first of these chapters, I start with an analysis of how solidarity was mobilized and how the notion of a 'welcome culture' translated into concrete practices of refugee support on the ground (Chapter 2). In the third, fourth and fifth chapter, I investigate how solidarities and related practices then became subject to the (de)politicizing interventions of different actors, including the state government of Baden-Württemberg, political activists and the asylum seekers themselves. In the sixth chapter, I investigate how solidarities might eventually dissolve and ultimately be broken again. This outline takes into account the wide range of actors involved in the contestation of solidarities and thus offers a multi-perspective view on practices of refugee support. The chapters focus on the solidarity networks that were forged between different groups and individuals (Chapter 2) or on how solidarities and related practices of refugee support were governed through governmental actors (Chapter 3), politicized by those acting in support of refugees (Chapter 4), recast by the asylum seekers themselves (Chapter 5), and eventually broken by refugee activists (Chapter 6).

The second chapter, *Mobilizing Solidarity*, investigates how the notion of a 'welcome culture' became enacted in a small town in the area of my field research and how it translated into immediate practices of refugee support on the ground. I illustrate how different actors mobilized, forged and shaped relationships of solidarity with refugees. My investigation also sheds light on the differing social imaginaries at play as well as on the positionalities and interests of different actors involved. For the purpose of this chapter, I take as my case study the small Swabian town of Ellwangen, which saw the establishment of a new initial reception centre that had to cope with up to 5,000 asylum seekers at a time. The practices of refugee support that developed in this specific context responded to *a moral imperative to act* and *a need to help* that crucially shaped the humanitarian imaginaries at play. The mobilization of such a humanitarian imaginary came with quite contrasting antipolitical and political meanings and effects, ranging from a complicity in the local governance of asylum seekers to the promotion of alternative political and religious world views.

The third chapter, *Governing Solidarity*, analyses how the state government of Baden-Württemberg intervened in order to organize, regulate and coordinate practices of refugee support. Guided by the idea that refugee support requires governmental interference in order to be 'effective', governmental actors launched numerous policies and programmes targeting the section of 'civil society' concerned with refugees. Around the long summer of migration, thus, solidarity with refugees became a major site of governmental intervention. Put differently, the state government sought to govern the rising numbers of asylum seekers through extended state-citizen networks that put an emphasis on humanitarian help and compassion. These *depoliticizing* interventions sought to make committed citizens complicit in the governance of migration, reordered tasks and responsibilities between the entities imagined as 'civil society' and 'the state', and restricted the space for disagreement between the two. Yet, those who engaged in practices of refugee support were often quite critical of these interferences in their role and conduct. Thus, this chapter also illustrates how solidarity with refugees proved to remain to a certain extent ungovernable.

The fourth chapter, *Politicizing Solidarity*, investigates the manifold political possibilities emanating from the practices of refugee support that emerged around the long summer of migration. It sheds light on how different actors or individuals *politicized* the social imaginaries at play, put forward alternative visions of a 'better society' and voiced dissent at governmental policies. What proved to be of particular importance for the purpose of this chapter were my observations at the regular conferences of the Refugee Council of Baden-Württemberg, the umbrella association of citizens' initiatives across the state. This non-governmental organization served as an important platform for volunteers for elaborating political positions towards the governmental handling of asylum seekers. Building on the insights of my field research, I argue that those who supported refugees engaged in a *politics of presence* that sought to bring about change while emphasizing *co-presence*, the physical act of 'being there'. Thus, this chapter investigates how 'the local' became an important means for political claims-making around the long summer of migration.

The fifth chapter, *Recasting Solidarity*, analyses the possibilities for asylum seekers to contest the conditions of their reception and to have a stake in the relationships of solidarity that emerged around the long summer of migration. In the course of my field research, asylum seekers repeatedly staged acts of protest in makeshift reception facilities that were established during the long summer of migration. However, their scope for political agency proved to be contingent on the *intermediation* of the actors involved in their reception, including those who engaged in practices of refugee support. Through their (de)politicizing responses to the protests, these actors influenced whether the asylum seekers' acts were regarded as meaningful political action or emptied of political content. Food, in this context, gained important political meanings: while it served as a means for the asylum seekers to draw attention to their reasons of protest, actors involved in their reception reduced the protests to a distaste for German cuisine. In the course of this chapter, I show how the protesting asylum seekers nonetheless *recast* the social imaginaries of those who engaged in practices of refugee support in a variety of ways.

The sixth chapter, *Breaking Solidarity*, investigates the elusive nature of relationships of solidarity and illustrates how they dissolve and might eventually be broken again. I draw on an intriguing case study in Schwäbisch Gmünd, a small town in the area of my field research. From 2012 to 2015, it became the site of repeated conflicts and disputes between a group of self-described 'refugee activists' and local actors, including citizens supporting refugees in town. My analysis of these moments of conflict illustrates how the social imaginaries pertaining to relationships of solidarity can be so contrasting and conflictive that it becomes impossible to find a common denominator. While the refugee activists accused the local volunteers' initiative for its 'deceptive solidarity', volunteers eventually withdrew all offers of help and support that were previously made to the refugee activists.

The concluding section summarizes the findings on the contested solidarities that emerged around the long summer of migration in Germany. It argues that these findings are telling in regards to wider disputes concerning the parameters of living-together in an increasingly heterogeneous and diverse society. I thus sketch out three lines of contestation in contemporary migration societies that crystallize over the course of this book.

2. MOBILIZING SOLIDARITY: Building Local 'Welcome Culture' through a Moral Imperative to Act

2.1. The Notion of a 'Welcome Culture' and its Mobilizing Effects

Peter Bauer greeted me in his office with a heavy Swabian dialect and a friendly smile when I met him for an interview in April 2015. The grey-haired man in his fifties had been working for the local authority of Ellwangen for several decades. Shortly before I met him for an interview, he was internally relocated to the newly established office of "Refugee Commissioner" ("Flüchtlingsbeauftragter"), meaning that he took on responsibility for all matters concerning the reception and accommodation of asylum seekers in the town. Such offices were introduced in many places in the area of my field research from 2014 onwards, when the arrival of asylum seekers increased and received growing public attention. During my fieldwork in Ellwangen, the small town on the edge of Baden-Württemberg that became a locus of my field research in 2015 and 2016, Peter Bauer was a central contact person, one I met several times to discuss the recent developments surrounding the reception of asylum seekers in the town.

At the first of our meetings in April 2015, I questioned him about the attitudes amongst local residents towards the rising number of asylum seekers arriving in the town. He replied that citizens had shown an extraordinary level of compassion and a remarkably great willingness to "help" the newcomers. Ellwangen, he asserted, presented a particularly successful example for the local implementation of a "welcome culture". He put this as follows:

> "People simply want to help the refugees and that's something I think is really great here in Ellwangen [...] there are so many people volunteering because they see how bad the situation is in their country of origin and because

they see that, here in Ellwangen, they have support. And I always say that the *welcome culture* really means something here."[1] (Interview with Peter Bauer: 16/4/2015, emphasis added)

What remained unspoken during our first conversation, however, was the fact that the arrival of asylum seekers was also accompanied by a remarkable rise in hostile attitudes amongst residents. In late 2014, a new Facebook group protesting against the reception of asylum seekers in Ellwangen gained thousands of members within a few weeks. And yet, Ellwangen's Refugee Commissioner presented the town as a particularly positive example for the creation of a local 'welcome culture'.

Throughout 2015, the notion of a German 'welcome culture' circulated widely across the media and among the public (see for instance Die Zeit: 12/9/2015)[2]. In a nutshell, this vague catchphrase denoted a generally positive or supportive attitude towards the reception of asylum seekers among German citizens (cf. Hamann & Karakayali 2016; Fleischmann & Steinhilper 2017; Karakayali 2017; Sutter 2019). It presented German society as being characterized by a remarkable level of open-mindedness, hospitality and compassion for those in search of refuge and asylum. In the course of my field research in southern Germany, I soon realized that this idea of a 'welcome culture' was also evident at a local level, where it played out in manifold practices of refugee support and was appropriated by a wide range of actors involved in the reception of asylum seekers (cf. Turinsky & Nowicka 2019). Many people emphasized that their town, neighbourhood or village represented a particularly positive example for the creation of a 'welcome culture'.

In this empirical chapter, I investigate how the notion of a 'welcome culture' played out in a specific local context. Taking the small Swabian town of Ellwangen as a case study, I provide insights into the practices of refugee support that emerged around the long summer of migration, illustrating how they became embedded in social imaginaries that framed the reception of asylum seekers in humanitarian parameters. Through a multi-perspective view,

---

1 Translation by LF. German original: "Man will den Flüchtlingen einfach helfen und das find ich einfach bei uns in Ellwangen klasse [...] da gibt es einfach so viele Leute, die sich sozial engagieren, einfach weil sie sehen, wie schlecht es denen im Heimatland geht und weil sie einfach sehen, hier in Ellwangen haben sie Unterstützung und ich sag immer, die Willkommenskultur wird hier einfach groß geschrieben.".
2 See: http://www.zeit.de/2015/37/willkommenskultur-deutschland-fluechtlinge-zeitge ist (last accessed 1/8/2020).

I scrutinize how practices and discourses of refugee support were mobilized, appropriated and shaped by different actors and individuals. This will demonstrate that, on the one hand, the notion of a 'welcome culture' opened up political possibilities to insert change and transformation towards a different alternative. On the other hand, it functioned as a means for governmental actors to take hold of committed citizens and to shape their conduct in ways that benefitted the governments' aims in the reception of asylum seekers.

My local case study of Ellwangen should be read as an extraordinary and intensified example of the developments that unfolded in the course of the long summer of migration. The town sparked my interest in early 2015, when it became the focal point of political and public debates surrounding the reception of asylum seekers in Baden-Württemberg. Shortly before, the government of this south German state had announced its plans to open a new initial reception centre ('Landeserstaufnahmestelle') – or "*LEA*" as my interlocutors called it for short – in the abandoned military barracks of Ellwangen (Baden-Württemberg: 2/10/2014)[3]. The government chose these premises since they could be easily converted into accommodation for a projected 500 to 1,000 asylum seekers, which equated to a capacity of several thousand processed asylum seekers over the course of a year. During the so-called 'refugee crisis', however, these numbers were easily exceeded and the facility was hopelessly overcrowded, hosting more than 5,000 asylum seekers at a time. Within a short period, this small town with a population of 25,000 thus came to play a major role in the reception of asylum seekers not only in Baden-Württemberg but in Germany as a whole. Initial reception centres across the country fall under the jurisdiction of the German *Länder*, Germany's 16 federal states, which in the case of the LEA Ellwangen meant Baden-Württemberg. These facilities served as the initial point of contact for asylum seekers entering the country; it was where they registered their asylum claim, where they received a health screening and where they lived during the first weeks after their arrival, until their transfer to a shared accommodation facility ('Gemeinschaftsunterkunft') in one of the districts of the federal state or their relocation to another federal state[4] (cf. Nettelbladt & Boano 2019: 81).

---

3   See: https://www.baden-wuerttemberg.de/de/service/presse/pressemitteilung/pid/pl aene-fuer-landeserstaufnahmestelle-in-ellwangen-vorgestellt/ (last accessed 1/8/20 20).
4   Asylum seekers within Germany are distributed among the 16 federal states according to the "Königsteiner Schlüssel" (literally "Königstein Key"). This distribution quota is calculated on an annual basis and determines the share of asylum seekers received

The decision to establish the new LEA in Ellwangen was taken at short notice. In mid-2014, the state government of Baden-Württemberg came under increasing pressure to restructure and extend its modes of reception.[5] Around this time, the LEA in Karlsruhe, previously the central reception facility for asylum seekers in Baden-Württemberg, became the subject of media controversy. With the rapidly rising number of asylum seekers since at least 2012, the facility had become hopelessly overcrowded, hosting up to 2,700 individuals at a time (see KA-News: 22/9/2014)[6]. Various media articles reported "chaos" at the facility, a "measles outbreak" among its inhabitants (Bild: 18/7/2014)[7], people sleeping outside due to a lack of spare beds (see KA-News: 8/8/2014)[8], and other examples of deteriorating conditions. Paradoxically, in the years prior to these reports, capacities for asylum seekers had been subject to strategic cutbacks, until, in late 2014, the state government announced plans to decentralize and extend its initial reception capacities in order to bring "urgently needed relief" to the Karlsruhe facility (Baden-Württemberg: 10/3/2015)[9]. One of these new reception centres opened its doors in Ellwangen in April 2015.

I visited the LEA in Ellwangen for the first time in May 2015, just a couple of days after its official inauguration. In the course of my field research the following year, I then returned to the town several times. I was thus able to observe the developments that occurred in Ellwangen before, during and after the long summer of migration. I conducted interviews with diverse actors involved in the reception of asylum seekers, including volunteers, local government representatives, a Catholic priest, employees of social welfare organizations, and the manager of the LEA. In addition, I attended various seminars

    by each *Land* (see BAMF: 1/10/2016). These numbers are calculated based on the tax receipts and populations of the respective states. Accordingly, the state of Baden-Württemberg was allocated 12.9 per cent of all asylum seekers arriving in Germany in 2016 (ibid.).
5   This was illustrated in a discussion at the regional parliament on 17th July 2014.
6   See: http://www.ka-news.de/region/karlsruhe/asyl-karlsruhe./LEA-Chaos-in-Karlsruhe-Es-geht-nicht-so-geordnet-zu-wie-es-sollte;art6066,1481005 (last accessed 1/8/20 20).
7   https://www.bild.de/regional/stuttgart/kritik-an-stuttgart-wegen-unterbringung-von-36872940.bild.html (last accessed 1/8/2020).
8   See: http://www.ka-news.de/region/karlsruhe/asyl-karlsruhe./Karlsruher-Fluechtlings situation-Es-ist-eine-Katastrophe-was-gerade-ablaeuft;art6066,1452907 (last accessed 1/8/2020).
9   See: https://www.baden-wuerttemberg.de/de/service/presse/pressemitteilung/pid/land-organisiert-erstaufnahme-von-fluechtlingen-neu/ (last accessed 1/8/2020).

and events in Ellwangen, such as internal meetings of LEA staff, public information events organized by the local authority, and a seminar for prospective volunteers at the LEA.

The following investigation into the contested solidarities that emerged in Ellwangen around the long summer of migration is structured in two parts. First, I analyse the march 'Ellwangen Shows its Colours' that took place in January 2015, when hundreds of residents took on the streets in support of the soon to be inaugurated LEA. Second, I scrutinize how the notion of a 'welcome culture' became translated into more structured and ongoing practices of refugee support: governmental actors and social welfare organizations mobilized local residents 'to help' as volunteers at the new initial reception facility. Both cases illustrate how the notion of a 'welcome culture' instilled *a moral imperative to act*, a perception that mobilized immediate practices of refugee support revolving around a humanitarian imaginary. These practices and discourses depicted the reception of asylum seekers in morally charged tones and generated feelings of compassion for those 'in need'. And yet, they were not devoid of political and antipolitical meanings, something I will illustrate in the course of this chapter.

2.2. Humanitarian Dissent: The Solidarity March 'Ellwangen Shows its Colours'

When the state government announced its plan to establish a new initial reception centre at the abandoned military barracks in Ellwangen in late 2014, right-wing groups were quick to stir up hostile attitudes among local residents. By the end of 2014, the newly founded Facebook group "No Asylum Seeker Accommodation at Reinhardt Barracks" ("Kein Asylheim in der Reinhardtskaserne") boasted several thousand members. And even before the first asylum seeker had moved into the LEA, right-wing groups were organizing a demonstration that would signal their opposition to the decision to open a reception facility in the town.

In this tense atmosphere, two initiatives joined forces in order to counteract the rise of hostile attitudes in the town, arranging a "solidarity march" ("Solidaritätszug") under the banner "Ellwangen Shows Its Colours" ("Ellwangen zeigt Flagge"). On a cold winter's day in January 2015, more than 1,000 people marched through the streets of Ellwangen in order to signal their support for the reception of asylum seekers and the development of a local 'welcome culture'. This 'solidarity march' was jointly organized by the well-known local peace group "Mahnwache Ellwangen" ("Vigil Ellwangen") and the hitherto unknown "Aktionsgruppe Solidarität" ("Solidarity Action Group").

Father Feldmann[10], an 80-year-old Catholic priest, was one of the organizers of the event and a member of the Mahnwache group. During one of my field trips to the town, I interviewed him at the premises of the Comboni order of Catholic missionaries, where he lived and worked. He told me that he remembered no other instance in the past years, maybe even decades, when as many citizens were mobilized to march through the streets of Ellwangen for a common purpose. Indeed, the organizers succeeded not only in mobilizing a high number of participants but also in bringing a broad range of around fifty groups and well-known individuals from the region to lend their support to the event. The resulting alliance joined major political parties, the town's mayor, church communities, local schools and a wide range of civil society initiatives ranging from the football fan club "Sankt Pauli Province Fanatics" to the Turkish-Islamic cultural association. In addition, the event attracted a high level of attention from local and regional newspapers.

In the following sections, I investigate the discourses and practices surrounding this solidarity march in more detail. I illustrate how the two organizing groups appropriated the notion of a 'welcome culture' and translated it into concrete action on the ground. During campaigning, the organizing groups mobilized a *moral imperative to act* and strategically embedded the event in an ostensibly 'apolitical' humanitarian imaginary in order to attract 'ordinary citizens' and a broad range of supporters. Looking behind the scenes, however, we find this event was not as free from political reasoning as it appeared: it figured as a means for the organizers to promote their religious and political beliefs and to voice dissent towards governmental decisions.

2.2.1. Mobilizing a Moral Imperative to Act

In order to mobilize participants for the solidarity march, the organizing groups designed and circulated "mobi material", as they called it short for "mobilization material", which included flyers, posters and the launch of a

---

10 Throughout this chapter, I refer to my interlocutor Paul Feldmann as "Father Feldmann" as this reflects how he identified himself and how others in the town referred to him ("Pater Feldmann").

website. Taking a closer look at this material, I soon realized that the organizers remained vague and unspecific about the political objectives and demands of the event. Rather than voicing political dissent, it appeared, the solidarity march aimed at sending a general message in support of the reception of asylum seekers in the town.

It was thus not so much the concrete (political) objectives or claims with which the organizers set out to mobilize people to join the march, but rather their evocation of moral sentiments. For instance, the official flyer of the event appealed to the citizens of Ellwangen with the following words:

"Ellwangen Shows its Colours – for a future for refugees based on solidarity and justice. We are calling on the citizens of Ellwangen to back this rallying cry and join us on a solidarity march through the centre of town. On 24th January 2015, we will take to the streets as a broad alliance of people in support of this cause. Together, we will send a clear message that those who have fled war, hunger, poverty and discrimination are welcome here!"[11] (Official flyer of the solidarity march, January 2015)

By presenting the solidarity march in such a way, I would argue, the organizers invoked a *moral imperative to act*, a feeling of being obligated to stand up for those who are worse off, in this case suffering asylum seekers arriving in Ellwangen. Observations on the mobilizing qualities of moral sentiments have been made in other academic works. Scholars writing on the practices of refugee support that emerged around the long summer of migration have repeatedly emphasized the role of emotions, such as compassion, for mobilizing and recruiting new volunteers (Karakayali 2017; Kleres 2018; Sirriyeh 2018; Armbruster 2019; Doidge & Sandri 2019; Gomez, Newell & Vannini 2020; Maestri & Monforte 2020). This emphasis on emotions and moral sentiments also connects strikingly to works on humanitarian action. Ticktin, in her book *Casualties of Care*, argues that an emphasis on human suffering triggers morally mandated humanitarian responses. She illustrates how, in

---

11 Translation by LF. German original: "Ellwangen zeigt Flagge – Für eine Zukunft Geflüchteter Menschen in Solidarität und Gerechtigkeit. Mit dieser Zielsetzung rufen wir zu einem Solidaritätszug durch die Ellwanger Innenstadt auf. Am 24. Januar 2015 wollen wir mit einem breiten Bündnis für dieses Anliegen auf die Straße. gehen und gemeinsam mit der Ellwanger Bevölkerung ein Zeichen setzen, welches deutlich macht, dass Menschen, die vor Krieg, Hunger, Armut und Diskriminierung flüchten müssen, bei uns willkommen sind!".

the context of the reception of asylum seekers in France, "a moral imperative to relieve suffering" had emerged, a notion that inspired the formation of "regimes of care" spanning both governmental and civil society actors (Ticktin 2011: 2). Chouliaraki (2012: 11) argues that 'doing good' is quite often driven by a moral imperative to act for the vision of a "suffering-free humanity", while, in his monograph *Humanitarian Reason* (2012), Fassin outlines how "moral sentiments" generate compassion and prompt immediate actions for the sake of others.

In the case of the solidarity march in Ellwangen, the mobilization of a *moral imperative to act* was based on two specific framings. Firstly, the organizers portrayed the event as an "expression of humanity" and, secondly, they claimed that it would be "outside" or "above" politics. This particular social imaginary promoted by the organizers is encapsulated in an online news report on the press conference held by the organizers:

"Chairman Paul Feldmann made clear that the various groups do *not aim to send a political message* but, as a broad alliance standing above party lines and rooted in the centre ground of society, want to offer an *expression of humanity*." (beobachternews.de: 21/1/2015, emphasis added)[12]

The local media echoed this imaginary in the run-up to the event. For instance, an article in a local newspaper quoted the town's mayor, who backed the solidarity march with the words: "It is never too early to speak up for an *act of humanity*" (Gmünder Tagespost: 7/1/2015, emphasis added)[13]. Another local newspaper article asserted that the march was about "underlining that [...] the establishment of a new initial reception centre at the former barracks of Ellwangen is a *natural act of humanity*" (Schwäbische Post: 22/1/2015, emphasis added)[14]. Thus, the act of marching through the streets of Ellwangen in support of asylum seekers was depicted not as a political message but as

---

12 See: http://www.beobachternews.de/2015/01/21/nonnen-an-der-seite-der-antifa/ (last accessed 1/8/2020). Translation by LF. German original: "[...] machte der Versammlungsleiter Paul Feldmann deutlich, dass die verschiedenen Gruppen keine politische Aussage zum Ziel hätten, sondern als 'breites, überparteiliches Bündnis aus der Mitte der Gesellschaft' ein Zeichen der Menschlichkeit setzen wollten".
13 See: http://www.gmuender-tagespost.de/p/781918/ (last accessed 1/8/2020).
14 See: http://www.schwaebische-post.de/p/784179/ (last accessed 1/8/2020). Translation by LF. German original: „verdeutlichen dass [...] die Einrichtung einer Erstaufnahmestelle in der ehemaligen Kaserne in Ellwangen ein selbstverständlicher Akt der Menschlichkeit ist".

a "moral endeavour based on solidarity with other members of humanity" (Terry quoted in Scott-Smith 2016).

Works in the anthropology of humanitarianism and beyond have discussed how the notion of a shared identity of humanity figures, alongside the principles of neutrality and impartiality, as a key characteristic of humanitarian action (see Nyers 2006a: 27; Barnett 2011; Fassin 2012). Calhoun (2010: 31) describes this conception as the notion of "a mass of individuals equally entitled to care, and a sense of ethical obligation based on common humanity, rather than on citizenship or any specific loyalty". The mobilizing qualities of the idea of humanity are also stressed by Fassin (2012: 2) who argues that the impetus for humanitarian action stems from the "concept of humanity" since it comes with an "affective movement drawing humans toward their fellows". Similarly, I would suggest that the notion of the solidarity march as an 'act of humanity' generated compassion among the residents of Ellwangen and a feeling of being obligated to stand up for asylum seekers.

At the same time, the organizers framed the march as an 'apolitical' and 'impartial endeavour'. The article on beobachternews.de cited above quoted my interlocutor Father Feldmann, who emphasized that the event "did not aim to send a political message", but rather stood "above party lines" and was rooted in the "centre ground of society". In doing so, he presented the public demonstration of a supportive stance towards the reception of asylum seekers in Ellwangen as an apolitical practice that transcended political positions. This claim to stand 'outside' or 'above' politics, I would argue, was critical to the mobilization of a high number of participants: it assured them that they were not taking political sides or causing agitation. Through such means, the organizers depicted the demonstration of welcoming attitudes towards asylum seekers as 'natural' common sense.

Works in social anthropology and beyond have discussed how a claim of 'apolitical' action represents another key premise of a humanitarian imaginary (Feldman & Ticktin 2010; Bornstein & Redfield 2011a; Fassin 2012; Ticktin 2014). Ticktin (2011: 19) remarks that "those who act in the name of the moral imperative generally claim to be apolitical – beyond or outside politics". Nyers (2006a: 27) argues that politics and humanitarianism are generally thought of as occupying two opposing poles: "humanitarian action and political action are cast as two distinct and separate modes of acting and being-in-the-world". While the former carries negative connotations, such as being cynical, self-interested or amoral, the latter is framed as its positive counterpart – as compassionate, principled or impartial (ibid.). In practice, however, this distinction is clearly not as straightforward as it might appear. Scholars have discussed public demonstrations – such as the 'solidarity march' in Ellwangen – as a 'classical' performative tool for voicing political dissent, and thus as a form of political action (see Butler 2011; Butler 2015). And yet, the organizers of the solidarity march in Ellwangen framed it as an 'apolitical' endeavour.

The idea of the solidarity march as a symbol of humanity that existed 'outside' or 'above' politics was underlined by the emphasis placed on the broad range of actors behind the march. The mobilization material repeatedly stressed that the event aimed to unite a 'broad coalition' that together would support the welcoming of asylum seekers to Ellwangen:

> "Let us, *as a broad alliance*, raise awareness of the present situation in Ellwangen, which does not signal the downfall of the Occident, but instead represents opportunity and enrichment. Let us [...] show what Ellwangen is really about: open-mindedness, social commitment and solidarity!" (Official flyer of the solidarity march, emphasis added)[15]

This excerpt indicates how the organizers established an 'us', an inclusive subjectivity of which the reader is assumed to be part. The official list of supporters, which features at the bottom of the flyer, did indeed seem quite impressive. Around 50 groups and individuals were named, spanning remarkably diverse fields and interests, various civil society initiatives, religious groups and church parishes, left-wing activist groups, local high schools and other public institutions, trade unions, political parties and local government representatives. The organizers' ability to win such a broad alliance of supporters, I would argue, reassured potential participants that by getting involved they would not be taking political sides. In fact, they might even have feared that as non-participants they would risk being seen as outsiders. This significance of a 'broad alliance' points to what Agustín and Jørgensen (2019: 31) consider a key characteristic of solidarity: "alliance building is a crucial aspect of solidarity". In a similar vein, alliance building was central to the mobilization of solidarity with refugees in Ellwangen.

Several newspaper articles also took up this theme of a broad and unusual alliance when reporting on the upcoming event. For instance, the online news

---

15   Translation by LF. German original: "Lasst uns deshalb als breites Bündnis ein Bewusstsein schaffen, dass unsere aktuelle Situation in Ellwangen nicht den Untergang des Abendlandes bedeutet, sondern eine Chance und Bereicherung darstellt. Lasst uns [...] Ellwangen als das zeigen, was es ist: solidarisch, weltoffen und engagiert!".

platform beobachternews.de published an article with the eye-catching headline "Nuns and Antifa activists side by side", highlighting the heterogeneity of the actors involved in an almost ironic way. Another article in a regional newspaper speaks of a "solidarity march of the centre of society" ("Ein Solidaritätszug der Mitte") (Schwäbische Post: 19/1/2015). This notion of a socio-political "centre ground of society" that backed the march was repeatedly evoked during campaigning since it reinforced the notion of 'apolitical' action. It reassured people that participation in the march would not be 'extremism', that it was simply a march of ordinary Ellwangen citizens in which their next door neighbours might also take part.

In his study on the 2006 mega-marches in the United States, Gonzales (2009) notes a similar pattern. These marches brought millions of people onto the streets of major American cities, people taking a stand for the rights of undocumented immigrants. They were among the biggest public demonstrations in the history of the U.S.. According to Gonzales, the unprecedented success of these mobilizations was founded on their ability to unite a broad alliance of actors in support of undocumented migrants, what he terms a "counter-hegemonic moment" in reference to the work of Antonio Gramsci (1971). According to Gramsci, the struggle for hegemony is ultimately a "struggle of objectivity" (Gramsci quoted in Riley 2011) through which views are presented as objective truth. In a similar vein, the two organizing groups portrayed supportive acts for the reception of asylum seekers in Ellwangen as an 'objective truth' that transcended political positions and interests. At closer examination, however, the march was clearly not as devoid of political messages and interests as it first appeared. I will look at this in more detail in the following section.

2.2.2. Behind the Scenes of 'Apolitical' Action

If we look behind the scenes, the political positionalities and interests of the two organizing groups turn out to be a key cornerstone of the solidarity march. By claiming to be apolitical, however, they intentionally concealed these positionalities in order to mobilize a larger number of participants and to generate a higher level of public attention. My insights into their behind-the-scenes negotiations, which I present in the course of this subsection, are based on my interview with Father Feldmann, who was a leading member of "Mahnwache Ellwangen". Since I was unable to detect the members of the second initiative, "Aktionsgruppe Solidarität", and win them for an interview during my field research, these findings are however partial and tentative.

It was some days before Christmas 2014, Father Feldmann remembered, when he and the fellow members of the Mahnwache peace group received unusual visitors. A group of young "adolescents" – in the eyes of the 80-year-old priest and the other mostly retired members of the group – addressed them regarding an urgent matter. They were deeply worried about the rise of hostile attitudes in light of the decision to open a new initial reception centre in the town, as my interlocutor recalled. The group consisted of a handful of students who were born and raised in Ellwangen and had moved to cities in eastern Germany to study. They called on the peace initiative with the aim of working together in order to "do something" about these rising right-wing attitudes and raised their idea of organizing a public demonstration in Ellwangen. Since some of the members of the Mahnwache group, including Father Feldmann, had recently been very active in support of asylum seekers in the town, they shared the students' concerns about rising hostility and eventually agreed to "give their support" to these "dedicated young people" (Interview with Paul Feldmann: 15/3/2016). The main incentive in initiating what the organizers would later label a solidarity march was thus the desire to counteract hostile attitudes towards asylum seekers and agitation by right-wing groups in the town. The organizers may have presented the march as an 'apolitical' humanitarian endeavour, but they evidently did aim to send a message regarding political attitudes in Ellwangen.

To my surprise, Father Feldmann recalled during our interview that, at their first meeting, the students introduced themselves as members of the 'Antifa'. This short form of 'antifascist action' stands for a loosely connected network of anarchist and autonomous groups who clearly identify themselves as left-wing political activists (for more information see Schuhmacher 2015). These left-wing political positions, however, were not made public, with the activists campaigning under the name "Action Group Solidarity" in the run-up to the event and thus deliberately concealing their left-wing, activist identity.

The shared incentive to organize a solidarity march in Ellwangen thus brought together a rather unusual and contrasting pairing of initiatives. The young antifascist activists may have represented left-wing political positions but, as Father Feldmann stressed, the Mahnwache peace group was determined not to take political sides. Instead, my interlocutor told me, members of the initiative "advocated for peace" and maintained a "pacifistic" position. Each Saturday morning, when the town centre is packed with week-end shoppers, members of the group gather at Fuchseck, the town's central square, my interlocutor explained. They discuss what was in the newspapers that week and raise awareness of various issues, including conflicts such as the war in Iraq or Syria, the arms trade, or the Charlie Hebdo terror attacks in Paris. Due to their regular public visibility, Father Feldman stressed, the Mahnwache group was well known and respected by many in the town. This esteem was enhanced by the fact that most of its members were part of the "intellectual bourgeoisie" ("Bildungsbürgertum") of Ellwangen, including retired physicians and priests as well as the chairperson of the local branch of the left-wing political party Die Linke. However, my interlocutor emphasized, the Mahnwache initiative is neither religious nor political but rather "transcends these boundaries" (Interview with Paul Feldmann: 15/3/2016). Apparently, however, this intention did not always work out in practice, as was illustrated by Father Feldmann's remark that passers-by sometimes took the Mahnwache group for a religious cult: "Some maybe confuse us with Jehova's Witnesses or something like that" (ibid.). I would suggest that parallels could be drawn between the group and the German peace movement of the 1980s (see Schmitt-Beck 1990), while the term 'Mahnwache', which roughly translates as 'vigil', dates back to at least the 1950s and signifies a peaceful public gathering intending to raise awareness of a social problem (Otto 1977). More recently, the term received renewed attention when several groups, primarily in eastern Germany, chose it as the label for their own activities, which they often claimed to be outside of politics (Daphi et al. 2014).

Despite their differences, the collaboration between the left-wing political activists and Mahnwache Ellwangen offered important synergistic effects. For instance, this is apparent from the following statement by Father Feldmann:

"And they said: 'As Mahnwache, you have a certain pool of interest that you can motivate and we motivate via Facebook around 150. If you mobilize 100 more, so together we can attract 250 people, then we organize something in the town [...] and then we said: if the youth are taking the initiative over something like this themselves, then we want to give them our support."[16] (Interview with Paul Feldmann: 15/3/2016)

The collaboration was thus partly based on the perception that each of the groups was able to mobilize a distinct "pool" of participants and target groups for the event. While Mahnwache was more likely to recruit local actors and participants to the event, the antifascist activists were able to mobilize additional support from outside the town's boundaries via their activist networks on Facebook. During our interview, Father Feldmann put forward another reason why the young activists had sought support from the Mahnwache group: the high standing of its members in the town and the initiative's ostensibly politically neutral position would lend the solidarity march greater respectability. By contrast, if the activists had organized the march on their own and by openly identifying themselves as left-wing activists and members of the antifascist movement, "ordinary citizens" would have been "put off" from participating in the march. My interlocutor explained this as follows:

LF: "Why do you think reading 'Antifa' would have put people off?"
PF: That's just the way it is today. Left- and right-wing, both of them, they put ordinary citizens off [...] They associate them with stone-throwing or such like. So it is important to us, if I can put it like this [...] we are not against this, but, with our peace campaigning, we aim to speak to those in the centre ground"[17] (Interview with Paul Feldmann: 15/3/2016)

In Father Feldmann's eyes, an explicit political position would have been associated with deviant, dangerous or criminal behaviour such as the "throwing of stones" while "ordinary citizens" would not have wanted to associate themselves with such behaviour. During campaigning, the organizers thus strate-

---

16   Translation by LF. German original: "Und die haben gesagt: 'Ihr habt von der Mahnwache, ihr habt einen gewissen Interessenpool, den ihr motivieren könnt und wir machen über Facebook, wir motivieren auch bis zu 150 und so weiter. Wenn ihr nochmal 100 zusammenkriegt, dann sind wir 250, da können wir schon was machen in der Stadt [...] da haben wir gesagt: ‚Mensch, wenn Jugendliche für sowas selber die Initiative ergreifen, dann wollen wir ihnen auch ihre Unterstützung geben'.".
17   Translation by LF. German original: LF: "Warum meinen Sie, das hätte die Leute verschreckt, wenn sie 'Antifa' gelesen hätten? PF: "Das ist heute genauso. Sowohl das linke als auch das rechte Spektrum, egal ... schreckt den Normalbürger [...] Damit assoziiert man Steine werfen oder so etwas. Wir wollten also ... es ist uns schon wichtig, ich möchte das mal so sagen [...] wir haben da nichts dagegen und möchten mit unserer Friedensarbeit möchten schon die Mitte der Bevölkerung ansprechen.".

gically concealed the left-wing political leanings of the young antifascist activists in order not to put off 'ordinary citizens', Father Feldmann recalled. In her seminal work on *The Politics of Volunteering*, Eliasoph (2013: 43) observes a similar pattern: she argues that 'political activism' commonly evokes negative feelings and connotations, while 'volunteering', in contrast, is mostly treated in positive terms. She puts this as follows: "In our shared imagination, the volunteer feels comfortably warm, while the activist either feels too coolly intellectual or too hot-headed. In our collective imagination, the nice, agreeable volunteer reads to pre-schoolers, while the activist pickets and shouts" (ibid.). As she goes on to argue, this "makes activism look potentially too difficult and risky for ordinary people" (ibid.). In an attempt to avoid these negative preconceptions with 'ordinary people', the young activists thus strategically disclosed their political alignment to the public.

In the term "solidarity" they found a positive alternative; a common denominator that was deemed acceptable by both organizing groups. This crystallized in two behind-the-scenes negotiations that underpinned the collaboration between the organizing groups and aimed for a positive and less-biased public image. Firstly, the activists campaigned as "Aktionsgruppe Solidarität", which, according to Father Feldmann, was a new and therefore less partisan name. Secondly, the event was promoted not as a 'demonstration' or 'protest' but as a "solidarity march", an unusual term for a public demonstration. Father Feldmann explained the reasoning as follows:

> "Yes, this solidarity march, there was a discussion as to whether we should say a 'protest march'. So we said, we don't want to call it a demonstration, because then you think of being against something and, we said, we don't want to be against anything; we want take to the streets to show our support for a welcome culture for refugees. And so we tried to bring on board as many people as possible – churches, associations [...]"[18] (Interview with Paul Feldmann: 15/3/2016)

---

18 Translation by LF. German original: „Ja dieser Solidaritätszug, es war eine Diskussion, ob wir es Protestmarsch nennen sollen. Also wir haben gesagt, wir wollen nicht ‚Demonstration' sagen, da assoziiert man ja irgendwas dagegen und da haben wir gesagt, wir wollen ja eigentlich nicht gegen, sondern wir wollen für eine Willkommenskultur für Flüchtlinge auf die Straße gehen. Und da haben wir halt versucht, alles so irgendwie möglich ins Boot zu holen, die Kirchen, die Vereine [...]".

Although the initial motivation for organizing the march was to act *against* right-wing tendencies, the organizers decided to present the event as a march *for* solidarity and a local "welcome culture" – and thus *for* a common purpose. This sending of a positive message, Father Feldmann remarked, enabled the organizers to attract a broader range of supporters and participants to the event. They avoided the words "protest march" and "demonstration" since these were more likely to be associated with a specific political position and, instead, decided to employ new and less partisan terms. In the eyes of the organizers, the chosen labels "Action Group Solidarity" and "solidarity march" were both free from political preconceptions. I would thus argue that such a framing was critical to the success and high public profile of the event.

These behind-the-scenes insights into the solidarity march in Ellwangen indicate that an 'apolitical' humanitarian imaginary may be strategically invoked by certain actors in order to promote their own interests and to open up political possibilities on the grassroots level. Existing works on humanitarianism, however, have often investigated how an 'apolitical' humanitarian imaginary becomes complicit in forms of domination and governing 'from above' (see for instance Bornstein & Redfield 2011b; Ticktin 2011). I would argue that such an emphasis on the adverse effects of humanitarian action risks neglecting the diverse and contested reasonings and interests behind an 'apolitical' framing. This resonates with the writings of Redfield (2011: 56) who points to these often overlooked dimensions of 'apolitical' action: "The refusal of political positioning not only has political effects, it is also a political strategy". He thus regards a claim of 'apolitical' action not as being devoid of politics but instead as a political tool. Similarly, Hilhorst and Bram (2010: 1118) highlight that an 'apolitical' positioning may be "strategically or tacitly used by different actors to advance or legitimize their respective interests, projects or beliefs". Vandevoordt and Verschraegen (2019: 124) thus speak of "subversive humanitarianism", which they conceive as "a form of direct action that gains political momentum precisely through its apolitical appearance". This becomes even clearer when we take a closer look at how the actual solidarity march served as a platform for promoting and performing the organizers' political and religious worldviews.

2.2.3. The Political Messages of the Solidarity March

Although the organizers presented the solidarity march as an "apolitical expression of humanity" during campaigning, they did not shy away from sending out their own particular messages on the day of the event. On the one hand, the young left-wing activists marched through the streets of Ellwangen bearing 'Antifa' flags, chanting political songs and proclaiming their political demands through a megaphone. On the other hand, Father Feldmann promoted his Christian beliefs and values among participants at the event. Both organizing groups thus used the actual solidarity march as a means to send out covert messages that responded to their own interests. This becomes strikingly illustrated, when we take a closer look at their speeches to the march's roughly 1,000 participants at the day of event.

The members of the 'Aktionsgruppe Solidarität' not only took a stand against right-wing attitudes and groups but also voiced dissent towards the government and its asylum laws. Repeatedly, the young activists criticized specific policies and laws that they deemed discriminating while advocating for the rights of asylum seekers. The following excerpt from their speech offers one example:

> "It is often forgotten that the Residence Obligation and work bans deny the refugees any possibility of work and self-fulfilment. These people want to participate in our society, but they are being hindered by the state."[19] (Speech by Aktionsgruppe Solidarität: 24/1/2015)

As this quote shows, these covert antifascist activists did not hesitate to take a stand *against* "the state" and openly voiced criticisms of existing laws and policies such as the "Residence Obligation", which declares that asylum seekers must remain within a defined geographical area and thus substantially restricts their movement (see also Chapter 6). The activists blamed the German state for directly "hindering" the inclusion of asylum seekers into German society. Later on, their speech also denounced both German and European asylum policies for being "racist" and for distinguishing between "useful" and "useless" refugees (Speech by Aktionsgruppe Solidarität: 24/1/2015).

Furthermore, the activists called attention to the wider capitalist context in which the reception of asylum seekers in Ellwangen unfolded. They claimed that "we live in a world of global violence and exploitation" and called for the breaking down of all boundaries and territorial borders (ibid.). Moreover,

---

19   Translation by LF. German original: „Hier wird oftmals vergessen, dass Residenzpflicht und Arbeitsverbote den Flüchtlingen jegliche Form von Arbeit und freier Entfaltung nehmen. Gerade diese Menschen sind es, die an unserer Gesellschaft teilhaben wollen, aber von staatlicher Seite daran gehindert werden".

they directly blamed the German government for producing "causes of flight", claiming that the German arms trade and the uneven distribution of capital were forcing asylum seekers to leave their countries of origin. By doing so, they placed the solidarity march in a wider context of global inequalities and exploitation while voicing their dissent towards the status quo. The ostensibly 'apolitical' march in support of asylum seekers thus served as a means for the activists to promote their anti-capitalist world views.

The activists also voiced their dissent towards the local political context that surrounded the implementation of a new initial reception centre at the abandoned military barracks in Ellwangen:

> "For us, it goes without saying that we will follow decisions concerning the LEA and, if necessary, raise awareness of any irregularities. For instance, in connection with the commissioning of European Homecare. This company, which has been publicly criticized over the abuse of asylum seekers, should no longer be given responsibilities in refugee accommodation or initial reception centres."[20] (Speech by Aktionsgruppe Solidarität: 24/1/2015)

With this statement, the activists painted themselves as critical observers and declared that they would not hesitate to take a stand *against* governmental decisions concerning the LEA, even though the solidarity march had, during campaigning, been portrayed as a general expression of support *for* the establishment of the facility.

The solidarity march served as a political platform not only for the antifascist activists but also for Father Feldmann, whose speech contained various messages promoting his Christian beliefs and values. He linked these beliefs and values with criticisms of social and political developments surrounding the reception of asylum seekers. Interestingly, Father Feldmann did not speak on behalf of Mahnwache Ellwangen but instead addressed the audience in his own name. This might be explained by the fact that, in his speech, he clearly positioned himself as a Catholic priest and member of the Catholic congre-

---

20 Translation by LF. German original: "Für uns ist klar, dass wir Entscheidungen, welche die LEA betreffen, begleiten und, wenn nötig, auf Missstände aufmerksam machen. Zum Beispiel bezüglich der Beauftragung von European Homecare. Dieses Unternehmen, welches öffentlich in der Kritik bezüglich der Misshandlung von Asylsuchenden steht, darf keine Aufgaben in Flüchtlingswohnheimen und Landeserstaufnahmestellen mehr bekommen.".

gation, a stance that would perhaps not have tallied with the peace group's 'apolitical' identity.

Father Feldmann's speech was filled with religious metaphors and anecdotes. In it, the 80-year-old priest and member of the Comboni order of missionaries repeatedly cited lines from the Bible and referred to "his Christian belief" and "his Christian values" (Speech by Paul Feldmann: 24/1/2015). A particularly clear example of this came when he referred to the Christian confirmations taking place at the Catholic church of Ellwangen at the same time:

> "By the way, a confirmation service is taking place right now at St Wolfgang's Church. In terms of meaning and substance, confirmation fits very well with the purpose of this rally. It is about responsibility in the world."[21] (Speech by Paul Feldmann: 24/1/2015)

This quote aptly illustrates how Father Feldmann linked his Christian beliefs with the purpose of the event. In other words, he used his speech at the solidarity march not only to foster a positive attitude towards the reception of asylum seekers but also to promote the values of confirmation, a key rite in most Christian denominations.

He also linked his religious beliefs directly with recent political and social developments surrounding the reception of asylum seekers in Germany, while taking a clear stance and voicing dissent. For instance, at the beginning of his speech, Father Feldmann referred to the nativity story and jokingly asserted that, if you were to take out all those figures who originated from the Orient rather than the Occident, there would be nobody left around the crib except the donkey (ibid.). Through this anecdote, he implicitly criticized the right-wing Pegida movement, which claims to represent the 'Occident', i.e. the Christian world. Pegida had been promoting hostile attitudes towards asylum seekers and Muslims since late 2014, attracting thousands of people to its weekly marches across the country. Later in his speech, Father Feldmann also blamed Pegida explicitly for misapplying Christian symbols. To the Catholic priest, a proper Christian belief should take its cue from Jesus Christ, who promoted compassion and hospitality towards strangers. In this context, he put forward his own interpretation of what a proper Christian position towards the reception of asylum seekers would be:

---

21   Translation by LF. German original: "Übrigens ist gerade jetzt zu dieser Stunde Firmungsgottesdienst in der Wolfgangkirche. Vom Sinn und Gehalt her passt Firmung und diese Kundgebung sehr gut zusammen. Es geht ja um Verantwortung in der Welt.".

"I would take strangers to mean not only 'war refugees' in the narrow sense of the word but also those who want to leave a poor country that offers no prospects. These young people have their lives in front of them too. Who can blame them for this wish? Our society will change. The unknown is always alien to us. When we get to know it, it becomes familiar."[22] (Speech by Paul Feldmann: 24/1/2015)

Speaking from the position of a Catholic priest, he thus took a clear political stand on the reception of asylum seekers. This connects strikingly with what Wyller (2019) outlines: around the long summer of migration, some churches and religious organizations did not hesitate to resist and counteract governmental policies and actions they deemed unjust. The quote illustrates how Father Feldman also openly criticized the government's distinction between 'genuine' and 'bogus' asylum seekers, between refugees who fled war-torn countries and those deemed economic migrants (see also Ratfisch 2015). In doing so, he called on participants of the solidarity march to give asylum seekers in the town an unconditional welcome.

Furthermore, Father Feldmann voiced his dissent towards governmental decisions surrounding the implementation of the new initial reception centre in Ellwangen. In the final part of his speech, he directly addressed "those responsible in the state government and on the local council", asking them for direct changes in the plans for operating the soon to be inaugurated facility.

Taken together, the mobilization of a *moral imperative to act* served as a political tool for the organizers to promote their left-wing worldviews and religious messages. The case of the solidarity march thus clearly illustrates the powerful political potentials stemming from the notion of a 'welcome culture' and its humanitarian imaginary: it was appropriated by political groups and civil society initiatives with the aim of promoting social and political transformations on a grassroots level. There is, however, another side of the coin. In the following section, I take a closer look at how the notion of a 'welcome culture' became translated into more long-term volunteering practices at the new initial reception centre in Ellwangen. In this case, governmental actors

---

22　Translation by LF. German original: "Ich möchte unter Fremden nicht nur Kriegsflüchtlinge im engeren Sinn verstehen, sondern auch solche, die aus der Perspektivlosigkeit in einem verarmten Land herauskommen wollen. Auch diese jungen Leute haben ein Leben vor sich. Wer kann ihnen den Wunsch verdenken? Unsere Gesellschaft wird sich ändern. Alles, was wir nicht kennen, ist uns fremd. Wenn wir es kennen, wird es uns vertraut.".

appropriated a humanitarian imaginary in order to make committed citizens complicit in the local governance of asylum seekers.

2.3. Humanitarian Governance: Volunteering with Refugees in Ellwangen

Soon after its inauguration in March 2015, the initial reception centre in Ellwangen was operating far beyond its limits. In the course of 2015, employees and officials in charge of the LEA were increasingly unable to provide for even the most basic needs of the new arrivals. This situation also presented an extraordinary challenge for Peter Bauer, the local authority's Refugee Commissioner. During our second interview in March 2016, he recalled how he had been increasingly under pressure to mediate between the actors involved and the local population in Ellwangen. He also recounted how the relationship between the local council and the state government of Baden-Württemberg, which was formally in charge of the reception centre, had become increasingly conflicted in the latter half of 2015: the mayor of Ellwangen had urged the state government to come up with solutions for relocating asylum seekers to other towns and districts.

This emergency situation, Peter Bauer emphasized repeatedly, could not have been managed without citizens' extraordinary willingness 'to help' as volunteers at the facility. The following statement is a case in point:

"You can't say it often enough to people who volunteer what an important job they do. I always say, this is the *backbone of society*, if I can put it like that. If there wasn't such a willingness to volunteer, you wouldn't be able to run such a facility."[23] (Interview with Peter Bauer: 7/3/2016, emphasis added)

From the perspective of the local authority, thus, the volunteers at the LEA played an essential role in the reception of asylum seekers in town. Indeed, as I realized in the course of my field research, volunteers and governmental actors often formed a symbiosis in response to the emergency situation that

---

23 Translation by LF. German original: "Das muss man aber immer wieder auch den Leuten sagen, die wo ehrenamtlich arbeiten, sagen, was für eine wichtige Arbeit die leisten. Ich sag immer, das ist ja eigentlich das Rückgrat einer Gesellschaft, wenn man das so ausdrücken darf. Wenn es so ein Ehrenamt nicht gäbe, dann könnte man eine solche LEA nicht betreiben.".

characterized the second half of 2015: While volunteers stepped in where local authorities were unable to provide for the basic needs of asylum seekers, volunteers had their efforts honoured and their individual interests rewarded by governmental actors. In the following sections, I scrutinize how the notion of a 'welcome culture' was translated into volunteering activities on the ground. I show how governmental actors and social welfare organizations appropriated a humanitarian imaginary in order to mobilize a *need to help* among local residents, making them part of a symbiotic relationship.

2.3.1. Mobilizing a Need to Help

Soon after its opening, hundreds of local residents became actively involved at the LEA through regular volunteering activities. These included, for instance, teaching German language classes at the facility, organizing social activities for the new arrivals, sorting and distributing tons of donations and assisting at the 'Baby Room', a childcare centre and nursery. Volunteering at the facility, however, was not possible on an independent or self-organized basis. Instead, the state government of Baden-Württemberg had commissioned the social welfare organization "Caritas", which is affiliated to the Catholic Church, to coordinate and manage the activities of volunteers at the facility. Caritas received funding in order to employ three "Volunteer Coordinators", who served as primary contact persons for all volunteers at the LEA.

One of these volunteers was Bernhard Thiele, a retired teacher in his late sixties who wore his age well. We met at the premises of the LEA in Ellwangen for an interview in March 2016. Finding my way through the confusing maze of buildings at the former military site, I eventually came to our arranged meeting point: the small building where volunteers had established a 'German school' for asylum seekers wanting to learn German. Bernhard Thiele was one of several volunteers who twice a week helped with the teaching of German language classes at the facility. He told me that he had always loved his job as a teacher at an Ellwangen high school, where he had worked for more than forty years. For decades, he had also been a member of the local SPD, the German Social Democratic Party and, ever since, had been active in contributing to the 'public good' in the town, for instance, through his position as a representative of a residential neighbourhood ("Ortsvorsteher"). When Bernhard Thiele went into retirement, he and his wife sought a way to spend their considerable free time "meaningfully" that would also enable them to participate in day-today life. It was for this reason, my interlocutor recalled, that he first started working as a volunteer driver for the local food bank "Die Tafel".

In mid-2015, however, Bernhard Thiele decided to give up his work at the food bank and volunteer at the new initial reception centre in Ellwangen instead. It was the notion of an urgent *need to help* that drove him to act. He put this as follows:

> "Then, when the numbers exploded in July, August, September, with 3,000, 4,000 and almost 5,000 [asylum seekers]. Then it was clear to me that help was needed" (Interview with Bernhard Thiele: 15/3/2016)

To Thiele, the increased numbers of asylum seekers arriving in Ellwangen meant that "help" was urgently "needed". This reasoning epitomizes a pattern I encountered repeatedly during my fieldwork: many volunteers in the area of my field research told me that, in light of the events in the second half of 2015, they felt "obligated" to step up and help. During this time, the image of a "European refugee crisis" was circulating widely across national and international media (cf. Collyer & King 2016; Holmes & Castañeda 2016; Kallius, Monterescu & Rajaram 2016). This acute emergency also became visible in the small Swabian town of Ellwangen, where rapidly growing numbers of asylum seekers had to be accommodated. Several of my interlocutors told me about the deteriorating conditions at the facility during this time. Bernhard Thiele recalled how all of the common rooms and various offices and corridors were filled with mattresses so that people did not have to sleep outside. Tents were set up in outdoor areas of the former barracks in order to accommodate additional new arrivals, among them children and elderly people. Another volunteer recalled how she was deeply affected by the shocking conditions at the facility. For instance, she told me, 300 people had to share one toilet and hundreds had no access to showering facilities. Only from December 2015 onwards, due to the rigorous closure of the European Union's external borders, did the number decline again to below 1,000 asylum seekers (Südwest Presse: 12/1/2016).[24]

The mobilizing effects of the 'crisis' in late summer 2015 were also stressed by Helga Maurer, one of the Volunteer Coordinators employed by the social welfare organization Caritas at the initial reception centre in Ellwangen. During our interview, she recalled that it was the desire to be part of this "historic

---

24   See: http://www.swp.de/crailsheim/lokales/region/wie-sich-die-stadt-ellwangen-dur ch-die-lea-veraendert-11766590.html (last accessed 1/8/2020).

moment" that provoked hundreds of citizens to engage in volunteering practices. She compared this to the situation after the "Hundred Year Flood" in central Europe in 2002, which saw an extraordinarily high willingness to assist the disaster victims through donations or practical action. Interestingly, she thus paralleled the man-made 'refugee crisis' to a natural catastrophe, thereby presenting it as a non-political phenomenon and furthering an 'apolitical' humanitarian imaginary. Moreover, Helga Maurer recalled how, during the time of the 'refugee crisis', she and her colleagues had been constantly overworked since they served as the primary contact point for the growing numbers of residents seeking to help at the facility.

Academic works across the social sciences have discussed the mobilizing qualities of situations deemed humanitarian emergencies. Calhoun (2010: 33) outlines how the "idea of emergency" is immanently connected to a moral incentive to act. At the same time, he criticizes how the use of crisis metaphors puts emphasis on the event itself while diverting attention away from its causes. Others have outlined how the topic of asylum is more generally framed through alarmist perceptions of emergency and risk (cf. Malkki 1995; Nyers 2006a). As Calhoun (2010: 44) puts it: "Refugees became the focus of a global emergency response in the 1930s, and indeed, it is from this point on that the association of refugees and emergencies became consistent". Authors often discuss this relationship between the reception of refugees and the image of crisis by drawing on the works of Giorgio Agamben (see for instance Agamben 1998, 2005). Seen from such a perspective, refugees are caught in a permanent "state of exception" that enables the sovereign state to insert biopolitical modes of governance in which asylum seekers are confined to a marginalized position (cf. Ophir 2010; Vandevoordt 2020). To Fassin and Pandolfi (2010: 15f) such a "state of exception" forms "the basis for a government that is at once military and humanitarian, resting on a logic of security and a logic of protection, on a law external to and superior to law, rooted as it is in the legitimacy of actions aimed at protecting life". Scholars have also critically discussed this merging of humanitarian action and government (see for instance Bornstein & Redfield 2011b; Ticktin 2011; Fassin 2012). They problematize the effects of a humanitarianization of policy domains, such as the reception of asylum seekers (see Fassin 2009, 2010; Williams 2016; Cuttitta 2018). For instance, Nyers (2006a: 30) argues that humanitarian imaginaries "work to establish the refugee phenomenon as a nonpolitical occurrence". Fassin (2016) outlines how, in the course of 2015, the topic of asylum had become increasingly framed as a moral endeavour rather than as a political issue, an imaginary that shifted the reception of asylum seekers "from right to favour". Scholars have thus pointed to the intimate connection between the image of the 'crisis', the governance of asylum seekers and humanitarian action.

This also became visible in Ellwangen, where governmental actors framed the reception of asylum seekers not as a political question but as a humanitarian one. I would argue that this framing played a pivotal role in mobilizing a need to help among local residents. The following quote by the mayor of Ellwangen illustrates this strikingly:

> "I am delighted that, by receiving refugees, Ellwangen has the opportunity to make a *humanitarian* contribution and to offer people *practical help*. The citizens of Ellwangen have shown a great willingness to volunteer in support of refugees. With the establishment of the initial reception centre, Ellwangen [...] is demonstrating its open-mindedness and desire to help."[25] (Press release from the state government of Baden-Württemberg: 6/5/2015, emphasis added)

In this statement, the mayor not only framed the reception of asylum seekers in the town as a humanitarian matter but also as a way to provide "practical help". At the same time, he praised the willingness of local residents to engage in volunteering practices. In doing so, he blurred the distinction between governmental responsibilities and humanitarian helping.

Governmental actors also engaged in direct efforts seeking to mobilize local residents for volunteering activities in Ellwangen. Through different incentives, they called on citizens to volunteer at the new reception facility. For instance, my interlocutor Bernhard Thiele recalled how he had started volunteering in response to an appeal from the local council in the official bulletin. In many localities in the area of my field research, local authorities or social welfare organizations published such appeals in newspapers or bulletins, asking residents to help and calling on them to volunteer. Often, such appeals invited citizens to participate in so-called "kick-off events" that were organized

---

25 Translation by LF. German original: "Ich freue mich, dass Ellwangen mit der Aufnahme von Flüchtlingen einen humanitären Beitrag leisten und Menschen konkret helfen kann. In der Ellwanger Bevölkerung gibt es eine große Bereitschaft, sich ehrenamtlich für die Flüchtlinge einzusetzen. Ellwangen [...] zeigt sich mit der Einrichtung der Landeserstaufnahmestelle weltoffen und hilfsbereit." Available online at: https://www.baden-wuerttemberg.de/de/service/presse/pressemitteilung/pid/landeserstaufnahmeeinrichtung-fuer-fluechtlinge-in-ellwangen-vorgestellt/ (last accessed 1/8/2020).

by governmental actors. This was also the case in Ellwangen. In March 2015, shortly before the new initial reception centre was inaugurated, governmental actors organized a public "kick-off event for volunteers" that attracted more than 80 interested persons. At this occasion, governmental and political representatives held speeches talking about the possibility of and necessity for people to help out at the new reception facility (see Schwäbische: 19/3/2018)[26].

The government's efforts to mobilize citizens to get involved as volunteers proved quite successful. Like Bernhard Thiele, many volunteers in the area of my field research told me that they had decided to get involved in response to published appeals or kick-off events in their town. In many places, such instances brought together a group of newly recruited volunteers who, in the aftermath of the event, founded "circles of helpers" ("Helferkreise"), self-organized local initiatives supporting refugees. This, however, was not the case in Ellwangen, where citizens who volunteered at the LEA were coordinated through the Catholic social welfare organization Caritas.

To sum up, in parallel to the rising numbers of asylum seekers arriving in Ellwangen, governmental actors actively mobilized local residents into volunteering with refugees. As I will illustrate in the next section, this often resulted in the forging of a symbiotic relationship that offered mutual rewards to both the local government and the new-born volunteers.

2.3.2. Volunteering as a Symbiotic Relationship

Founded in 1542, the *Roter Ochsen*, a restaurant serving local Swabian specialities and house-brewed craft beer, is known as the oldest and most traditional establishment in Ellwangen. It is also one of the "most prestigious places" in town, where usually "the richest" and "most pre-eminent" come to dine on special occasions, as the volunteer Bernhard Thiele remarked during our interview. On an evening in late March 2016, the restaurant's rustic spaces were filled with more than 200 citizens who had been formally invited to dinner by the mayor of Ellwangen and by representatives of the state government of Baden-Württemberg. Almost one year after the new initial reception centre opened its doors to asylum seekers, it was time to "say thank you" and "to recognize" the extraordinary commitment of the citizens of Ellwangen, my interlocutor Peter Bauer, the local Refugee Commissioner, told me. For this

---

26 See: http://www.schwaebische.de/region_artikel,-Freiwillige-koennen-sich-in-fuenf-Bereichen-der-LEA-engagieren-_arid,10198048_toid,290.html (last accessed 1/8/2020).

reason, the government decided to invite those who had volunteered at the LEA over the previous months to a "Helper's Feast" or "Thank-You Feast", during which the invited guests could enjoy a three-course menu and listen to a local musician playing the harmonica. In the course of the evening, the town's mayor, other local government representatives and the regional head of the social welfare organization Caritas all gave moving speeches expressing their deep thanks to those who had been volunteering at the LEA.

This "Helper's Feast" was just one example of the manifold efforts that governmental actors made to honour volunteers who were actively involved in the reception of asylum seekers in Ellwangen. In the course of my field research, I came across numerous similar events that aimed to recognize practices of refugee support. This included, for instance, a "Summer Festival" organized for the volunteers at the LEA in 2015, which brought prominent governmental representatives to the town, such as the Minister of Integration of the state of Baden-Württemberg. The local council of Ellwangen also established a monthly "Stammtisch", a social evening at which volunteers could meet and mingle at a local pub. I witnessed similar initiatives to reward volunteers for their efforts in various places across the area of my field research. Often, the local authority invited volunteers to dinner parties at which they formally thanked them for their efforts. In other instances, special ceremonies were held at which volunteers received a medal or an award in recognition of their help.

Such instances, I would argue, rewarded those volunteering activities that backed governmental aims and objectives in the reception of asylum seekers. Put differently, they served as a means for governmental actors to foster a symbiotic relationship with committed citizens, while mobilizing new ones. The Refugee Commissioner of Ellwangen, Peter Bauer, described how the local authority aimed to promote volunteering with their efforts to honour volunteers:

> "It is important to express our appreciation of the volunteers and, besides, if we want to *promote volunteering*, then it has to be via some sort of word-of-mouth recommendation, so that somebody says: 'Hey, this is so much fun, maybe you could also volunteer once a week?'"[27] (Interview with Peter Bauer: 7/3/2016; emphasis added)

---

27 Translation by LF. German original: "Man muss einfach zeigen, die Wertschätzung gegenüber dem Ehrenamt ausdrücken und was vielleicht dazu kommt, wenn wir dann vielleicht Werbung machen für das Ehrenamt, dann muss das so eine Mundpropa-

This connects to Malkki's (2015) seminal work on *The Need to Help*. Malkki argues that helping is less a selfless endeavour and more an activity that responds to and rewards the particular needs of the helpers. Governmental efforts to recognize the help of committed citizens in Ellwangen could thus be read as a means of rewarding them by engendering positive feelings, such as 'having fun'.

Vice versa, I also came across instances when volunteers voiced their desire to reward governmental actors with their volunteering activities. Some even appeared to be driven much more by a desire to assist governmental actors than by an urge to help the asylum seekers. A striking illustration of this came up in my interview with the retired teacher Bernhard Thiele. When I asked about his motivation to help at the LEA, he replied:

> I appreciate what the state has invested in me in terms of my education, my forty years as a teacher with a decent salary and a decent pension. That makes you want to give something back, I think"[28] (Interview with Bernhard Thiele: 15/3/2016)

My interlocutor thus perceived his volunteering at the LEA as a means of "giving something back" to the state. From his point of view, it was not primarily the asylum seekers that he sought to support but rather the state and what he saw as its welfare responsibilities: it would simply be "too costly", he remarked, for the government to employ professional German teachers at the LEA in order to do the work he performed voluntarily. Just as the authorities felt a duty to "reward" committed citizens for their activities, volunteers such as Bernhard Thiele felt obligated to help the state fulfil its welfare responsibilities.

These examples from my field research demonstrate that governmental actors sought to foster symbiotic relationships with the newly committed volunteers in many places in the course of 2015. Scholars have emphasized this entangled nature of governmental and humanitarian actors, depicting it as "humanitarian government" (Fassin 2012) or "regimes of care" (Ticktin 2011). According to Peter Nyers (2006a), this complicity may even lead to forms of

---

ganda sein. Der andere sagt dann quasi ‚Mensch, das macht Riesenspaß, könntest du nicht vielleicht auch einmal in der Woche mitarbeiten?'".
28 Translation by LF. German original: "Ich weiß es zu schätzen, was der Staat in mich investiert hat in Form von Ausbildung und in Form von 40 Jahren Lehrer-Dasein und ordentliches Gehalt, ordentliches Ruhegehalt, dass man dem ein bisschen was zurück gibt, denke ich.".

"humanitarian violence" that occur when humanitarian and governmental actors work in perfect synergy. In the following subsection, I scrutinize the role of social welfare organizations in governing volunteers and driving them into a symbiotic relationship with the state.

2.3.3. The Role of Social Welfare Organizations

An outgoing and self-confident woman in her early forties, Helga Maurer was a trained social worker and one of three Volunteer Coordinators working at the LEA in Ellwangen. Before the facility opened its doors to asylum seekers in March 2015, the state government of Baden-Württemberg, which was officially in charge of the facility, decided to commission Caritas with the management of local residents' efforts to get involved; this the Catholic social welfare organization did by employing three Volunteer Coordinators. In the course of my field visits, I met Helga Maurer several times in order to speak to her about the volunteering activities at the reception facility. Each time, she seemed deeply stressed out by her work and emphasized how demanding it was to "look after" one hundred committed volunteers. In the course of our conversations, I realized that Helga Maurer and her colleagues played a central role in directing the volunteers and shaping their conduct according to governmental needs and objectives. They determined what was the 'right' conduct of support and vetoed those forms of volunteering deemed unbeneficial.

Helga Maurer and her fellow two Volunteer Coordinators were the first contact persons for all local residents seeking to help at the new initial reception centre. There was no way for prospective volunteers to circumvent these 'gatekeepers' if they wanted to access the highly securitized facility and engage in volunteering practices. During our first conversation, I asked Helga Maurer why such coordinators were needed at the LEA. She gave me a simple answer: "volunteers need supervision", she replied (Interview with Helga Maurer: 16/4/2015). Such supervision was, to her, essential to the efficiency and success of volunteering activities. In one of our interviews, she described her role at the facility as follows:

> "As social workers, we have the training for this, to say: let's bring a little order to all of this and see who has what kind of resources. [...] Where are the resources, how can we deploy them, where can we mobilize further resources,

what are the needs, how can we bring needs and resources together. And that is something that needs doing."[29] (Interview with Helga Maurer: 15/3/2016)

My interlocutor thus saw herself as having an important ordering function, one that would enable the efficient implementation of volunteering activities. She and her colleagues determined the assignment of volunteers to tasks that would meet the "needs". These needs were defined not by the volunteers or the asylum seekers themselves, but by the social welfare organization and the governmental actors who had commissioned it with coordinating the volunteers.

Based on his field study in Zambia, Kirsch (2017) outlines how the local Caritas branch attempted to control and monitor the volunteers under its supervision. In order to "domesticate partisan volunteering", he argues, Caritas employees used different strategies that sought to deal with volunteers who had 'gone astray', for instance, by "being selective in the question which volunteer would be deployed in which of the programmes" (ibid.: 3). In parallel, my observations at the LEA in Ellwangen illustrate the social welfare organization's role in 'domesticating' those wanting to volunteer at the new initial reception centre. For instance, Caritas employees defined the 'needs' and 'resources' and determined how both could be met. By doing so, they shaped the conduct of volunteering in ways that were deemed beneficial to the governance of asylum seekers while co-opting other practices of refugee support.

My findings also connect with Muehlebach's (2012, 2013) writings on volunteering and care work in Italy. She illustrates how Catholic charity is complicit in a neoliberalization of the welfare state. She terms this as a movement towards the "moral neoliberal", which she describes as follows: "The state, while withdrawing its welfarist functions, mediates its own withdrawal by mobilizing thousands of volunteers into caring about and for the less fortunate" (Muehlebach 2013: 454). Seen from this perspective, the Catholic welfare organization Caritas might have played a pivotal role in mobilizing volunteers in Ellwangen to fulfil responsibilities previously implemented by the government.

In order to shape the conduct of the volunteers under their guidance, the Volunteer Coordinators at the LEA structured and controlled their activities in

---

29   Translation by LF. German original: "Und wir sind da einfach geschult als Sozialpädagogen, dass wir sagen: das ordnen wir ein bisschen, so eine Arbeit, dass wir sagen, wir gucken, wer hat welche Ressourcen. [...] Wo sind die Ressourcen, wie kann man die einsetzen, wo kann man weitere Ressourcen mobilisieren, wie ist der Bedarf, wie bringen wir den Bedarf und das Angebot zusammen. Und das braucht es eigentlich schon.".

various ways. In a first step, all prospective volunteers had to schedule a personal appointment with one of the coordinators. Helga Maurer summarized this initiation process as follows:

"They get in touch either via mail or via our contact form or via telephone. Then we schedule an appointment and they come for an initial chat, then in the chat we ask them about their motivation and what moved them [to help], but that's always a bit wishy-washy [...] Then we present the different work areas and, over time, you get a really good eye for it: 'He's one for the clothing store, he's one for the Baby Room, language [teaching] [...].'"[30] (Interview with Helga Maurer: 15/3/2016)

This statement demonstrates how the coordinators were in full charge of the actual volunteering activities. Local residents willing to volunteer could not freely choose how to help and what to do but were assigned to set work areas, such as teaching German language classes, working in the clothing store, at which donated clothes were sorted and handed out, caring for children at the "Baby Room", and working at the "cafeteria", the facility's volunteer-run common room.

Before prospective volunteers could start working at the LEA, the coordinators also briefed them on the guidelines and requirements for volunteering at the facility. For instance, prospective volunteers had to provide a police record attesting that they did not hold any previous criminal convictions. Then they had to sign a "Contract of Honour" ("Ehrenkontrakt"), a non-binding and symbolic contract with Caritas. Helga Maurer commented that its aim was to make sure that prospective volunteers respected the "principle of humanity" during their activities as well as the principles of the Catholic Church, and that they would not harm or sexually assault persons under their guidance. These requirements and the symbolic concluding of a contract, I would argue, are a clear indication of how Caritas sought to influence the 'right' conduct of volunteers and brought them under its control and supervision.

---

30 Translation by LF. German original: "Ja und dann ist das so, dann melden die sich entweder über die Mail oder über unser Kontaktformular oder über's Telefon, dann machen wir einen Termin aus und dann kommen die zum Infogespräch, dann fragen wir in dem Gespräch auch zur Motivation und was sie so bewegt, aber das ist immer sehr wischiwaschi [...] dann stellen wir die Bereiche vor und man hat dann mit der Zeit einen echt guten Blick: der ist eher was für die Kleiderkammer, der ist eher was für Babyzimmer, Sprache [...]".

Moreover, the Volunteer Coordinators directly intervened when volunteers did not comply with the "rules". Helga Maurer told me that she was also responsible for dealing with volunteers who showed "problematic" or "anomalous" behaviour. For instance, some would reject the tasks assigned to them, when it came to helping to sort and give out clothing donations to the asylum seekers. Others would get "too involved" and forge personal relationships with the asylum seekers, a tendency indicating that they suffered from "helper syndrome" (Interview with Helga Maurer: 15/3/2016). According to Helga Maurer, such volunteers did not know their "limits" and spent too much time at the LEA. If she noticed such symptoms, she would immediately schedule an appointment with the relevant volunteers and ask them to reduce their involvement. This would spare volunteers the "immense frustrations" that would occur without their interventions, Helga Maurer stressed. Through such interventions, I would suggest, the coordinators also sought to prevent practices of refugee support that were considered unbeneficial to the smooth management and governance of asylum seekers. For instance, the forming of close affective ties was considered a risk factor that might eventually lead volunteers to object deportations.

The long summer of migration thus illustrated the important role of social welfare organizations in the management of asylum seekers. At the new initial reception centre in Ellwangen, the state government of Baden-Württemberg commissioned Caritas, the German Red Cross and other organizations with the fulfilment of various tasks and responsibilities. This was also the case in many other places, where governmental actors increasingly outsourced responsibilities and tasks to such organizations. Besides the coordination of volunteers, this included the management of entire reception facilities and the social and legal counselling of asylum seekers. Officially, social welfare organizations work independently of governmental actors, concerning themselves with the 'public good' and the provision of care to those in need[31]. In German constitutional law, the outsourcing of tasks to ostensibly independent welfare organizations is inscribed as one of the key pillars of the German welfare state and dates back to the Weimar Republic. Nowadays, German wel-

---

31 See for instance the website of the "Bundesarbeitsgemeinschaft der freien Wohlfahrtspflege", the umbrella association of German welfare organizations: http://www.bagfw.de/ueber-uns/freie-wohlfahrtspflege-deutschland/selbstverstaendnis/ (last accessed 1/8/2020).

fare organisations are "large and highly professionalised social service organisations", as Mayer (2017: 6) notes.

However, I also came across a couple of incidents when social welfare organizations took a critical stance towards governmental actors and their decisions. For instance, in September 2015, the heads of the social welfare organizations at the LEA in Ellwangen composed a "Warning letter" ("Brandbrief"). This letter was addressed to the state government of Baden-Württemberg and called for immediate solutions to the "crisis situation", which had led to deteriorating conditions that were "no longer bearable" and "risked escalating at any minute" (Warning letter: 18/9/2015). In other places, employees of social welfare organizations circumvented or actively boycotted governmental decisions in the reception of asylum seekers. In spite of these cases, I would still argue that the organizations' antipolitical effects dominated around the long summer of migration.

2.4. Concluding Remarks: Practices of Solidarity between Dissent and Co-Optation

This chapter scrutinized how the widely circulating image of a German 'welcome culture' played out on the ground; how it became appropriated by different local actors; and how it mobilized immediate practices of refugee support. Based on a case study in Ellwangen, I illustrated how the notion of a 'welcome culture' instilled *a moral imperative to act*, a feeling that action was morally mandated to alleviate human suffering, among residents in town. This moral imperative mobilized manifold practices of refugee support, including a public march and more long-term volunteering activities. Both examples revolved around a humanitarian imaginary that depicted the reception of asylum seekers in morally charged tones and generated feelings of compassion for those 'in need' – a framing that presented practices of refugee support as natural and ostensibly 'apolitical' 'expressions of humanity'. In late summer 2015, this humanitarian imaginary was given further impetus by the notion of an extraordinary emergency situation and the widely circulating image of a 'refugee crisis'. Such crisis metaphors had important mobilizing effects on local residents, many of whom sought to help and to be part of this 'historic moment'.

The practices of solidarity that I investigated in the course of this chapter brought together a wide range of local actors and individuals with differing positionalities and interests. They included left-wing political activists, local governmental actors and political representatives, social welfare organizations, religious leaders and established residents. All of these actors and individuals became involved in the mobilization of solidarities in one way or another. They all shaped the conduct of refugee support according to their peculiar interests and worldviews – thus, they participated in the contestation of migrant solidarity.

The practices of solidarity in Ellwangen came with diverse (anti)political meanings and effects. At times, volunteers became complicit in the governance of asylum seekers and formed a symbiosis with governmental actors. There were also moments, when practices of refugee support opened up new political possibilities on a grassroots level, possibilities to challenge the status quo, to voice dissent and to foster change towards a more inclusive and egalitarian alternative.

These findings raise questions and indicate avenues for the remainder of this book. In the following third chapter, I investigate in more detail how practices of solidarity became a site of governmental intervention and control. In Chapter 4, I then focus on how practices of refugee support opened up political possibilities to bring about change and transformation in migration societies.

3. GOVERNING SOLIDARITY: Volunteering with Refugees as a Field of Governmental Intervention

3.1. Governmental Interventions in the Conduct of Volunteering with Refugees

At the height of the 'refugee crisis' in October 2015, I attended the third "Forum for Refugee Help" ("Forum Flüchtlingshilfe"), one of a series of conferences organized by the state government of Baden-Württemberg. Gisela Erler, a Green party member and the state's first "Counsellor for Civil Society and Civic Participation" gave the introductory address to the event. In her speech, she lauded the outcomes of her efforts to enhance and support the growth in volunteering with refugees. "You won't find another product anywhere in the world as participatory as this one in this field!", she remarked enthusiastically (Field notes: 16/10/2015). The State Counsellor waved a small, yellowish booklet in the air so that everyone in the room could catch a glimpse of it. "It has been extremely successful!" she announced. Developed under her auspices and in the name of the state government, it was designed as a "practical guidebook" for citizens seeking to help refugees across the state. According to Gisela Erler, the government had given out more than 30,000 free copies within the few weeks since its publication date.

During my field research among volunteers in Baden-Württemberg, I came across this booklet on numerous occasions. It appeared to be an important source of information for many of my interlocutors. As stated on its title page, it aims to "give answers to key questions at a glance", features "good examples" and practical advice for volunteers, for instance on how to found a citizens' initiative in support of refugees, and contains information on the legal situation of asylum seekers and refugees. The booklet begins with a short commentary by Gisela Erler, who introduces the handbook entitled *Welcome! A Handbook for Voluntary Help for Refugees in Baden-Württemberg*[1] with the following words:

"Volunteering is of the highest importance when it comes to our humanitarian obligations. For this reason, we took a decision together with the volunteer helpers on the ground to provide a compass. A compass with which you and the refugees entrusted to you can navigate the confusing landscape of federal, state and communal laws, decrees, and responsibilities."[2] (Handbook: 2015, p. 3)[3]

Around the long summer of migration, governmental actors assigned committed citizens an important role in the 'humanitarian reception' of asylum seekers. They fuelled the notion that help was urgently needed and actively mobilized practices of refugee support among local residents. By doing so, they sought to integrate committed citizens into a symbiotic relationship that offered mutual rewards (see Chapter 2). At the same time, governmental actors felt a growing need to influence, support, motivate, enhance and coordinate citizens seeking to help refugees. The handbook for committed citizens is a striking case in point. It illustrates how the state government of Baden-Württemberg felt a need to provide a 'compass' that, metaphorically speaking, pointed volunteers in the right direction and ensured they would remain on the desired path.

In the course of 2014 and 2015, governmental actors introduced numerous other programmes and instruments that aimed to shape the conduct of newly committed citizens. Their efforts were underpinned by the notion that volunteers needed governmental guidance, coordination and support in order to work effectively – a notion that I repeatedly encountered in the course of my field research. The state government of Baden-Württemberg,

---

1 German original: "Willkommen! Ein Handbuch für die ehrenamtliche Flüchtlingshilfe in Baden-Württemberg".
2 Translation by LF. German original: "Das Ehrenamt hat bei unseren humanitären Verpflichtungen höchsten Stellenwert. Deshalb haben wir gemeinsam mit vielen ehrenamtlich Helfenden vor Ort beschlossen, einen Kompass bereitzustellen. Einen Kompass, mit dem Sie sich und die Ihnen anvertrauten Flüchtlinge durch eine zuweilen unübersichtliche Landschaft von Bundes-, Landes- und Kommunalgesetzen, Verordnungen und Zuständigkeiten lotsen können.".
3 See: https://www.fluechtlingshilfe-bw.de/fileadmin/_flh/Praxistipps/Handbuch-Fluechtlingshilfe-3.Aufl-WEB-DB.pdf (last accessed 1/8/2020).

for instance, provided special training schemes, introduced financial support programmes, published a regular newsletter and launched a website (www.fluechtlingshilfe-bw.de) featuring practical information for volunteers. It also held regular "Forum for Refugee Help" conferences that aimed to facilitate networking and dialogue among volunteers and other actors in the field. Furthermore, so-called "Volunteer Coordinator" positions were introduced in almost all municipalities and district councils across the area of my field research. A similar tendency unfolded at social welfare organizations, who were given responsibility for implementing additional efforts to coordinate and support citizen engagement around refugees – a responsibility for which they received increased funding from the state government.

This chapter investigates the rationalities behind governmental efforts to intervene in volunteering with refugees. I also provide insights into the mechanisms and techniques with which actors set out to shape the 'proper' conduct of refugee support. The manifold programmes that were introduced around the long summer of migration, I will argue, not only extended governmental control over committed citizens but also aimed to shape their practices of refugee support in a way that served the state's interests in the governance of migration. They shifted governmental responsibilities to the individual and placed an emphasis on self-government, a development that Lessenich (2011: 316) calls "governing the self in the name of society". Yet, it is important to keep in mind that certain volunteers also constantly exceeded and defied governmental attempts to shape their 'proper' conduct. By doing so, they remained to a certain extent ungovernable.

The following analysis is deeply influenced by a Foucauldian perspective on government and governmentality (Foucault 1982, 1991). Following Foucault, I understand government as the "conduct of conduct" that is "constituted by all those ways of reflecting and acting that have aimed to shape, guide, manage or regulate the conduct of persons [...] in the light of certain principles or goals" (Rose 1996: 41). My analysis also draws on works that outline how ostensibly 'apolitical' humanitarian interventions have become increasingly entangled with and complicit in the governance of marginalized groups of society, such as irregular migrants and asylum seekers (Ticktin 2006; Fassin 2007; Bornstein & Redfield 2011a; Ticktin 2011). For instance, Fassin (2007: 509) scrutinizes the development of a new mode of governing based on humanitarian premises, arguing that "humanitarianism and politics are tending to merge – in governmental, intergovernmental, and nongovernmental spheres". This chapter contributes to these works by investigating how state actors set out to shape the conduct of grassroots humanitarian action in order to increase their influence in domains commonly considered non-governmental. By doing so, I will argue, they seek to govern migration societies through extended state-citizen networks veiled in a cloak of humanitarianism.

I draw on field research conducted between late 2014 and mid-2016 in various localities across the southern German state of Baden-Württemberg. During this period, I spoke to numerous governmental representatives from the level of the state to the level of municipalities. Moreover, I participated in conferences, training schemes and other events that governmental actors organized for volunteers supporting refugees across Baden-Württemberg.

This chapter consists of five parts. In the following section two, I scrutinize how the programmes launched by governmental actors shifted, challenged and (re)produced the contested boundary between 'state' and 'civil society', while (re)ordering responsibilities in the reception of asylum seekers. Section three explores the discourses and practices with which governmental actors intervened in the self-conduct of volunteers in order to shape 'socialized selves'. In section four, I illustrate how governmental actors positioned themselves in relation to what one of my interlocutors called kinds of 'uncomfortable engagement' through which volunteers expressed their dissent towards governmental decisions and policies. I conclude with reflections on the role of governmental actors in the contested solidarities that emerged around the long summer of migration.

3.2. (Re)Ordering Responsibilities in the Reception of Asylum Seekers

In his seminal essay on the limits of the state, Mitchell (1991) argues that what we think of as "the state" only gains meaning in relation to what is defined and understood as "(civil) society". He thus calls on scholars to reflect on the processes of boundary-making between what appear to be two distinct entities: "Rather than searching for a definition that will fix the boundary, we need to examine the detailed political processes through which the uncertain yet powerful distinction between state and civil society is produced" (ibid.: 78). In this section, I investigate how the long summer of migration brought about important – but necessarily contested – (re)negotiations of the role and responsibilities of "active citizens" vis-à-vis "the state" in migration societies. I scrutinize how the programmes launched by governmental actors shifted, challenged and (re)produced the contested boundary between 'state' and 'civil society', while (re)ordering responsibilities in the reception of asylum seekers.

3.2.1. The Birth of 'Civil Society' as a Responsible Actor

From late 2014 onwards, the state government began to present volunteering with refugees as a particularly important task of 'civil society', one that needed special guidance and support. This came through very clearly in my interview with a member of the State Ministry of Social Affairs in Baden-Württemberg, Marlies Vogtmann. I met the friendly and good-humoured woman in her forties in April 2016. As a trained lawyer, she had been working as one of the ministry's deputy secretaries for civil society and citizen participation for two years. In this role, she was involved in the design and implementation of governmental programmes aimed at citizen engagement in support of refugees. During our conversation, she asserted that the design and implementation of these programmes resembled a "process of invention" (Interview with Marlies Vogtmann: 20/4/2016), a process that had begun when the state cabinet decided to allocate funding to such efforts in late 2014. This she summarized as follows:

> "Help for refugees through citizen engagement is something that didn't really exist before … so we didn't have a support programme or such like. Before, we were more focussed on citizen engagement in general; that is, after all, part of our mandate. Of course, we are still committed to that issue too, but it's just down to what's happening in society that we are now paying so much attention to the refugee issue and that we have launched a dedicated programme."[4] (Interview with Marlies Vogtmann: 20/4/2016)

The implementation of "dedicated programmes" was thus a response to the particular developments in late 2014, when the number of citizens willing to volunteer with refugees began to increase sharply. My interlocutor Marlies Vogtmann even claimed that citizen engagement with refugees "didn't really

---

4 Translation by LF. German original: "Flüchtlingshilfe durch bürgerschaftliches Engagement gab's davor in dem Sinne nicht … also wir hatten kein Förderprogramm oder sowas. Also wir waren vorher wirklich auf bürgerschaftliches Engagement allgemein fokussiert, was eben auch unser Auftrag ist. Das Thema haben wir natürlich nach wie vor sozusagen parallel laufen, das ist einfach durch die Ereignisse in der Gesellschaft, dass uns jetzt das Flüchtlingsthema so stark beschäftigt und dass wir da eben ein Extraprogramm aufgelegt haben.".

exist before". During my field research, however, I encountered groups and individuals who had been supporting refugees for decades – often with faith-based or more explicitly activist motivations. And yet, practices of refugee support only became visible as a potential field of intervention for the state government from 2014 onwards.

In an interview, the personal assistant to Gisela Erler, Baden-Württemberg's State Counsellor for Civil Society and Civic Participation, explained this impetus for implementing dedicated programmes for refugee support as follows:

> "Civil society plays a critical role and so the State Counsellor is, of course, interested in ensuring these structures are explained and managed in a clear way that makes civil society and citizen engagement easier and more pleasant. So, this is the main impetus, how can we [...] contribute so that more people take an interest, so that more people get involved, and so that the integration of refugees or fellow citizens [...] will be a success."[5] (Interview with Gisela Erler and Annette Brüderle: 17/4/2015)

In the course of 2015, the state government thus began ascribing 'civil society' a critical role in the successful reception and social integration of asylum seekers. At the same time, it felt responsible for "managing" and "explaining" this process, thereby portraying itself as being in charge of the situation. These efforts might thus be read as means to (re)gain control over both the management of asylum seekers as well as the growing numbers of volunteers committed to refugees.

The programmes and instruments, which addressed practices of refugee support across Baden-Württemberg from 2014 onwards, were developed in a specific political context. It was the ruling coalition of Greens and Social Democrats that designed and introduced most of these programmes. Right from the start of its legislative period, it declared enhancing citizen participation in governmental decisions to be one of its top priorities (cf. Stuttgarter

---

5   Translation by LF. German original: "Da kommt natürlich der Zivilgesellschaft dabei eine ganz wesentliche Bedeutung zu und da interessiert sich die Staatsrätin natürlich insbesondere, wie können die Strukturen so verdeutlicht oder klar geregelt werden, dass Zivilgesellschaft und bürgerschaftliches Engagement leichter und angenehmer möglich ist. Also das ist eigentlich die Triebfeder, was können wir [...] dazu tun, damit mehr Menschen sich interessieren, damit mehr Menschen sich engagieren und Integration auch von Flüchtlingen oder Menschen und Mitbürgern [...] besser gelingt.".

Zeitung: 5/11/2013).[6] During campaigning for the 2011 election, the Greens focused heavily on citizen engagement, something that may even have contributed to its successful election result. Around this time, plans for a new central train station in Stuttgart, the capital city of Baden-Württemberg, gave rise to an unexpected protest movement. Thousands of citizens protested on the streets of Stuttgart for months, demanding that this huge construction project, which was set to cost the state billions of euros, be stopped. These "Stuttgart 21" protests not only received a high degree of media attention across the country but also triggered more general discussions on the extent of citizen participation in governmental decision-making processes (for more information on the Stuttgart 21 protests see Brettschneider & Schuster 2013; Gabriel, Schoen & Faden-Kuhne 2014). The Greens were the only political party in the Baden-Württemberg state parliament to take a stand *against* the construction project from the outset and call for it to be scrapped (cf. Grüne BW: 2010).[7] This might be partly explained by the historical origins of the party, which arose out of the anti-nuclear, women's rights and peace movements of the 1970s (see for instance Schmid 1990). Nowadays, the party sees itself as "ecological, social and cosmopolitan" (Grüne BW: 2017)[8] and is often classified as left of centre.

This background partly contributed to the extraordinary success that the Greens achieved in the Baden-Württemberg state elections in 2011, in which the party won 24 per cent of the vote, compared to 12 per cent in the previous election (Statistisches Landesamt BW: 2016).[9] This percentage was also substantially higher than the party's vote share at a federal level: in the 2009 and 2013 elections to the federal parliament, the Greens won around 10 per cent of the vote (Bundeswahlleiter: 2017).[10] With this success in the 2011 state elections, the Greens became the governing party of Baden-Württemberg for the first time in their history, forming a coalition with the Social Democratic Party (SPD, "Red"). In Winfried Kretschmann, they also had the first ever Green first minister of a German federal state. The formation of a Red-Green government

---

6 See: http://www.stuttgarter-zeitung.de/inhalt.buergerbeteiligung-gruen-rot-laesst-die-buerger-mitentscheiden.23934955-9780-420a-98b4-e826ad410104.html (last accessed 1/8/2020).
7 See: https://www.gruene-bw.de/stuttgart-21-stoppen/ (last accessed 1/8/2020).
8 See: https://www.gruene-bw.de/partei/wer-wir-sind/ (last accessed 1/8/2020).
9 See: https://www.statistik-bw.de/Wahlen/Landtag/LRLtW.jsp (last accessed 1/8/2020).
10 See: https://www.bundeswahlleiter.de/bundestagswahlen/2009.html (last accessed 1/8/2020).

coalition thus marked an important shift in the history of the state: since 1953 the ruling government of Baden-Württemberg had been formed by the conservative Christian Democratic Union (CDU).

Right from the start of its legislative period, the Green-SPD government introduced various measures seeking to enhance citizen participation across the state – at that time, however, they were not yet specifically targeted at the section of 'civil society' concerned with asylum seekers. This included, for instance, the creation of the special office of "State Counsellor for Civil Society and Civic Participation" by the first minister. In 2014, the state government then published a "Civic Engagement Strategy", ("Engagementstrategie") which, in more than 100 pages, outlined the concrete steps needed to foster an active 'civil society' (Sozialministerium BW: 2014). And yet, the entire document contained not a single reference to the topic of 'asylum seekers' or 'refugees'. This indicates that, when the document was published in 2014, the reception and social integration of asylum seekers was not yet considered a particularly important or noteworthy responsibility of 'civil society'.

These insights illustrate how, from late 2014 onwards, a section of 'civil society' encompassing citizens supporting refugees was born and institutionalized as an actor that is, together with the state, responsible for the reception of asylum seekers. Meanwhile, the government presented citizen engagement in support of refugees as a section of 'civil society' that needed special guidance and intervention. In the following subsection, I outline how this development shifted responsibility to committed citizens – a tendency that, however, remained highly contested among the volunteers themselves.

3.2.2. "Civil Society is the Music between the Notes": The Impetus for Meaningful Cooperation

The programmes and instruments, which addressed practices of refugee support across Baden-Württemberg from 2014 onwards, built on the notion that the successful reception and integration of asylum seekers could only be achieved if 'civil society' and 'the state' were willing to cooperate and collaborate effectively. This came across clearly in my interview with Gisela Erler, Baden-Württemberg's State Counsellor for Civil Society and Civic Participation, and her personal assistant Annette Brüderle. At the beginning of our interview, I asked about the role of committed citizens in the reception of refugees in Baden-Württemberg. Annette Brüderle replied as follows:

"Yes, civil society, of course, plays a very big part, because the state and the municipalities can put lots of things in place concerning accommodation [...], concerning possibilities and finances, how to take care of them and how to integrate them. But the actual integration, of course, needs to come about through civil society. It has to come about through neighbours, through schools, through kindergartens, through church parishes – in other words, through all the different areas in which civil society is active and involved. *In that sense, civil society is a bit like what you find between two musical notes: the music.*"[11] (Interview with Gisela Erler and Annette Brüderle: 17/4/2015, emphasis added)

According to my interlocutor, 'the state' produces the notes while 'civil society' is responsible for transforming what might be perceived as noise into music. In other words, while 'the state' is responsible for more technical matters, such as finances or accommodation, and thus lays the groundwork for the reception of asylum seekers, 'civil society' is deemed responsible for the step of "the actual integration". As our interview proceeded, Annette Brüderle also stressed the role of 'civil society' in producing "acceptance", thereby putting further emphasis on the impetus for meaningful cooperation:

"Acceptance can only be reflected by civil society. But the authorities [...] they, of course, need to see that there is transparency, participation from an early stage ... i.e. to work with lots of different instruments that make for a situation where acceptance can develop or be created."[12] (Interview with Gisela Erler and Annette Brüderle: 17/4/2015)

---

11 Translation by LF. German original: "Ja, die Zivilgesellschaft spielt natürlich eine ganz große Rolle, weil sowohl das Land als auch die Kommunen letztendlich viel vorgeben können an Unterkünften [...] an Möglichkeiten und Finanzierung, wie man sie betreut und integriert. Aber der eigentliche Schritt der Integration muss natürlich über die Bürgerschaft kommen. Der muss über die Nachbarn kommen, der muss über die Schulen kommen, die Kindergärten, die Kirchengemeinden, also die vielen Bereiche auch in denen Zivilgesellschaft aktiv ist und sich einbringt. Insofern ist die Zivilgesellschaft eigentlich das, was man in der Musik vielleicht zwischen zwei Tönen findet: die Musik.".

12 Translation by LF. German original: "Die Akzeptanz kann nur durch die Zivilgesellschaft widergespiegelt werden, aber die Verwaltungen [...] die müssen natürlich schauen, dass sie dann Transparenz, frühzeitige Beteiligung ... also mit vielen Instrumenten arbeiten, die dann dazu führen, dass diese Akzeptanz dann auch entstehen kann oder hergestellt werden kann.".

To my interlocutor, thus, the primary initiator of the smooth reception of asylum seekers was 'the state', while 'civil society' bore responsibility for creating "acceptance" of asylum seekers and governmental decisions. Such narratives, which I repeatedly encountered among governmental actors in the area of my field research, clearly depicted 'the state' as being the one who determines the key tenets of migration management 'from above', while 'civil society' was responsible for effectuating these decisions 'on the ground'.

By doing so, I would argue, governmental actors sought to shift responsibility from 'the state' to committed citizens. Lemke (2002: 11) regards such a tendency as part of a wider shift in techniques of governing:

> "What we observe today is not a diminishment or reduction of state sovereignty and planning capacities but a displacement from formal to informal techniques of government and the appearance of new actors on the scene of government (e.g. NGOs), that indicate fundamental transformations in statehood and a new relation between state and civil society actors." (Lemke 2002: 14)

According to Lemke, the state is thus increasingly extending its power over ostensibly non-governmental and civil society actors while modes of governing are becoming "informal". Others read the outsourcing of governmental responsibilities to domains commonly considered non-governmental as a process of neoliberalization. Seen from such a perspective, the welfare state is increasingly withdrawing from certain sectors, such as the provision of care to those in need, and outsourcing them to what has been called the "third sector" or to private companies (Lemke 2001; Carey, Braunack-Mayer & Barraket 2009; Muehlebach 2012). The developments in the long summer of migration might have contributed to these wider shift in techniques of governing in that they outsourced responsibilities in the reception of asylum seekers from 'the state' to committed citizens.

At the same time, governmental authority over the reception of asylum seekers was reinforced, for instance, by the image of *verticality*. I encountered one particularly clear example of this in February 2016 at the conference "Together. Diverse. Colourful" ("Gemeinsam. Vielfältig. Bunt."), which was organized by the state government of Baden-Württemberg. The event brought together not only volunteers' initiatives but also governmental representatives from across the state. In his introductory speech, Gerd Maler, the mayor of a medium-sized town in Baden-Württemberg, opened the conference with the following words:

"The motto of this event is not something that can be dictated *from above*, it has to come *from below.*" (Field notes: 22/2/2016; emphasis added).

With this statement, the mayor implicitly drew a line between 'state' and 'civil society' while placing the two on a vertical scale. By 'below', he most likely meant 'civil society', while 'above' was presumably the state government. According to the mayor, 'together', 'diverse' and 'colourful' were therefore attributes for which 'civil society' was responsible. Later in his speech, the mayor further argued that in order for the integration of asylum seekers to develop "from below", the requisite space needed to be provided "from above" (Field notes: 22/2/2016). He thus placed 'the state' and 'civil society' in relation to each other on a vertical scale, while shifting power to the state government.

In their essay on the "spatialization of the state", Ferguson and Gupta (2002) point out how 'the state' reifies itself as an enclosed entity and source of power by using spatial metaphors, such as the "image of verticality" that imagines 'the state' to be 'above' an entity called 'civil society' (ibid.: 982). These spatial metaphors, they argue, hold a strategic function as sources of power and domination. They put this as follows: "[These images of verticality] help to secure their [the states'] legitimacy, to naturalize their authority and to represent themselves as superior to, and encompassing of, other institutions and centres of power" (ibid.). In a similar vein, I would argue, governmental actors in the area of my field research sought to extend control and power over volunteers supporting refugees.

This tendency, however, did not go uncontested by the committed citizens themselves. I came across various moments when volunteers did not accept governmental interventions in their role and conduct. A striking example of this came in October 2015, when I attended the third "Forum for Refugee Help", a series of conferences organized by the state government. One of the topics of the conference was the integration of asylum seekers and refugees into the labour market. Examples of 'best practice' were introduced in which volunteers had – from the perspective of governmental actors – successfully placed asylum seekers in jobs. Eventually, a woman in the audience voiced her concerns in this regard. She identified herself as a committed volunteer and recalled with apparent frustration how she had tried her best to integrate asylum seekers into the local labour market, but failed each and every time because of the "Proof of Precedence" ("Vorrangprüfung"). This national law stipulated that employers hiring non-European nationals residing in Germany had to prove that they could not find suitable applicants of German or

EU nationality for the position[13]. With this regulation, the woman declared, 'the state' was directly hampering her voluntary work and her efforts to integrate refugees into the labour market. The comment sparked a discussion among several volunteers in the audience who also voiced their criticisms of governmental regulations. For instance, a volunteer in the audience asserted that her efforts to integrate asylum seekers had failed due to the "anti-integration policies" of the state (Field notes: 16/10/2015). Another one remarked: "We need to advocate for the abolition of the Proof of Precedence!". These dissenting voices made clear that they were not solely responsible for the integration of asylum seekers, while criticizing their legal exclusion and marginalization. They asserted that the inclusion of asylum seekers into society also needed to be 'ordained from above' through laws and regulations that were beneficial to the volunteers' efforts rather than hampering them. Such instances clearly indicated that some citizens were neither prepared to silently accept the basic tenets of the governance of migration nor to cooperate uncritically with 'the state'.

Despite the government's efforts to shift responsibility and extend power, the relationship between 'state' and 'civil society' thus remained open to disagreement and contestation. In the following section, I investigate in more detail how the long summer of migration (re)opened this boundary for negotiation.

3.2.3. Negotiating the Boundary between 'State' and 'Civil Society'

During the final minutes of our interview, Marlies Vogtmann, the Deputy Secretary for Civil Society and Citizen Participation at Baden-Württemberg's Ministry of Social Affairs, shared some personal insights into the challenges of her work. She acknowledged that there was a central question that she herself repeatedly struggled with:

> "I keep thinking that this is a really tantalizing question: how far should the state's sphere of action extend and how useful is it if civil society assumes certain responsibilities – because you have to also take on board people's

---

13   In August 2016, around one year after these frustrations were voiced in relation to the "Proof of Precedence", the German government suspended this law for a period of three years in order to ease refugees' access to the German labour market. See for instance: http://www.spiegel.de/karriere/vorrangpruefung-erleichterungen-fuer-fluechtlinge-am-arbeitsmarkt-a-1162174.html (last accessed 1/8/2020).

personal attitudes towards these issues if you say: "Okay, that's the responsibility of civil society". In other words, if you ask yourself how far should the welfare state extend [...] or is this, in fact, an area where we should work with volunteers – not only because they are cheaper, but also because we believe that this is a fundamental aspect of civil society and such a civil society is a defining characteristic of our society."[14] (Interview with Marlies Vogtmann: 20/4/2016).

My interlocutor thus struggled to draw a clear line between 'the state' and 'civil society' in the context of her work. She acknowledged that this distinction and the responsibilities ascribed to both sides were not straightforward but instead open to interpretation. On the one hand, she related this question to the issue of how far-reaching the welfare state should be. If 'civil society', on the other hand, assumed certain responsibilities, it would be "cheaper" but you would have to "take on board" citizens' personal attitudes, she acknowledged.

As our interview proceeded, Marlies Vogtmann also problematized the taking over of governmental tasks by 'civil society'. If volunteers step in to provide support where they "notice a deficiency", she argued, governmental reforms aimed at addressing this deficiency become redundant. The central question for Marlies Vogtmann was therefore: in what areas should 'civil society' withdraw assistance so that "the state" will finally "do its job"? (Interview with Marlies Vogtmann: 20/4/2016).

This uncertainty pertaining to the boundary between 'state' and 'civil society' has often been discussed in academic studies (Burchell, Gordon & Miller 1991; Ferguson & Gupta 2002; Gudavarthy 2013). For instance, Mitchell (1991: 88) asserts that "the edges of the state are uncertain, societal elements seem to penetrate it on all sides, and the resulting boundary between state and

---

14 Translation by LF. German original: "Das ist auch ne wahnsinnig spannende Frage, finde ich immer wieder: bis wohin sollte der Staat handeln und wie wertvoll ist es eigentlich, dass bestimmte Bereiche dann wiederum von der Zivilgesellschaft wahrgenommen werden, denn die persönlichen Einstellungen der Menschen zu diesen Themen, die man sich ja dann eben mitkauft, wenn man sagt: ‚ok, das ist eine Aufgabe für die Zivilgesellschaft'. Also wenn man fragt ‚wie ausgeprägt sollte der Sozialstaat sein [...] oder ist das eigentlich auch etwas, wo wir gern mit Ehrenamtlichen arbeiten nicht nur weil sei billiger sind, sondern weil wir finden, dass das eine ureigenste Aufgabe der Zivilgesellschaft ist, dass das unsere Gesellschaft auch ausmacht, dass wir das als Zivilgesellschaft leisten.'".

civil society is difficult to determine". He thus suggests analysing the contested processes of boundary-making as mechanisms through which power is generated and a given social and political order is maintained (ibid.: 90). Baker-Cristales (2008: 352) points to the co-constitutive nature of conceptions of 'state' and 'civil society: "Civil society does not exist as a prior and primordial unit; rather, civil society is formed in and through the same discourses and practices that create that artificially bounded postulate, the state". The long summer of migration, I would argue, brought this boundary under renewed scrutiny and (re)opened it for contestation and interpretation.

An issue that repeatedly stirred negotiation processes on where to draw the boundary between 'state' and 'civil society' was the question of payment. Both volunteers and governmental representatives problematized the merging of volunteering with forms of paid employment. At a conference organized by the state government of Baden-Württemberg in March 2015, for instance, a governmental representative stressed that volunteering must not replace municipal "administration work" (Field notes: 14/3/2015). Governmental representatives were also critical of moments when the distinction between professional care work and volunteering became blurred. As Marlies Vogtmann, Deputy Secretary for Citizen Engagement at the state government's Ministry of Social Affairs, put it:

> "And there's one area where we are always very critical, when a mixture of volunteering and employment arises [...] A hypothetical example: the Red Cross says 'We need helpers for the supervision of children's groups on the ground' [...] they then get expenses of four euros per hour but they also have to sign that they will always turn up at 3 p.m. and, suddenly, you have a mixture of work and volunteering. To me, that's very problematic."[15] (Interview with Marlies Vogtmann: 20/4/2016)

This problematic nature of blended forms of volunteering and employment was often explained with particular advantages arising from unpaid volun-

---

15   Translation by LF. German original: "Und an einer Stelle sind wir auch immer ganz kritisch, wenn dann so eine Vermischung von Ehrenamt oder bürgerschaftlichem Engagement und Arbeitsverhältnis entsteht, so dieses Thema, also als theoretisches Beispiel jetzt, das Rote Kreuz fängt an, sagt ich brauch viele Helferlein für die Betreuung von Kindergruppen vor Ort [...] also kriegen die jetzt eine Aufwandsentschädigung von 4 Euro pro Stunde, dafür müssen sie dann aber unterschreiben, dass sie immer um 15 Uhr da sind und schon ist man in so einer Mischform von Arbeit und Ehrenamt. Finde ich ganz schwierig.".

tary work. As the statement by Marlies Vogtmann indicates, governmental representatives often asserted that – rather than responding to obligations and strict rules such as fixed working hours – volunteers were more flexible and therefore able to react more immediately to changes or problems that arose in the reception of asylum seekers. Paid employees, in contrast, needed to adhere to bureaucratic procedures and regulations and were therefore not as spontaneous as volunteers in reacting to the uncertainty pertaining to the migration of asylum seekers. This came out clearly in my interview with Gisela Erler, the State Counsellor for Civil Society and Civic Participation. She explained that volunteers followed a particular intrinsic "logic":

> "These are not part-time employees that you hire, they are volunteers with their own logic based for the most part on motivation and reliability, though that is something that's generated not by an apparent straitjacket of rules but by other means ... I believe that it works, and until now people have been doing it perfectly well ... Only now is there this wave of 'We have to regulate all of this'. So you've got this conflicted relationship between a need to regulate and the logic of volunteering."[16] (Interview with Gisela Erler and Annette Brüderle: 17/4/15)

With this statement, Gisela Erler pointed to a central issue in the context of her work: on the one hand, volunteering would follow an intrinsic logic that is not based on imposed rules and thus defies governmental control to a certain degree. On the other hand, governmental actors see a 'need to regulate' volunteers and thus attempt to extend control over their activities. From her perspective, there was a 'thin line' between regulating volunteers through governmental programmes and crushing volunteers with rules and obligations. It was thus the shaping of the volunteers' self-conduct that gained priority in the course of the long summer of migration – something I will illustrate in more detail in the following section.

---

16 Translation by LF. German original: "Das sind keine Teilzeitarbeitskräfte, die du einstellst, sondern das sind Ehrenamtliche mit ner eigenen Logik und das beruht im Wesentlichen auf Motivation und Verlässlichkeit, die aber anders hergestellt wird als durch ein scheinbar festes Regelkorsett, ja ... ich glaube, dass das geht und bisher haben das die Leute ja auch immer gemacht ... erst jetzt kommt die Flut von ‚Wir müssen das aber alles regeln. Also das ist so das Spannungsverhältnis zwischen Regelungsbedarf und der Logik von Ehrenamt.".

3.3. (Re)Shaping the Self-Conduct of Committed Citizens

The manifold programmes that intervened in citizen commitment around the long summer of migration also served as a means to gain governmental control over the self-conduct of committed citizens. They normalized a certain way of acting and being in relation to the 'public good' and produced volunteers as responsible citizen-subjects within 'the state'. In the following sections, I explore these discourses and practices with which governmental actors intervened in the self-conduct of volunteers supporting refugees in more detail. To start off, I outline how governmental actors promoted an understanding of volunteering as a self-rewarding activity – a framing that laid the ground for their attempts to influence the volunteers' self-conduct.

3.3.1. "Volunteering Makes You Happy": Promoting the Personal Benefits of Volunteering

Around the long summer of migration, governmental actors in the area of my field research put special emphasis on the personal benefits of volunteering with refugees. A striking example came up in my conversation with Johannes Mayer, the Deputy Secretary for Citizen Engagement at the "Städtetag Baden-Württemberg" (approximately "Association of Cities and Towns in Baden-Württemberg"). The Städtetag is a state-level governmental agency that holds an intermediary position between the state government and its city councils. My interlocutor's job was to give advice to local authorities on how to foster an active 'civil society' on the ground. During our interview, he told me about a recent speech he gave in several localities across the state entitled "Ehrenamt [approximately volunteering] makes you happy". He offered the following description of its content:

> "The good within human-beings, you can call it Christian or atheistic or whatever ... but the key point is that people don't just communicate with each other but also build relationships ... The "Ehrenamt makes you happy" speeches I give – in Biberach, I held one and more than 100 persons attended. It really does make you happy. Because when you engage as a volunteer, you also benefit yourself, and you should feel good in the process

and see that it can really change something."[17] (Interview with Johannes Mayer: 20/4/2016)

This quote indicates how my interlocutor promoted the personal rewards of 'Ehrenamt' (literally 'honorary office') by asserting that volunteers become 'happier' in the process. In doing so, he put forward an understanding of volunteering that underlines how it makes those willing to volunteer "feel good", rather than what it does for its ostensible beneficiaries.

Many of those who supported refugees in the area of my field research identified themselves as "Ehrenamtliche" (approximately 'holders of an honorary office') and were identified as such by governmental actors. Although I use the English term 'volunteer' throughout this book, it is important to note that this translation is unable to depict all the contextual meanings of the specific German term 'Ehrenamt' along with its counterpart 'Hauptamt' (literally 'main office') (for more information see for instance Krimphove 2005). Roughly, the term 'Ehrenamt' means a voluntary activity that contributes to the public good without monetary rewards and that is executed for the 'honour' that one receives in return. Traditionally, this spans a wide range of community work, for instance, offices at local sports clubs or volunteering with a local church. The term is often defined through its demarcation from what is understood as 'Hauptamt', vaguely referring to paid employees in the care sector, for instance, in social welfare organizations. Together, 'Ehrenamt' and 'Hauptamt' are often depicted as important pillars of the German welfare state (cf. Koch 2007).

A good illustration of how governmental actors framed the term 'Ehrenamt' can be found in the 'Civic Engagement Strategy', a strategy paper published by the state government of Baden-Württemberg in 2014, shortly before I started my field research in the area:

> "The most traditional term is of course 'Ehrenamt'. Its current meaning can be traced to the more than 200-year-old practice of local self-government. In its basic meaning, it represents a clearly defined task (Amt), which is to

---

17 Translation by LF. German original: "Das Gute was im Menschen drin ist – kann man jetzt christlich nennen, oder atheistisch oder ist mir wurst ... Aber hauptsächlich, dass die Menschen miteinander nicht nur kommunizieren sondern auch in Beziehung gehen. Meine Vorträge, die ich halte: 'Ehrenamt macht glücklich', da hab ich in Biberach einen Vortrag gehalten, da waren über 100 Leute da, das macht echt glücklich. Weil Bürgerengagement hat immer auch einen Benefit für ein selber und da muss er sich dabei wohlfühlen und dann muss er auch sehen, dass es auch wirklich was verändert.".

be executed by a selected person who in return receives social recognition (Ehre). Historically, 'Ehrenamt' is the contribution of the citizen (in the literal sense) to the functioning of the common good."[18] (Civic Engagement Strategy: 2014, p. 9)

This quote outlines the historical dimensions of the term 'Ehrenamt'. It asserts that 'Ehrenamt' is directed at the "common good" ("Gemeinwohlorientiert") by contributing to its "functioning". The activities related to such 'honorary offices', however, are neither presented as altruistic acts of selfless giving nor as charity towards needy others. Instead, taking up an 'Ehrenamt' is regarded as engaging in a reciprocal process of giving and receiving, not in the form of monetary rewards but via "social recognition". Holders of such offices, the paper tells us, have a higher social capital than inactive members of society.

During the long summer of migration, governmental actors in the area of my field promoted these self-rewarding qualities of volunteering with refugees. Rather than as acts of selfless and generous assistance, they framed practices of refugee support as primarily benefitting those who offer the help and support. In other words, it is not the sake of refugees that lies, in this interpretation, at the heart of such voluntary work, but the personal self-improvement of those doing the volunteering. This conception of volunteering with refugees came through very clearly in my interview with Marlies Vogtmann, the Deputy Secretary for Citizen Engagement at the state government's Ministry of Social Affairs. She explained to me that there were two different understandings of volunteering or 'Ehrenamt', with the "old-fashioned" one now co-existing with a new one that has emerged in recent years. The more traditional understanding, she specified, followed a logic of "me for you" while the newer one was about "we together for us" (Interview with Marlies Vogtmann: 20/4/2016). This newly emerging understanding of citizen engagement, my interlocutor emphasized, creates social bonds and fosters relationships at a time when "families are no longer extended family networks" (ibid.). She thus stressed the social effects of this 'new'

---

18   Translation by LF. German original: "Der traditionsreichste Begriff ist gewiss das Ehrenamt, dessen heutige Bedeutung auf die mehr als 200 Jahre alte kommunale Selbstverwaltung zurückgeht. Von seinem Grundverständnis her bezeichnet es eine klar umrissene Aufgabe (Amt), die von einer ausgewählten Person zu leisten ist und für die diese im Gegenzug gesellschaftliche Anerkennung (Ehre) erhält. Das Ehrenamt ist historisch der Beitrag des Bürgers (im Wortsinn) zum Funktionieren des Gemeinwesens.".

understanding of volunteering while suggesting that altruistic acts of giving were old-fashioned.

Works on the historical development of 'Ehrenamt' have identified a similar change in its more recent understandings (see Hacket & Mutz 2002). For instance, Neumann (2016) analyses how the common understanding of 'Ehrenamt' has recently shifted from an altruistic to a reciprocal definition:

> "While, in the past, a voluntary activity had been understood mostly as an expression of charitable duty or family tradition, in surveys of volunteers conducted from the beginning of the 1990s, it developed into an openly communicated exchange in which volunteers, besides fun and social contacts, sometimes also expect an improvement in their professional employability."[19] (Neumann 2016: 10; Translation from German by LF)

This new conception of 'Ehrenamt' foregrounds the individual rewards of volunteering and does so not primarily in terms of its recipients but of those doing the volunteering. Corsten, Kauppert and Rosa (2008) also stress the social dimensions of citizen engagement in Germany. They argue that, through practices of volunteering, a "sense of community" ("Wir-Sinn") is generated and the volunteer becomes more socially integrated in the community or gains social recognition from it. The authors thus regard 'Ehrenamt' as a "form of social communitization" ("Form sozialer Vergemeinschaftung") (ibid.: 10).

Works in social anthropology have long emphasized the importance of reciprocity in acts of gifting (Mauss 1990 [1925]; Liebersohn 2011; Mallard 2011; Coleman 2015). These works take their cue from the writings of Marcel Mauss (1990 [1925]) who outlined how gift-exchange functions as a means to foster social coherence. Building on Mauss's conceptualizations, Heins and Unrau (2018) argue that volunteering with refugees around the long summer of migration in Germany had a similar function. They conceptualize practices of helping as a form of gift-exchange and outline how they came with an emphasis on reciprocity. Kolb (2014) also stresses the personal rewards of helping

---

19   Translation by LF. German original: "Während eine ehrenamtliche Tätigkeit in der Vergangenheit überwiegend als Ausdruck karitativer Pflichterfüllung oder familiärer Traditionen galt, avancierte freiwilliges Engagement in den seit Anfang der 1990er Jahre durchgeführten Freiwilligenbefragungen zum offen kommunizierten Tauschgeschäft, von dem sich die Freiwilligen mitunter auch eine Verbesserung ihrer beruflich verwertbaren Qualifikation erwarten.".

in his monograph on victim advocacy and counselling in the US, something he calls "moral wages":

> "[Those] who don't enjoy extrinsic benefits like pay, power, and prestige – are sustained by a different kind of compensation [...] They earn a special type of emotional reward reserved for those who help others in need: moral wages." (Kolb 2014: title page)

During my field research, the self-rewarding qualities of helping were also stressed by the volunteers themselves, who often had quite personal motivations for their engagement around refugees. One of the most thought-provoking instances in this regard occurred during my field visit to a small town in southern Baden-Württemberg. At a meeting of a local citizens' initiative supporting refugees, I met a middle-aged woman who had been volunteering with the initiative for several months. Giving me a ride to the train station after the meeting, she told me the very personal story that had led her to getting involved. She explained that she lost her husband, the father of her two children, in a car accident some years ago. After the tragic death, she decided to start anew and move back to the small town in southern Germany where she had grown up. She had, however, lost most of her personal contacts there. It was her involvement with the local citizens' initiative supporting refugees, the woman told me, that allowed her to re-integrate herself into the local community, to forge new contacts and to process the loss of her husband.

Summing up, volunteering with refugees was not primarily presented as an altruistic but as a self-rewarding activity in the area of my field research. As I will illustrate in the following section, this emphasis on the wellbeing of the volunteers paved the way for governmental actors to gain influence over their self-conduct.

3.3.2. Shaping 'Socialized Selves'

In the area of my field research, governmental attempts to intervene in volunteering with refugees were often based on the notion that there was a need to educate and train volunteers. Via the programme "Qualified.Engaged" ("Qualifiziert.Engagiert"), the state government of Baden-Württemberg spent millions of euros on the provision of training schemes for volunteers supporting refugees across the state. In addition, it provided substantial funding to third parties, such as social welfare organizations or the Refugee Council of Baden-Württemberg, in order to develop additional training schemes for volunteers. I also came across numerous instances when municipalities organized and funded training seminars for volunteers on the ground. In a similar way, the "Handbook for Voluntary Help for Refugees", which was published by the state government of Baden-Württemberg in 2015, included various examples of 'best-practice' and aimed to 'educate' committed citizens on the 'proper' way of volunteering.

Governmental actors rewarded committed citizens directly for their efforts to educate themselves. When volunteers successfully completed a training scheme, they often received certificates testifying to their successful completion of the training. I encountered a striking example of this in a small village in Baden-Württemberg in April 2016. The municipality organized a training day entitled "Asylum Driving Licence" ("Asylführerschein") for volunteers willing to help refugees on the ground. According to its official description, it aimed to "provide a basic understanding of three areas: the legal situation of refugees in Germany; intercultural communication; the right degree of help plus support through social networks" (Arbeitskreis Asyl Affalterbach: 2016)[20]. At the end of the day, participants received their "Asylum Driving Licence", which was formally handed over by the mayor of the village in the presence of the local press.

Through these manifold instruments encouraging the qualification of volunteers, I would argue, governmental actors sought to shape the conduct of committed citizens, employing a notion of self-improvement and self-management. By doing so, they normalized a certain way of acting and being in relation to the public good. These observations connect to Lessenich's writings (2011: 315) on the activation of "socialized selves". He argues that governmental actors increasingly attempt to foster "pro-active behaviour" among citizen-subjects: "Through social policies of 'activation', individuals are guided towards taking responsibility not only for themselves, but for society at large". Lessenich conceives of these tendencies as mirroring a broader transformation in the workings of Western 'welfare states' (see also Evers & Wintersberger 1990). He summarizes this as follows:

---

20   Translation by LF. German original: "Dieser Führerschein vermittelt Grundwissen in drei Bereichen. Es geht um die Rechtslage von Flüchtlingen in Deutschland; um interkulturelle Kommunikation; das rechte Maß des Helfens und um die Unterstützung durch soziale Netzwerke". See also: http://ak-asyl-affalterbach.de/ehrenamtliche-helfer-gesucht-kostenlose-fortbildung-asylfuehrerschein/ (last accessed 1/8/2020).

"At the end of the twentieth century and the beginning of the twenty-first, however, a reformed, activating welfare state has been constituting itself as the new mode of political self-justification of society vis-à-vis its individual members, constructing active subjects as bearers not of social rights, but of social obligations – as *socialized selves* obliged not only to be responsible for themselves, but for society and its welfare as a whole." (Lessenich 2011: 306 emphasis in original)

Instead of the welfare state, he argues, it is the citizen who is increasingly held responsible for actively contributing to the public good. In a similar vein, Rose (1996: 41) argues that 'the state' is seeking to govern "through the regulated choices of individual citizens, now construed as subjects of choices and aspirations of self-actualization and self-fulfilment". This development, Rose argues, comes with new practices of governing that "seek to shape individuality in particular ways" (ibid.: 45). Dean (1996), meanwhile, proposes turning attention to the forms and practices by which our own conduct and the conduct of others is shaped. My observations during the long summer of migration, I would suggest, mirrored a similar development in the context of the reception of asylum seekers: through their attempts to educate volunteers, governmental actors sought to shape 'socialized selves'. In this way, they increased their influence in domains commonly considered non-governmental, while governing migration societies through extended state-citizen networks.

Beyond training schemes, governmental actors used numerous other techniques for shaping and activating 'socialized selves'. For instance, in 2014 and 2015, they directly facilitated the founding of local citizens' initiatives supporting refugees via the organization of "kick-off events". Another example of such attempts to activate 'responsible' citizens came up in my conversation with Daniel Hayat, a member of the Stuttgart Regional Council (Regierungspräsidium Stuttgart), whom I met for an interview in March 2016. He summarized the council's attempts to facilitate the involvement of citizens through an open day in Ellwangen, where a new initial reception centre had been established, as follows:

LF: "So, you tried to promote citizen engagement from the very beginning?"
DH: "In October, when the decision [to establish the reception centre] was taken, we immediately organized a citizens' gathering. In November, we had a second [...] In January, we then organized an open day. I think it was very useful that we brought citizens on board early on. People were able to go inside as early as January, the facility then opened in April. Thousands of

people came, had a look around the premises [...] We tried to inform them and demonstrate transparency."²¹ (Interview with Daniel Hayat: 11/3/2016)

The Regional Council thus aimed to include citizens in the reception of asylum seekers from the very beginning. Through means such as an open day, it sought to instil a sense of responsibility among local residents and, thus, to activate 'socialized selves'.

This focus on self-conduct and self-activation is also illustrated in the "Civic Engagement Strategy" published by the state government of Baden-Württemberg in 2014, even before volunteering with refugees appeared on its agenda. The paper stated that an active commitment to the public good presented a means for reintegrating those who have become "isolated" from society, for instance through unemployment:

"Civic engagement can help citizens to test themselves, restore their confidence and regain a visible place in the community. It is important, though, that they don't miscalculate their own energies or expect too much of themselves and thus overextend themselves again.²² (Civic Engagement Strategy: 2014, p. 12)

The strategy paper thus depicts citizen engagement as something that cannot only contribute to the 'public good' but, at the same time, shapes the behaviour and conduct of citizens themselves. This is made even more explicit in the paper's assertion that volunteering could "change outdated patterns of thought" and "correct societal images" (literally "Gesellschaftsbilder korrigieren") (Civic Engagement Strategy: 2014, p. 12). For instance, the paper asserts, age-related

---

21 Translation by LF. German original: "LF: Also hat man da dann auch von Anfang an darauf geachtet, dass man versucht Bürgerbeteiligung dann schon auch mitaufzubauen?" DH: "Also im Oktober, als dann die Entscheidung gefallen war, hat man dann gleich noch ne Bürgerversammlung gemacht. Im November war dann die zweite [...] Im Januar haben wir dann Tag der offenen Tür gemacht. Ich denke das war auch gut, dass man da viele Leute schon recht früh miteinbezogen hat. Also schon im Januar konnten die Leute rein, im April hat sie geöffnet. Da waren tausende da, haben sich die Räumlichkeiten angeschaut [...] also wir haben versucht zu informieren und Transparenz zu zeigen.".
22 Translation by LF. German original: "Bürgerschaftliches Engagement kann dabei helfen, sich zu erproben, Zutrauen zurückzugewinnen und wieder einen sichtbaren Platz in der Gemeinschaft zu finden. Dabei ist darauf zu achten, dass nicht durch falsche Einschätzung der eigenen Kräfte und durch übergroße Erwartungen an die eigene Person erneute Überforderung entsteht".

images could be "corrected" via citizen engagement: where old age had previously been "interpreted as a phase of passivity, of well-deserved rest or of impending infirmity", it could now be seen "as a gainful time of life which is to be used actively" (ibid.: 12). This chimes with Lessenich's (2011: 312f) writings on "socialized selves": he argues that governmental actors portray the pro-active behaviour of citizens as being beneficial both to the individual *and* to wider society. Thus it is "self-interested" and "pro-social" at the same time (ibid.).

The sharp increase in citizens supporting refugees in 2014 and 2015, I would suggest, presented a means for governmental actors to institutionalize such an understanding of citizen engagement as simultaneously 'self-interested' and 'pro-social'. This was most evident in the case of the proclaimed ability of volunteering to "correct" age-related images. Many of those seeking to help refugees in the area of my field research were retirees, people in their sixties looking for ways to take part in social life and spend their retirement actively and meaningfully. This development appears to be in line with what the state government asserted in its Civic Engagement Strategy of 2014, namely an activation of retired parts of society into volunteering for the 'public good' and a 'correction' of age-related social images.

In the following section, I will focus on one of the governments' techniques to intervene in the self-conduct of volunteers in more detail, namely efforts to coordinate volunteering activities on the ground.

3.3.3. Coordinating Volunteers through Professionals

Governmental representatives in the area of my field research often told me that volunteers needed the guidance and supervision of professionals. "Ehrenamt is in need of Hauptamt" (Field notes: 14/3/2016) is a claim I heard countless times at state-organized conferences or meetings. Those professionally employed in the reception of asylum seekers would make the actions of volunteers "effective", they argued. This notion came with an impetus to organize and coordinate committed citizens on the ground. Marlies Vogtmann, the Deputy Secretary for Citizen Engagement at the state government's Ministry of Social Affairs, made clear reference to this drive to "coordinate" volunteers:

"When this big issue of helping refugees emerged, they [the state government] obviously said we need to make sure that municipalities intervene in a coordinating capacity. Citizen engagement always needs professional coordination, professional partners. At the moment, there is nowhere near enough manpower behind it ... We can help there, we thought, set up a good support programme, so we set up our support programme."[23] (Interview with Marlies Vogtmann: 20/4/2016)

In response to the rising numbers of citizens actively supporting refugees, the state government thus felt a need "to intervene in a coordinating capacity". In consequence, new Volunteer Coordinator positions were established in 2015 and 2016 in almost all municipalities and district councils across the area of my field research. These coordinators served as a first point of contact for those seeking to help refugees on the ground, they formed a link between committed citizens and local authorities, and they influenced volunteering activities on the ground. Thus, Volunteer Coordinators were often in quite a powerful position. They acted as 'gatekeepers' when it came to accessing reception centres, and receiving funding or information concerning local developments surrounding the reception of asylum seekers. Although many municipalities in the area of my field research already had existing offices for facilitating citizen engagement, it was only around the long summer of migration that they began to establish dedicated offices for citizens supporting refugees. Such efforts to intervene in a coordinating capacity also occurred in social welfare organizations (see Chapter 2). Many organizations employed Volunteer Coordinators who, in a similar way, aimed to intervene in the activities of volunteers on the ground.

Professionals and governmental representatives often explained the need to intervene in a coordinating capacity by the psychological well-being of the volunteers. Without professional coordination, they asserted, volunteers would become 'frustrated' and eventually drop out. Many also claimed that volunteers were in risk of being 'overburdened' or getting 'too involved', a notion that was expressed by a Volunteer Coordinator I interviewed in a medium-sized town in central Baden-Württemberg. When I asked her about the significance of coordinating professionals, she replied:

---

23 Translation by LF. German original: "Da war klar, als das große Flüchtlingshilfe-Thema aufkam, sie gesagt haben, da müssen wir gucken, dass die Kommunen koordinierend eingreifen. Bürgerschaftliches Engagement braucht immer hauptamtliche Koordination, hauptamtliche Partner. Da ist im Moment viel zu wenig manpower dahinter ... ähm, da können wir helfen ein gutes Förderprogramm auflegen und da haben wir unser Förderprogramm aufgelegt.".

"This volunteering is a really sensitive thing. Put bluntly, *you have to keep people's spirits up*. That's just the way it is – because there is often a lot of frustration among the volunteers, because they say: 'We do so much and it's not really recognized, and now I'm fed up of it.'"[24] (Interview with Jana Farkas: 18/2/2016, emphasis added)

The Volunteer Coordinator thus highlighted the need "to keep people's spirits up". At the same time, she regarded it as her responsibility to ensure volunteers derived personal benefits from volunteering and did not succumb to an undesirable self-conduct leading to their frustration. Building on Foucault, Lemke (2002) argues that such an emphasis on "self-care" functions as a means of governing, an argument he sums up as follows:

"The strategy of rendering individual subjects 'responsible' […] entails shifting the responsibility for social risks such as illness, unemployment, poverty, etc. and for life in society into the domain for which the individual is responsible and transforming it into a problem of 'self-care'." (Lemke 2002: 59)

This, I would argue, is echoed by the way the Volunteer Coordinators portrayed potential frustrations among volunteers as a matter of their "self-care". Through such means, they placed an emphasis on volunteers' self-conduct and legitimized intervening in their activities.

Volunteer Coordinators also played a key role in co-opting potential sources of dissent towards governmental decisions among the volunteers under their supervision. My interview with the social worker Jana Farkas illustrated this strikingly. Since 2015, she had been employed as Volunteer Coordinator by a social housing association that was majority owned by the local municipality. In this position, she served as the first contact point for all those seeking to support asylum seekers at the two new reception facilities in the neighbourhood. She assigned tasks, moderated meetings and was thus a person of considerable authority for local volunteers. During our interview, she repeatedly referred to her "boss" when talking about her work. For instance, I asked her whether there were volunteers under her guidance who publicly voiced discontent with the governmental handling

---

24 Translation by LF. German original: "Diese Ehrenamtsgeschichte ist ne ganz sensible Geschichte, also salopp gesagt muss man die Leute bei Laune halten, es ist einfach so, weil es ist auch immer wieder eine ganz große Frustration dabei bei den Ehrenamtlichen, weil sie sagen: 'Wir machen doch so viel und das wird nicht richtig angenommen und jetzt hab ich auch keine Lust mehr was zu tun.'".

of asylum seekers. She replied in the negative and asserted that her "boss" would "not like that at all" (Interview with Jana Farkas: 18/2/2016). After I pressed her for more information on her "boss", she told me that he was not only the head of the housing association but also the local mayor. This illustrates, I would suggest, how my interlocutor served as the 'extended arm' of the mayor, co-opting and depoliticizing practices of refugee support that took a more critical stand on local authorities' actions. In many other places, the establishment of Volunteer Coordinators presented a means for local governmental actors to exercise control over potentially dissenting behaviour among volunteers supporting refugees.

And yet, governmental efforts to organize and coordinate committed citizens did not go uncontested. In the course of my field research, I came across many instances when volunteers voiced their dissent towards the perceived "mushrooming" of Volunteer Coordinators who set out to intervene in their actions. Some told me that they felt increasingly patronized by efforts to coordinate their activities. Others also problematized and questioned the notion that they were at risk of becoming 'overburdened' and 'frustrated' by their volunteering activities. I repeatedly witnessed such critical discussions among volunteers attending the regular conferences of the Refugee Council Baden-Württemberg, the non-governmental and independent umbrella association of local volunteer initiatives across the state. For instance, in November 2015, the introductory address to the convention reflected critically on "attempts by local administrations to intervene in volunteering" (Field notes: 21/11/2015). The speaker was the "Asylum Priest" of the Protestant church of Baden-Württemberg, the official "priest for refugees and helpers" (Stuttgarter Zeitung: 18/11/2015)[25]. His critical remarks on governmental interventions in volunteering activities eventually sparked a heated discussion among the volunteers present. Numerous others also voiced their dissent towards the manifold attempts to 'coordinate' their voluntary work, which they regarded as an erosion of their independence. For instance, a middle-aged man remarked: "That volunteers are overburdened is only ever said by professionals!" (Field notes: 21/11/2015). Another audience member argued: "Only agreeable activities are promoted while others are hindered" (ibid.). Evidently, these volunteers were upset about governmental interferences on their work and per-

---

25 See Stuttgarter Zeitung (18/11/2015): http://www.stuttgarter-zeitung.de/inhalt.asylpfarrer-joachim-schlecht-pfarrer-fuer-geflohene-und-helfer.419b8484-8eb9-46d4-a0db-52299ac2cf1c.html (last accessed 1/8/2020).

ceived them as a means to shape their behaviour in ways that were beneficial to governmental actors.

To sum up, the manifold programmes that were introduced around the long summer of migration sought to extend governmental control and influence over the self-conduct of new volunteers. They did so by shifting responsibilities to committed citizens while seeking to shape their self-conduct in a way that served the governments' interests regarding the governance of migration. These interventions, however, did not remain unquestioned. Volunteers continuously contested their ascribed roles and responsibilities, voiced dissent towards governmental actors and demanded space for disagreement. These dissenting potentials of 'civil society', in turn, triggered depoliticizing reactions among governmental actors, something I will illustrate in more detail in the following section.

3.4. Depoliticizing "Uncomfortable" Practices of Refugee Support

Governmental representatives often emphasized that a smooth cooperation and meaningful division of responsibilities between 'state' and 'civil society' formed a prerequisite for the successful reception and social integration of asylum seekers. There was an aspect of refugee support that did, however, not sit well with this desire for meaningful cooperation. Certain groups and individuals also intervened critically, voiced dissent and highlighted deficiencies in the workings of 'the state' while calling for legal and political reforms in the management of asylum seekers. Such potentially dissenting behaviour among newly committed citizens, however, was "uncomfortable" to many governmental actors, as one of my interlocutors strikingly remarked. It presented a controversial element of 'civil society', one that put governmental actions, decisions and policies under critical scrutiny. In the following paragraphs, I illustrate how governmental actors in the area of my field research positioned themselves towards these 'uncomfortable' forms of refugee support and how they attempted to co-opt and depoliticize dissenting voices among citizens supporting refugees.

3.4.1. The Dark Side of 'Civil Society'

During my field research, I came across instances when volunteers uncritically accepted their ascribed role in the reception of asylum seekers and established a symbiotic relationship with governmental actors. However, there were also moments when volunteers opened up new political possibilities 'from below' by voicing dissent towards governmental actors and taking a stand towards perceived injustices in the reception of asylum seekers (see Chapter 2 and Chapter 4). The boundary between ostensibly 'apolitical' humanitarian helping and political action thus appeared rather blurred and was constantly exceeded by the practices of refugee support that emerged around the long summer of migration.

And yet, governmental representatives often considered humanitarian volunteering and political activism as distinguishable types of action, while seeking to restore a neat dividing line between the two. I came across many instances, when they clearly delineated activist forms of refugee support from the 'proper' conduct of volunteering with refugees. For instance, Marlies Vogtmann, the Deputy Secretary for Citizen Engagement at Baden-Württemberg's Ministry of Social Affairs, stressed that there were two distinct parts of 'civil society'. On the one hand, she identified those forms of citizen engagement that comprised practical projects that were "constructive" in relation to the governmental handling of asylum seekers. On the other hand, she claimed, there were those civil society groups that aimed to alter the fundamental conditions and workings of 'the state' through protest and political campaigning – practices of refugee support that were, in her opinion, "uncomfortable" (Interview Marlies Vogtmann: 20/4/2016). This dark side of 'civil society', she asserted, could not be classified as volunteering and therefore did not fall under her jurisdiction. She emphasized that volunteers should steer clear of such "uncomfortable" forms of engagement and should not allow themselves to "be stirred up" and thereby risk jeopardizing the successful collaboration with governmental actors. She put this as follows:

> "I think things can work quite well if you try and keep these two sections apart, so that you don't stir up those groups that aim to collaborate with the municipality for a common purpose. Because I think this can work quite well on the ground. Of course, that doesn't mean that, wherever the collaboration between volunteers and professionals works well, you have to keep your mouth shut. But I think that it's difficult if these are the same people [...] when protest turns destructive, for example, then it's difficult to have a foot in both camps."[26] (Interview with Marlies Vogtmann: 20/4/2016)

---

26 Translation by LF. German original: "Ich glaube, dass es allerdings ganz gut klappt, wenn man versucht diese beiden Teile auch ein bisschen auseinander zu halten, dass

Therefore, the state government made sure that it targeted those parts of 'civil society' with its manifold programmes and instruments that were conducive to its aims and decisions in the reception of asylum seekers. By silencing potentially dissenting and disagreeing voices among those seeking to support refugees, it simultaneously *depoliticized* the practices of migrant solidarity that emerged around the long summer of migration.

This connects to Ferguson's (1994) seminal work on discourses and practices of development aid in Lesotho. This "development apparatus", he argues, functions as an "anti-politics machine" that depoliticizes the reasons and effects of poverty. Rather than rendering their structural roots open for political discussion, disagreement and contestation, development aid reduces them to "a technical problem" and proposes "technical solutions to the sufferings of powerless and oppressed people" (ibid.: 256). This "anti-politics machine", Ferguson argues, comes with the side-effect of extending the power of the state, albeit in a hidden way. Similarly, I would suggest that the governmental impetus to intervene in volunteering with refugees around the long summer of migration also functioned as an 'anti-politics machine' in Ferguson's sense. The programmes launched by the state government of Baden-Württemberg served as a *depoliticizing* force that silenced the possibility for disagreements between 'the state' and 'civil society', while coming with a similar side-effect of extending state power over practices of refugee support.

However, the perception of a lack of a potential *space for disagreement* formed one of the major sources of frustration for volunteers in the area of my field research. I came across many instances when volunteers voiced their anger about the expectation that committed citizens had to accept governmental decisions and policies uncritically, while expressing a desire to participate in decision-making processes. This is an issue that was, for instance, repeatedly discussed at the regular conferences of the Refugee Council of Baden-Württemberg, the non-governmental umbrella association of citizens' initiatives across the state. For instance, volunteers repeatedly

> man nicht sozusagen Gruppen, die eigentlich das Ziel haben gut mit der Kommune zusammenzuarbeiten, für einen gemeinsamen Zweck dann aufzuwiegeln irgendwie, weil ich glaub tatsächlich, dass es vor Ort doch auch gut klappen kann. Das heißt natürlich nicht, dass überall, wo es gut klappt, die Zusammenarbeit zwischen Hauptamtlichen und Ehrenamtlichen, dass man dort dann den Schnabel halten müsste. Aber dass das halt glaube ich schwierig ist, wenn das die gleichen Leute sind, die dann [...] also wenn dann zum Beispiel der Protest destruktiv wird sozusagen, dass es dann irgendwie schwierig ist, dass man dann sozusagen auf beiden Hochzeiten tanzt.".

criticized how the municipalities appointed Volunteer Coordinators with the aim of controlling and determining their activities, something they perceived as a significant erosion of their independence and their ability to voice criticisms. Several volunteers also remarked that they were frustrated with local governmental representatives who did not take them "seriously" and did not include them in decision-making processes. For instance, one of my interlocutors, the head of a citizens' initiative supporting refugees, vented his irritation at the local council's lack of consultation in its decision-making, stating:

> "If the council says 'we need volunteers for our work', then, in my opinion, they also have to consult them on decisions and include them to a certain extent. Of course, we know that when the council hands out money, we're not the ones holding the purse strings. But they should at least say: 'Hey, what do you think? Are you okay with that?' And if we have objections, then we have to try and find a course that both parties can live with."[27] (Interview with Klaus Böhlen: 25/4/2016)

I talked to numerous other volunteers who insisted that they did not only want to engage in immediate helping practices but also object governmental decisions and policies if need be. Like Klaus Böhlen, many seemed quite frustrated if their own critical opinions were not considered in governmental decision-making processes.

The space of disagreement between citizens supporting refugees and governmental actors thus presented a highly contested issue during my field research. As I will outline in the following subsection, this became most visible in the context of deportation orders.

3.4.2. Deportations and the Contested Space of Disagreement

In October 2015, the newspaper *Stuttgarter Nachrichten* (20/10/2015) published an article with the headline: "Refugee brochure: Green-SPD asylum advice

---

27 Translation by LF. German original: "Wenn das Landratsamt sagt, wir brauchen die Ehrenamtlichen für unsere Arbeit, dann muss sie die Ehrenamtlichen eigentlich nach meinem Dafürhalten auch bei Entscheidungen fragen und in gewissem Sinne einbeziehen. Natürlich wissen wir, dass das Landratsamt, wenn es Geld rausrückt, dass wir da dann nicht am entscheidenden Hebel sind. Aber einfach zu sagen: ‚hey, wie seht ihr das? Ist das in Ordnung?' Und wenn wir Einwände haben, dann müssen wir schauen, dass wir eine Linie finden in der beide mitkönnen.".

astonishes opposition"[28]. Next to the article was a picture of Gisela Erler, the State Counsellor for Civil Society and Civic Participation and a member of the ruling Green party, holding the small yellowish booklet in the air. It is the "Handbook for Voluntary Help for Refugees" that the Green-SPD state government of Baden-Württemberg published in 2015. According to the newspaper article, this handbook angered both the conservative and the liberal opposition parties in parliament as well as various municipalities across the state. Their anger revolved around a short paragraph giving advice regarding the question "What are the possibilities if an asylum case is rejected?" (Handbook: 2015, p. 76). The handbook suggests the volunteers could take legal action against the rejection or, if all legal means were to fail, could organize "church asylum". The latter is a non-governmental form of temporary protection for asylum seekers afforded by local churches[29]. Apparently, this advice became a subject of intense debate in state politics in Baden-Württemberg. The newspaper article quoted Guido Wolf, the chairperson of the conservative CDU, who called on the state government "to withdraw the brochure" and claimed it was unacceptable for a state government "to call for civil disobedience against itself". The article also quoted a member of the liberal FDP, to whom the handbook represented a source of information on "how to block a deportation" and tied in with what he perceived as a generally weak record of the governing Green party in relation to the implementation of deportations. Furthermore, the article stated that municipalities across the state had criticized the handbook for complicating local efforts to manage the rising numbers of asylum seekers.

This debate illustrates that the question of how volunteers should react towards deportations often gave rise to controversial discussions and opinions in the course of my field research. Not only did it lead to ambivalent attitudes among volunteers themselves, it was also an issue for governmental actors. The newspaper article highlighted that there were contested views and controversies concerning deportations within 'the state'. On the one hand, the Green-SPD state government was giving advice on how to react when an asylum case was rejected, thus acknowledging that committed citizens did not

---

28   See: http://www.stuttgarter-nachrichten.de/inhalt.fluechtlingsbroschuere-gruen-rote-asyl-tipps-verwundern-opposition.2c96c64b-7f1c-4e71-944f-d9c5d11a5570.html (last accessed 1/8/2020).

29   For more information on church asylum in Germany, see for example the website of the German Ecumenical Committee on Church Asylum: http://www.kirchenasyl.de/herzlich-willkommen/welcome/ (last accessed 1/8/2020).

have to uncritically accept governmental decisions but could, in fact, disagree with and challenge them. On the other hand, representatives of opposition parties and municipalities framed such critical interventions in the context of deportations as inacceptable "acts of civil disobedience" or as a complication of local efforts in the management of asylum seekers. The *space of disagreement* ascribed to 'civil society' was thus contested among governmental actors.

The Green-SPD state government did, indeed, appear to be more receptive to dissenting positions among citizens supporting refugees. This came through in my interview with Gisela Erler, who stated that "uncomfortable conflicts" between volunteers and governmental actors around the issue of deportations would be unavoidable in the future (Interview with Gisela Erler and Annette Brüderle: 17/4/2015). For my interlocutor, the topic of deportations thus represented a potential but acceptable source of disagreement and contestation between 'civil society' and 'the state'. Our interview indicated that she herself held rather ambivalent views on the enforcement of deportations:

> "To be honest, we shouldn't be desperately trying to deport refugees, not even those from the Balkans ... we should really be focusing more on integration because we won't be able to deport the majority of them anyway."[30]
> (Interview with Gisela Erler and Annette Brüderle: 17/4/2015)

My interlocutor, the Green State Counsellor for Civil Society and Civic Participation, was thus herself critical of the rigorous enforcement of deportations. She voiced her understanding of and sympathy for those volunteers who refused to accept governmental decisions to deport certain asylum seekers and protested against them or opposed them in other ways. This more supportive stance towards the dissenting voices of committed citizens might in part be explained by the particular history of the Greens, a party that itself arose out of the anti-nuclear, women's rights and peace movements of the 1970s, and was thus formed in opposition to a ruling elite.

Such conflicts around the issue of deportations and the question of how volunteers should react 'properly' towards them, I would argue, are deeply political. Dissenting voices in the context of deportation orders shine a light

---

30 Translation by LF. German original: "Ehrlich gesagt müsste man auch diese Abschieberei nicht forcieren, weil auch die Balkanflüchtlinge ... man sollte wirklich mehr auf Integration setzen, weil wir kriegen eh einen Großteil nicht abgeschoben.".

on the injustices and uncertainties pertaining to the distinction between 'genuine' and 'bogus' refugees and, in doing so, call for the inclusion of groups who are excluded from protection. According to the French philosopher Jacques Rancière, "dissensus" or "dis-agreement" forms the true basis of the political (Battista 2017). To him, dis-agreement goes beyond the mere confrontation between opinions and occurs whenever a 'wrong' is voiced that challenges the partitioning of the dominant order in the name of 'a part of those who have no-part' (Rancière 1998, 2009). He expresses this as follows:

> "The essence of politics is *dissensus*. Dissensus is not the confrontation between interests or opinions. It is the manifestation of a distance of the sensible from itself. Politics makes visible that which had no reason to be seen, it lodges one world into another." (Rancière 2001: no page number; emphasis in original)

Following Rancière's conception, I would suggest that those moments when committed citizens contested the deportations of asylum seekers challenged the dominant order in such a way that *dissensus* arose. Such acts were deeply political, while attempts to suppress or silence them might be read as attempts to depoliticize practices of refugee support.

Scholars in the field of critical migration studies have also emphasized the significance of struggles over deportations (see De Genova 2010; Darling 2014). Nyers (2010a: 415) argues that they might be "read in terms of contemporary disputes over who has the authority to protect, and under what terms and conditions. Such activism can reveal new problematizations as well as new ways of thinking and acting politically". Other works highlight that deportations of rejected asylum seekers have a strategic function for governments in that they reinforce sovereign power (Nyers 2010b; Ilcan 2014). For instance, Mountz and Hiemstra (2013: 388) outline how the enforcement of deportations serves as a means for governmental actors to seemingly bring "order to chaos". Tyler and Marciniak (2013: 145) point out how the risk of being deported contributes to the criminalization of 'undesirable migrants' and functions as an important source of domination in the governance of migration. Volunteers' criticisms and protests around the issue of deportations might thus also be read as a contestation of sovereign power and of the basic tenets of the governance of migration.

During the long summer of migration, governmental actors sought to impede such possibilities for politicization around deportations through different means. For instance, the state government emphasized the need for "returnee counselling" ("Rückkehrberatung") for rejected asylum seekers. Governmental representatives repeatedly stressed that the 'proper' way for volunteers to respond to deportation orders would be to advise the affected on how to 'successfully' return to their country of origin. During my field research, I encountered an example for this emphasis on returnee counselling at the conference "From Refugee to Fellow Citizen" organized by the Baden-Württemberg Greens in March 2015. Several speakers at the conference emphasized that, along with efforts to integrate accepted refugees, "qualified returnee counselling" for those asylum seekers who had been rejected was an "equally important" responsibility for committed citizens (Field notes: 14/3/2015). For instance, the moderator of the conference problematized how volunteers will often have emotionally bonded with families whose asylum case is eventually rejected. He therefore asked a governmental representative in the audience about the 'right' way to respond in such instances. The governmental representative replied: "You need to move on to returnee counselling, even if the heart says otherwise" (ibid.). She thus made it clear that volunteers had to put their personal attachment to rejected asylum seekers aside, to accept the governmental decision, and to counsel returnees on practical matters. With this emphasis on returnee counselling, she left no space for disagreement and protest and, instead, asserted that 'civil society' had to uncritically accept and support governmental decisions to deport asylum seekers. Vandevoordt (2016) identifies a similar tendency in Belgium. He argues that, through the promotion of voluntary return to the migrants' country of origin, civil society actors became complicit in governmental objectives in migration management.

Despite these government's efforts to make committed citizens complicit in the governance of migration, volunteers did not cease to voice dissent and to demonstrate their disagreement, something I will illuminate in more detail in the subsequent fourth chapter of this book.

3.5. Concluding Remarks: The Government of Refugee Solidarity

This chapter looked at the manifold governmental interventions that aimed to enhance, coordinate or facilitate volunteering with refugees. Around the long summer of migration, governmental actors launched numerous programmes and instruments seeking to shape the volunteers' 'proper' conduct while extending their control over newly committed citizens. By doing so, they intervened in the contested practices of solidarity that developed around this time.

These interventions came with twofold effects. Firstly, they shaped the conduct of refugee support in ways that made citizens complicit in the governance of migration. Cloaked in humanitarian imaginaries, the introduced programmes and instruments backed those practices that were conducive to governmental decisions and policies in the reception of asylum seekers. At the same time, they depoliticized and silenced the dissenting potentials of refugee support. For instance, this crystallized in an emphasis on meaningful cooperation and harmony between 'state' and 'civil society'. While committed citizens were deemed responsible for the 'soft factors' of migration management, 'the state' was portrayed as being in charge of its key tenets, for instance via the making of laws and regulations. The emphasis on smooth cooperation also came with incentives to limit the space of disagreement between 'state' and 'civil society'. Thus, the state government sought to manage the rising numbers of asylum seekers through extended state-citizen networks that placed an emphasis on humanitarian compassion.

Secondly, governmental interventions shaped understandings of 'responsible' citizens in migration societies. Many programmes, such as the provision of training schemes and the employment of Volunteer Coordinators, promoted a focus on self-conduct and self-improvement. Governmental interventions in refugee support might therefore also be read as attempts to increase influence over the conduct of citizen-subjects while shifting responsibilities from the welfare state to 'responsible' citizens. The extraordinary increase in citizen engagement around the long summer of migration thus enabled governmental actors to engender a sense of responsibility towards the 'public good' and to exercise control over individual self-conduct and self-management in migration societies.

And yet, committed citizens did not uncritically accept governmental interventions in their role and (self-)conduct. Certain volunteers contested these efforts while demanding a space for disagreement and voicing a will to remain independent. They thus remained to a certain extent ungovernable. It was Michel Foucault who once remarked: "Where there is power, there is resistance" (Foucault 1978). I will turn to these dissenting and political dimensions of refugee support in the following fourth chapter of this book.

4. POLITICIZING SOLIDARITY: The Contested Political Meanings and Effects of Refugee Support

4.1. "We are also Political Volunteers!"

On a Saturday in March 2015, I attended one of the regular conferences of the Refugee Council of Baden-Württemberg ("Flüchtlingsrat Baden-Württemberg"), the non-governmental umbrella association of citizens' initiatives at the level of the state. Its regular meetings in Stuttgart, the capital city of the southern German state, take place every three months and are open to all interested. They aim to facilitate networking, information exchange and discussions among those supporting refugees across Baden-Württemberg. Participants attend workshops from morning until late afternoon, listen to 'expert talks', swap news and socialize during lunch and coffee breaks. Around the long summer of migration, these conferences were full to bursting, with around 200 persons crammed into a room at a church-run conference centre, the majority of them seemingly well past the age of fifty.

In the late afternoon of the conference in March 2015, an announcement by the steering committee of the Refuge Council caused a heated debate among the participants. In its closing plenary, it informed that, due to the increased budget provided by the state government for the year 2015, the Council aimed to implement new activities and programmes in the months to follow. One of these new activities caused the anger of numerous audience members: the steering committee's plan to implement a new training scheme for people supporting refugees across the state. For instance, a woman, introducing herself as a pastor working with refugees in a small town, openly questioned the value of such a training scheme, problematizing that "at the moment, there is a flood of trainings for people supporting refugees" (Field notes: 7/3/2015). A second woman commented that she was worried about the tendency that governmental actors and social welfare organizations were increasingly competing to provide seminars and trainings to volunteers in her town. Another participant then stated that such trainings had "clear preconceptions of what volunteers were allowed to do and what they were not allowed to do" (Field notes: 7/3/2015). Joining the debate, a man in his sixties argued that what volunteers really needed were seminars on asylum law and policies, whereas existing training schemes focussed merely on practical aspects of helping. Such seminars on the legal and political asylum system, he claimed, were undesirable to and sometimes even hindered by governmental actors because "they don't want educated volunteers!" (Field notes: 7/3/2015). During this heated discussion, I could clearly sense that many of the present volunteers were deeply critical of the rising number of governmental interventions in their role and conduct (see Chapter 3). After several minutes of debate, the head of the Refugee Council's steering committee eventually took over again. In an attempt to allay the growing anger among the audience, she argued: "The decision as to who trains whom should be made first and foremost by volunteers themselves!" (ibid.). She acknowledged that the discussion touched upon key questions for practices of refugee support, namely "What is a volunteer?" and "Do volunteers only provide bikes and clothing or do they also give legal advice to asylum seekers?" For the steering committee, the latter formed an essential part of refugee support, which is why the Refugee Council's new training scheme would include education on asylum policies and law. In a loud, confident voice, she then proclaimed: *"We are also political volunteers!"* (Field notes: 7/3/2015). The audience burst into applause.

This intriguing moment is a striking illustration of how, in the course of my field research, the distinction between forms of political action and ostensibly 'apolitical' humanitarian volunteering became increasingly blurry and untenable. Although governmental actors put much effort into promoting forms of volunteering they deemed beneficial to the governance of migration, many of the volunteers voiced a clear will to remain independent, to stay informed on asylum politics and law, and to oppose governmental actors when they perceived the necessity to do so (see also Fleischmann 2017). I also witnessed numerous instances during my field research when volunteers actively intervened in order to influence political decision-making processes, voiced dissent towards existing asylum laws and governmental policies or openly contested them through letters, campaigns or other more hidden forms of protest. While some claimed to be "apolitical", others acknowledged that they were "political volunteers", as illustrated in my observations at the conference of the Refugee Council. At the same time, many were quite uncomfortable with being classified as "left-wing" or "activist". And yet, some of their practices and positions were actually not that distinct from those of self-declared political activists. In her telling account on *The Politics of Volunteering*, Eliasoph (2013: 43) notes that 'volunteering' and 'political activism' are often thought of as distinct types of action, while they actually "blend and separate in many ways". Rather than being mutually exclusive, she argues, they frequently go hand-in-hand as a "mix of hands-on and abstract involvement" (ibid.: 61). Many times, she asserts, those who start out as 'volunteers' can also turn into 'activists' over time.

In this chapter, I take a closer look at the political dimensions of refugee support. My aim is to investigate how the manifold practices of refugee support that emerged around the long summer of migration were invested with political meanings. These political meanings were often situated *in-between* more radical calls for equal rights and mere complicity in the governance of migration. In what follows, I interpret practices of refugee support as *political* when they – intentionally or unintentionally – challenge the exclusions and discriminations of refugees and asylum seekers in migration societies and aim to bring about change towards what those engaging in relationships of solidarity consider a 'better' alternative. Such political forms of refugee support, I will argue, do not always form in direct opposition to the state nor do they necessarily emanate from individuals or groups that openly identify themselves as "political" or "activist". Rather, they often arise out of the impulse to change the status quo and to build a different alternative through hands-on interventions. In what follows, I thus explore the alternative visions of citizenship and belonging that were articulated and enacted through practices of refuge support.

I am also interested in moments when individuals and their practices become *politicized*, i.e. moments when actors try to shape the social imaginaries of refugee solidarity in ways that open up political possibilities and induce change towards a 'better society'. In the area of my field research, the Refugee Council played an important role in the *politicization* of those who became active as volunteers around the long summer of migration. For many, this non-governmental organization served as a key contact point and source of information. Its conferences, which I regularly attended between late 2014 and mid-2016, provided volunteers with an important platform for discussing problems and formulating positions relating to the most recent developments in the governance of refugees and asylum seekers. It should be acknowledged, however, that these conferences may have attracted those volunteers from across the state who were already more politically informed than others. Nonetheless, almost all of the citizens' initiatives I spoke to in the course of my field research considered the Refugee Council to be a central source of information. Besides organizing conferences, the Refugee Council also kept citizens informed about and expressed views on the latest local, national or European developments via regular email newsletters, its magazine and a website. In addition, it provided legal advice to volunteers, for instance via a counselling hotline, and also conducted lobbying work, representing the interests and concerns of citizens' initiatives at the level of the state government.

During my field research, I also came across instances of left-wing activist groups from across Germany intervening in a politicizing way in the practices and discourses of refugee support that emerged around the long summer of migration. Many of these groups had been committed to refugees for years, advocating for equal rights and freedom of movement (see Sasse et al. 2014). In the second chapter of this book, I illustrated how, in the small town of Ellwangen, a group of left-wing antifascist activists organized an ostensibly apolitical "solidarity march" in order to transmit their political worldviews and voice dissent towards governmental actors. I came across several similar instances when political activists aimed to influence the social imaginaries of newly committed volunteers or forged alliances with individuals who did not necessarily regard their actions as "political".

The investigation that follows draws on ethnographic fieldwork conducted between late 2014 and mid-2016 in the southern German state of Baden-Württemberg as well as in other localities across the country. I draw on interviews with volunteers and activists, on participant observations at conferences that brought together people engaging in refugee support, and analyse written documents such as flyers and websites. Of particular importance for the purpose of this chapter are my observations at the conferences of the Refugee Council Baden-Württemberg. Through these events, I gained insights into the discussions that developed between volunteers at the time.

The following chapter is divided into five parts. I start off by scrutinizing my analytical perspective on a *politics of presence*. With this terminology I grasp the political possibilities that unfold when alternative visions of society and belonging in migration societies are formulated and enacted, alternatives that revolve around the criterion of co-presence. These alternative visions, however, proved to be highly contested and debated among those who supported refugees in the area of my field research. As I will illustrate in sections three to five, people held differing and ambivalent standpoints in relation to a demand for equal rights (section three), a demand for a right to stay (section four), and a demand for a right to migrate (section five). In the concluding section, I summarize my findings on the political dimensions of refugee support around the long summer of migration.

4.2. Politics of Presence: Enacting Alternative Visions of Society

For the purpose of investigating the political dimensions of refugee support, I suggest to step back from clear-cut distinctions between ostensibly 'apolitical' forms of humanitarian volunteering and political activism. Instead, I look at practices of refugee support through the analytical perspective of a *politics of presence*. With this terminology I refer to the political possibilities that unfold when alternative visions of society and belonging in migration societies are formulated and enacted; alternatives to the exclusionary and discriminating effects of national citizenship that became increasingly pressing around the long summer of migration. I argue that these alternative visions centrally built on *presence*, i.e. the material act of being there, as the defining criterion for social membership. Nevertheless, as I will outline in more detail later on, these alternatives were highly contested among different groups and individuals and oscillated between a radical call for the universal inclusion of all those present on the ground to more conditional and hesitant views. In this section, I outline the conceptual contours of such a perspective on *politics of presence* in more detail. In the first part, I draw on works in the field of critical citizenship studies. In the second, I look in more detail at how 'presence' functioned as a (nonetheless contested) mode of belonging during the long summer of migration.

4.2.1. The Deficiencies of National Citizenship

Since the 18th century, the nation-state has formed the primary locus for political belonging and it still determines how we think about the political today (see Wimmer & Glick Schiller 2002). In more traditional understandings, national citizenship was depicted as a "contract" between state authorities and citizens, while the latter were said to hold certain rights and obligations towards the state (Marshall 1950). Such a perspective focussed mainly on the *inclusionary* dimensions of national citizenship. More recently, however, works in the field of critical citizenship studies began to stress the *exclusionary* dimensions of membership based on the nation-state (see Isin 2008; Isin 2011). They argue that the legal inclusion of some goes hand in hand with the definition of others as aliens or non-citizens who, although present on national territories, are excluded from political processes (see McNevin 2011). Through this logic, the nation-state produces unequal rights-holders within its own territorial confines.

This is all the more so in times of heightened global mobility, when populations are becoming increasingly heterogeneous (see Castles & Miller 1994; Cresswell 2006). Migrants – such as asylum seekers and refugees – lack access to citizen rights and are therefore kept in legal limbo, neither fully included nor fully excluded from the nation-state. Many of the works in the field of critical citizenship studies take their cue from Giorgio Agamben (2005), who outlines how the nation-state governs through the creation of "a state of exception" in which migrants and asylum seekers are deprived of fundamental rights. Others have stressed how, in the context of migration, the exclusionary dimensions of citizenship produce an exploitable labour force that is rendered vulnerable to the operations of government and market capitalism (Shachar 2009; Goldring & Landolt 2011; Aliverti 2012). In consequence, the relationship between the subjects residing within a nation-state and the polity is becoming "deterritorialized" (see Sassen 2003: 42). In sum, these works suggest that, in a globalized world where people are highly mobile, national citizenship is increasingly incapable of integrating a large proportion of the population as equal rights-holders.

In the field of critical citizenship studies, scholars have also outlined how national citizenship is continuously reworked, altered or contested in order to cope with the new circumstances (Ong 1999; Torpey 2000; Ong 2005, 2006; Staeheli et al. 2012). Such works put forward more flexible conceptions of citizenship that go beyond legal definitions and emphasize that citizenship is also socially (re)produced and contingent on acts and practices. A major influence here is Isin's work on "acts of citizenship". Isin emphasizes how subjects excluded from the dominant order nevertheless *enact* citizenship and, in doing so, make a claim to be counted (Isin 2008; Isin & Nielsen 2008; Isin 2012). Through such means, he argues, citizenship has historically become ever more inclusive and, since the Greek polis, has gradually integrated minorities that were formerly excluded from the dominant order, such as slaves and women (Isin 2002; Isin, Nyers & Turner 2008). Isin and Nielsen (2008) outline how "acts of citizenship" thus open up important political possibilities, writing:

> "Acts of citizenship [...] disrupt habitus, create new possibilities, claim rights and impose obligations in emotionally charged tones; pose their claims in enduring and creative expressions; and, most of all, are the actual moments that shift established practices, status and order." (Isin & Nielsen 2008: 10)

According to Isin and Nielsen, such "acts of citizenship" point towards alternative, more egalitarian forms of society; they shift established orders and are therefore highly political. Soysal (1994), meanwhile, argues that citizenship is increasingly going beyond national parameters, due to the development of what she calls "postnational citizenship". Such forms of citizenship, she reasons, blur the dichotomy between ostensible citizens and aliens through the multiplication of memberships:

> "What is increasingly in place is a multiplicity of membership forms, which occasions exclusions and inclusions that no longer coincide with the bounds of the nation(al)" (Soysal 2012: ; no page number).

Possibilities for transforming national citizenship can stem either from above or below the national level. On the one hand, scholars have discussed how forms of "transnational citizenship" (Bauböck 1994; Sassen 2003: 56) might alter and supplement national citizenship, for instance through European citizenship (see Balibar 2004; Soysal 2012). On the other hand, an emerging strand of literature investigates the tendencies that rework and challenge national citizenship "from below" through forms of "urban citizenship" (see Bauböck 2003) or "subnational citizenship" (Bhuyan & Smith-Carrier 2012).

The manifold practices of refugee support that emerged around the long summer of migration, I would argue, opened up such political possibilities for transforming and contesting national citizenship 'from below'. I will scrutinize these *politics of presence* that were opened up by practices of refugee support in more detail in the following section.

4.2.2. Presence as an Alternative Mode of Belonging

> "In the past year, something unbelievable happened: [...] When it became clear that state actors were not reacting adequately in order to provide the

most basic necessities to the newcomers, hundreds of thousands, maybe even millions of established residents reacted spontaneously and, together with the refugees, built structures of solidarity and understanding [...] Beyond established institutions, a broad and transnational process emerged that pointed to *a future society in which issues of fair distribution, belonging and social rights are redefined.*" (Call for Contributions, Welcome2Stay Conference, 10-12 June 2016 in Leipzig; emphasis added)[1]

On a sunny Sunday morning in June 2016, somewhere on the outskirts of the eastern German city of Leipzig, I made my way from the tramway station to the abandoned fairgrounds where the conference "Welcome2Stay" had taken place over the past two days. "Solidarity" was one of the buzzwords I heard countless times during these days. They were packed with thought-provoking workshops, discussion groups, plenary talks and social activities. The event aimed to bring together all kinds of different groups and individuals actively supporting refugees across Germany, including those who regarded themselves as "political activists" and those who sought to help refugees for ostensibly humanitarian reasons. Indeed, my approximately 800 co-participants seemed to be from diverse backgrounds and age groups.

On the morning of the third and final day of the conference, I opted to attend the last session of the scheduled programme, which was entitled "Visions, Networking, Political Perspectives, What Should We Do?". As usual, we started well behind schedule. When I entered the tent around the appointed time, people were still chatting or having their breakfast, supplied by the self-organized "solidarity kitchen", which had served food to the conference participants over the past days. With almost an hour of delay, a middle-aged moderator stepped up and welcomed participants to the last conference day. After some words of introduction, he kicked off a discussion among the audience by asking participants about the lessons they had learnt in the course

---

1 Translation by LF. German original: "Im letzten Jahr ist etwas Unglaubliches geschehen: [...] Als deutlich wurde, dass staatliche Stellen nicht angemessen handelten, um für die Neuangekommenen das Notwendige bereitzustellen, reagierten Hunderttausende, vielleicht sogar Millionen Alteingesessene spontan und schufen gemeinsam mit den Geflüchteten Strukturen der Solidarität und der Verständigung [...] Jenseits der etablierten Institutionen entstand ein breiter und transnationaler Prozess, der auf eine zukünftige Gesellschaft verwies, in der sich Fragen nach gerechter Verteilung, Zugehörigkeit und sozialen Rechten neu formulierten." See also: http://welcome2stay. org/de/aufruf-zur-beteiligung/ (last accessed 1/8/2020).

of the workshop and about their visions and ideas for future joint actions. After several people in the audience had shared their thoughts and ideas, the moderator took the microphone again and announced that he would like to put forward a proposition that, in his eyes, represented common ground for all of the participants. In a loud, confident voice, he asserted:

"Firstly, all of us here believe in the right to migration, no matter the origin – in a right to come, a right to stay and a right to leave! Secondly, all of us should have the same political and social rights! Including to education, housing and health." (Field notes: 12/6/2016)

These closing remarks, I would argue, are an example of the alternative visions of society, belonging and citizenship that were enacted and formulated through practices of refugee support around the long summer of migration. It epitomizes an aspiration for a society that does not make distinctions among its members based on pre-established ethnic or national criteria but, instead, grants equal rights to "all of us", i.e. to all those present on the ground.

The growing numbers of arriving asylum seekers made citizens more aware than ever that societies are becoming increasingly heterogeneous and mobile. This was due partly to the growing visibility of the cross-border movement of asylum seekers around the long summer of migration and partly to their accommodation in villages and neighbourhoods that had not previously received any asylum seekers. These developments, I would argue, led many volunteers to reflect on the deficiencies of national citizenship, to adopt critical positions towards them, and to enact alternative visions of belonging on the ground. Their practices of refugee support thus also responded to a need to incorporate newcomers with diverse backgrounds who were otherwise excluded from a membership based on national confines. Whether people considered their practices of refugee support as "political", "somewhat political" or "apolitical", questions of fairer distribution gained relevance for many during the long summer of migration. Quite connectedly, Schwiertz and Schwenken (2020: 418) argue that "practices, relationships, and institutions of solidarity take part in renegotiating modes of inclusion and exclusion inherent to citizenship in multiple aspects". Oosterlynck et al. (2016: 10) propose that "the growing ethnic and cultural diversity of the population makes it necessary to look for innovative forms of solidarity elsewhere, namely in the here and now of actual practices in particular places". They thus propose to shift attention "to the relationally constituted places where diversity is encountered and negotiated" (ibid.).

In his monograph *Give a Man a Fish*, Ferguson (2015: 33) considers such alternative forms of distribution building on the notion of a "rightful share" of existing resources for all, including marginalized sections of society. What is required, he says, is a "process of discovery and invention" in order to be "attentive to the ways that new conditions may be opening up new possibilities for politics and policy alike" (ibid.). Ferguson thus emphasizes the significance of forms of social assistance and argues that such practices entail a new way of thinking that is "associated with both new kinds of political claim-making and new possibilities for political mobilization" (ibid.: 14). In his lecture "Presence and Social Obligation: An Essay on the Share"[2], Ferguson (2017) proposed that such alternatives revolve around the theme of *presence*. They include whoever is 'here', present within a community, and thus focus on practical matters of distribution rather than on abstract membership based on the imagined community of the nation (cf. Anderson 1983). Co-presence, he suggested, comes with shared demands and provides the basis for more inclusionary forms of politics.

Building on Ferguson's works, I would argue that the practices of refugee support that emerged around the German migration summer came with a *politics of presence* that articulated and enacted new forms of distribution in an environment incapable of providing the newcomers with a 'rightful share'. As is the case for the mantra formulated in the closing session of the Welcome2Stay conference in Leipzig, these alternatives revolved around the theme of presence, i.e. the physical act of being there on the ground.

This emphasis on co-presence is in line with an emerging and growing interest in 'the local' as a spatial reference for political alternatives beyond the nation-state. For instance, Bauder has written extensively on the question of how political alternatives form 'below' the nation-state, on a local or urban scale (Bauder 2011, 2012, 2013, 2015, 2016). He suggests that a *jus domicile* principle might provide an emerging mode of imagining political membership beyond the national order (Bauder 2012). This principle would grant equal rights to all de facto residents in a community and thus enacts "a practical alternative for reconfiguring formal citizenship to include populations that are mobile across borders" (Bauder 2013: 3). Resulting forms of "domicile citizenship" would offer opportunities to decouple citizenship from the nation-state (ibid.). Writing with Austin, Bauder (2010: 12) emphasizes the significance of universality for such modes of belonging arguing that "*jus domicile* citizenship

---

2   Dahrendorf Lecture at the University of Konstanz, 5/7/2017.

should be a right and should not be conferred selectively on some residents and denied to others". In his writings on migrant solidarity, Bauder (2019: 7) also stresses that "the solidarities that emerge from migration give rise to 'place-based politics' [...] these politics relate to the local presence of international migrants and refugees". Similarly, the volunteers in the area of my field research often stressed the significance of implementing a more inclusive alternative in *their* neighbourhood, village or region and, in doing so, placed an emphasis on the local level.

Yet, scholars have also pointed to the contested nature of alternative modes of belonging that form 'below' the nation-state. There is a fruitful strand of literature that scrutinizes differing understandings of belonging (see for example Yuval-Davis 2006; Pfaff-Czarnecka & Toffin 2011; Yuval-Davis 2011). For instance, Youkhana (2015: 11) emphasizes that modes of belonging are subject to manifold contestations, opening up "a politics of belonging": "Belonging is produced beyond ethnic or national boundaries but is contested on interrelated sites, scales, and networks" (Youkhana 2015: 14). This contested nature of social membership is also emphasized by Soysal's works on postnational forms of citizenship: "Postnational rights are results of struggles, negotiations, and arbitrations by actors at local, national, and transnational levels and are contingent upon issues of distribution and equity" (Soysal 2012: no page number).

In a similar vein, the alternative visions of belonging that were articulated and enacted through practices of refuge support in the area of my field research also proved to be highly contested among different individuals and groups involved. They oscillated *in-between* calls for a radical egalitarian society and more conditioned and hesitant views. It is these diverse positions that I aim to grasp with the concept of a *politics of presence*. In the remainder of this chapter, I scrutinize the contested alternatives to national citizenship that emerged around the German migration summer, arguing that they revolved around a demand for equal rights (section three), a demand for a right to stay (section four) and a demand for a right to migrate (section five).

4.3. Contestations around Equal Rights

In his closing statement, the moderator at the Welcome2Stay conference put forward a demand for radical political equality: "[...] Secondly, all of us should have *the same political and social rights!* Including to education, housing and health" (Field notes: 12/6/2016, emphasis added). In his view, such a call for equal rights mirrored a demand shared not only by the audience members of the conference but by many that engaged in practices of refugee support. In contrast, I would suggest that a universal demand for equal rights for all those present on the ground was a highly contested claim among those who supported refugees. In the following subsections, I scrutinize the differing views towards such a demand among the individuals and groups I encountered in the course of my field research. Although some articulated and enacted a universal call for equal rights (first subsection), others made their efforts to integrate asylum seekers as equals contingent on certain categories and, thus, put forward more ambivalent and conditioned positions (second subsection).

4.3.1. Solidarity Cities: Universal Demands for Equal Rights

In the wake of the migration summer, incentives to implement "Solidarity Cities" emerged in many German cities. A striking example is the Solidarity City network in Freiburg, the second largest city in the southern German state of Baden-Württemberg. This network consisted of a loose alliance of individuals and groups supporting refugees in the city. The main impetus, however, stemmed from the group "Freiburger Forum aktiv gegen Ausgrenzung" (roughly "Freiburg Anti-Exclusion Forum"), as I discovered via its regular email newsletters, to which I subscribed. From mid-2016 on, the Solidarity City Freiburg became a major focus of the group's activities. In the course of my field research, I found the Freiburger Forum to be one of the most visible, well known and influential of the groups across Baden-Württemberg taking a critical stance on the situation of asylum seekers. The group openly voiced dissent with certain asylum policies through demonstrations, open letters and other campaigns that gained high public visibility. Although these actions might mark the group out as more politically informed than others, it neither presented itself as "activist" nor as acting from a leftist political position. This was also mirrored by the Solidarity City Freiburg network, which did not present itself as 'politically activist' but, instead, as an 'open alliance' of diverse groups and individuals.

The Solidarity City Freiburg campaign is a clear example of a group that put forward a radical call for equal rights for all those present within the confines of the city. This is best illustrated in the official flyer that promoted the Solidarity City idea and featured the silhouette of Freiburg in the background. In the foreground was the following statement:

"Our demands are simple: every person living in Freiburg ... should have a right to basic services; should have access to the infrastructure of the city; should be able to receive education; should be able to access medical health services; should be able to take part in political decision-making; should have the right to cultural participation; should have the right to stay! And these rights should be independent of the status of the individual person."[3] (Flyer, Solidarity City Freiburg, 2017)[4]

Solidarity, in this context, thus meant a vision of a socially and politically egalitarian society within the confines of the city. This vision is very much in line with what Schwiertz (2016) calls "radical egalitarian citizenship". The rights to be granted in this utopian Solidarity City include not only the right to equal access to the city's basic services but also the right to "take part in political decision-making processes", a right conventionally limited to those classed as national citizens. Furthermore, the Solidarity City project was presented as benefitting *all* and, thus, as a means to improve the city as a whole. This was reflected by the headline of the flyer, which proclaimed "an opportunity for a more just city" (Flyer, Solidarity City Freiburg: 2017).

The alternative understandings of belonging formulated by the Solidarity City Freiburg connect strikingly to the literature on forms of 'urban citizenship' (see Bauböck 2003; Varsanyi 2006; Lebuhn 2013). Different authors suggest that such forms of citizenship present an activist strategy that challenges the nation-state 'from below' by calling for equal rights for the inhabitants of a city (see Kalandides & Vaiou 2012; Canepari & Rosa 2017; Kandylis 2017). Many of these works refer to the writings of Henri Lefebvre (1996) and David Harvey (2012) on the 'right to the city', calling for all of a city's inhabitants to have the right to transform and participate in the reworking of its structures.

Drawing on these works, Purcell (2002: 100) outlines how demands on the 'right to the city' "offer an alternative that directly challenges and rethinks

---

3   Translation by LF. German original: "Unsere Forderungen sind einfach: Jede Person, die in Freiburg lebt [...] soll ein Recht auf Daseinsgrundversorgung haben; soll Zugang zu Infrastrukturen der Stadt gewährt werden; soll Bildung und Weiterbildung ermöglicht werden; soll medizinische Beratung und Versorgung in Anspruch nehmen können; soll politisch mitbestimmen dürfen; soll das Recht auf kulturelle Teilhabe besitzen; soll das Recht zu bleiben haben! Und diese Rechte sollen unabhängig vom jeweiligen Aufenthaltsstatus der Person sein.".
4   See: https://www.freiburger-forum.net/wordpress/wp-content/uploads/2017/06/solidaritycity-flyer-Freiburg.pdf (last accessed 1/8/2020).

the current structure of both capitalism and liberal-democratic citizenship". He thus argues that they not only articulate an alternative vision of social membership but also directly challenge the current status quo. This is also mirrored in the Solidarity City project in Freiburg: the flyer not only put forward a demand for a radical egalitarian alternative but also entailed a critical examination of current conditions of inequality affecting the inhabitants of the city. For instance, it drew attention to the marginalized political status of illegalized migrants, stating that "not all of our fellow citizens hold a German passport and not all have a secure residence status"[5] (Flyer, Solidarity City Freiburg: 2017). The flyer thus spoke out against the distinction between national citizens and aliens, a distinction that creates a situation of unequal rights on the ground. It also repeatedly criticized German asylum laws such as the "Asylbewerberleistungsgesetz", which determines the material and monetary benefits asylum seekers receive from the German state. This law, it claimed, resulted in a situation where asylum seekers were "even worse off" than those on social security benefits. Thus, the project highlighted various ways in which national laws produce inequalities on the ground.

Scholars have engaged more thoroughly with the Sanctuary or Solidarity City movement in the Anglophone world, in particular in Canada and the US (see Ridgley 2008; Ridgley 2011; Bauder 2017) but also in the UK (see Squire 2011b; Squire & Darling 2013). These works outline how such utopian projects challenge the exclusion of marginalized parts of society from national citizenship rights. Squire (2011b: 290), for instance, points out how their campaigns "enact a mobile form of solidarity based on participation through presence", cut across social hierarchies, and blur the distinction between 'guest' and 'host'. Others put forward a more sceptical view of the transformative power of Solidarity Cities. For instance, Bagelman (2013) argues that such imaginaries mobilize "a politics of ease" that is complicit in the existing asylum regime, deferring the debate about exclusionary mechanisms and laws that render asylum seekers vulnerable to the operations of the state.

In the German context, Solidarity Cities have not yet received the same attention as those in the United States. This might be partly explained by the fact that American cities have coped with a substantially higher number of undocumented illegalized migrants for years, from Central American countries for instance. And yet, the example of the Solidarity City network in Freiburg

---

5   Translation by LF. German original: "Nicht jede_r unserer Mitbürger_innen hat einen deutschen Pass, und auch nicht jede_r hat einen gesicherten Aufenthaltsstatus.".

clearly illustrates that such alternative imaginaries of urban citizenship have also started to take shape in Germany. In the wake of the long summer of migration, similar drives to implement Solidarity Cities emerged in various cities across the country, for instance in Berlin, Hamburg and Augsburg. Further research is needed in order to investigate their possibilities and limitations when it comes to enacting alternative visions of belonging.

To sum up, the example of the Solidarity City in Freiburg illustrated how alternative visions of society and belonging formed in response to the long summer of migration, alternative visions that revolved around a radical demand for equal rights for all those present on the ground. In the following subsection, I illustrate how many of the volunteers I spoke to in the course of my field research put forward more hesitant and conditioned views on a demand for equal rights. Nevertheless, they positioned themselves in manifold ways in relation to existing exclusions while forging new relationships that aimed to foster more egalitarian alternatives.

4.3.2. Ambivalent Positions and Conditional Hospitality

Many of the volunteers who engaged in practices of refugee support around the long summer of migration were mobilized by a desire to change the status quo in their local communities in favour of a different alternative. Nonetheless, they often refrained from a radical demand for equal rights. In order to illustrate this, I draw on an intriguing interview with two volunteers supporting refugees in the small village of Berglen. Birgit Frank and Julia Kuch were leading figures in the local citizens' initiative "Network for Refugees" ("Netzwerk für Flüchtlinge"), which had around 80 active members when I interviewed the two women in March 2016. This initiative formed in response to the allocation of around 100 refugees to Berglen in 2015, the first time the village had received asylum seekers. During our interview, I asked the women what had motivated them to get involved in practices of refugee support. Birgit Frank explained there was both a "human" and a "political component" behind her involvement. She explained the latter as follows:

> "I think it is also an opportunity for something to happen regarding social housing, and not just because of the refugees, but also for us to make sure that we don't pit the weak against the weak, that everyone has a minimum standard of living and that there is enough social housing. And that might also wake some of our politicians up to the fact that something has to be

done here because otherwise people really will vote AfD."[6] (Interview with Birgit Frank and Julia Kuch: 14/3/2016)

Quite similar to the Solidarity City network in Freiburg, Birgit Frank thus claimed to be motivated by a vision of society in which "everyone has a minimum standard of living", and equal access to benefits such as social housing. She also problematized the current situation of inequality, in which asylum seekers were pitted against others in "weak" positions, while depicting her actions as an opportunity to "wake up" politicians. I would argue that this clearly illustrates how my interlocutor regarded her helping practices as a means to enact a more egalitarian alternative in her local community, although she did not directly demand equal rights for the newcomers.

In contrast to Birgit Frank, her colleague Julia Kuch explicitly denied that her actions were "political". Nevertheless, she also emphasized her motivation to contribute to the public good in Berglen, saying:

"So from the beginning, I said: I'm not just doing it for the refugees, I'm doing it as much for the people of Berglen, just so that the two can live side by side more tolerably. In that sense, we see ourselves as intermediaries."[7] (Interview with Birgit Frank and Julia Kuch: 14/3/2016)

Julia Kuch thus aimed to change the situation in her local community by "intermediating" between newcomers and established residents. She regarded her practices of refugee support as a means to forge new relationships and to counteract exclusions and isolations on the ground. To Julia Kuch, helping refugees served as a way of ensuring everyone could live side by side and avoiding conflicts, while helping, to Birgit Frank, drew attention to the problems of 'weaker' groups. All the same, both volunteers sought to change their local community by enacting a 'better' alternative on the ground.

---

6   Translation by LF. German original: "Ich denk, das ist auch eine Chance, dass jetzt was Richtung Wohnungsbau net nur wegen den Flüchtlingen was passiert, sondern dass wir alle dafür sorgen müssen, dass nicht Schwache gegen Schwache ausgespielt werden, sondern dass wir alle einen Mindeststandard haben und genügend Wohnraum da ist und dass das auch manche politische Ebene wachrütteln wird, dass man was tun muss, weil sonst wird wirklich die AfD gewählt.".

7   Translation by LF. German original: "Also ich hab von Anfang an gesagt, ich mach das nicht nur für die Flüchtlinge, sondern ich mach das genauso gut für die Bevölkerung von Berglen, um einfach ein Zusammenleben zwischen beiden Parteien erträglicher zu machen. Insofern sehen wir uns schon so als Vermittler zwischen beiden.".

In their attempt to conceptualize the "role of individuals in creating change", Martin, Hanson and Fontaine (2007) pose the question: "What counts as activism?". They propose opening up the category of political activism to include not only actions that are conventionally considered 'political' but also everyday actions with a more limited geographic reach. They thus emphasize the significance of local and everyday forms of interaction:

> "activism [...] emerges from the everyday lived context (place) in which people are embedded; activism entails an individual making particular kinds of new connections between people that alter power relations within existing social networks" (Martin, Hanson & Fontaine 2007: 80)

Similarly, I would argue, many volunteers in the area of my field research aimed to foster new relationships within their community in order to alter and transform existing power imbalances – and thus engaged in forms of everyday activism. Nevertheless, the volunteers' positions regarding the question of how the more egalitarian alternatives should look like in practice were highly contested and debated. During my interview in Berglen, the two volunteers repeatedly argued when responding to my questions and apparently held quite different standpoints in this regard. To varying extents, their views also differed from the radical call for equal rights made at the Welcome2Stay conference and by the Solidarity City network.

Quite often, volunteers set certain limits on the inclusion of asylum seekers as fellow citizens within their local community and made their efforts to foster a more egalitarian alternative depended on certain categories. My conversation with Julia Kuch illustrated this strikingly: her practices of refugee support turned out to be conditional on the nationality, race and gender of the asylum seekers. This is illustrated by the following statement, in which she talked about the new accommodation centre that had been set up in a former schoolhouse in Berglen:

> "So, we are kind of very blessed here. Up there are many families, many children – they all give you a hug when you get there. If there were 60 black African men up there, that would be something quite different. Just in terms of the character, the potential, the appearance"[8] (Interview with Birgit Frank and Julia Kuch: 14/3/2016)

---

8   Translation by LF. German original: "Also wir sind halt schon auch verwöhnt, da oben sind viele Familien, viele Kinder, die nehmen einen alle in Arm, wenn man da oben ankommt. Wenn da oben jetzt 60 schwarzafrikanische Männer wären, dann

Most of the refugees who had arrived in Berglen, Julia Kuch told me, were families of Syrian or Iraqi origin. Therefore, they had good chances of being recognized as 'genuine' refugees in the course of their asylum process, while, in the long-run, they could be socially integrated as equal citizens in Berglen. However, if it had been "black African men" that would have been quite different, my interlocutor asserted. I came across many cases in the course of my field research, where people from Sub-Saharan African countries were depicted as 'bogus' asylum seekers who had claimed asylum for what were considered bogus economic reasons, a perception also mirrored in their generally low rates of recognition by the German government. My interlocutor Julia Kuch, along with her bluntly racist attitudes, thus also made her efforts to support refugees in Berglen contingent on governmental categorizations of 'genuine' and 'bogus' asylum seekers.

Furthermore, volunteers in the area of my field research often made the social integration of asylum seekers as equal members subject to certain rules of conduct. This became strikingly illustrated at the Welcome2Stay conference in Leipzig. As outlined above, the moderator of the final plenary discussion demanded equal rights for all in his closing statement. Yet, this demand also evoked sceptical reactions among audience members, some of whom commented critically on the moderator's proposition. Most strikingly, an elderly woman remarked that these demands were "too universal" and needed to be tied to certain conditions and obligations for the newcomers, such as respect for gender equality and non-patriarchal behaviour (Field notes: 12/6/2016). This comment, I would argue, epitomizes how many of my interlocutors tied their visions of a more egalitarian alternative to certain expectations concerning the behaviour of the present asylum seekers, such as gratitude.

Rather than supporting radical demands for equal rights, many of the volunteers in the area of my field research thus made their hospitality contingent on categories such as nation, gender or expected behaviours. These observations connect with Jacques Derrida's writings on the ethics of hospitality (see Derrida & Dufourmantelle 2000). Building on Kant, Derrida distinguishes between forms of "conditional hospitality" and "unconditional hospitality". The former, the unconditional reception of the foreigner, he argues, would always only present an ideal, a fiction that is impossible to implement in practice (Derrida & Caputo 1997: 110). Enacting hospitality, on the other hand, would

---

wäre es auch nochmal was Anderes. Schon allein vom Charakter, vom Potenzial, vom Auftreten.".

always require the imposition of certain conditions and terms upon it. The implementation of hospitality thus revolves around a "negotiation of the impossibility", as O'Gorman (2006: 54) remarks. This, I would argue, is also mirrored in the differing views among those volunteering with refugees in the area of my field research. While the Solidarity City network and the moderator of the Welcome2Stay conference issued a universal call for equal rights – for unconditional hospitality – those who sought to help refugees in their local communities, and thus practically enacted hospitality, often tied the integration of asylum seekers as fellow citizens to certain conditions. Nonetheless, all of them sought to enact a different alternative 'from below' the nation-state.

4.4. Contestations around a Right to Stay

Along with equal rights, the moderator at the Welcome2Stay conference in Leipzig demanded "a right to stay" (Field notes: 12/06/2016). During my field research, however, I realized that many of my interlocutors had quite ambivalent, and at times conflicting perspectives towards this demand. This was particularly evident in the context of deportations: whether or not asylum seekers whose asylum case was rejected should be granted a right to stay proved a central issue that regularly provoked discussions among those supporting refugees. In the following two subsections, I scrutinize how people in the area of my field research positioned themselves in relation to a demand for a right to stay.

4.4.1. Taking, or not Taking a Stand against Deportations

For many of my interlocutors, the question of whether all asylum seekers should be granted a right to stay or not was not an easy one. This became most apparent when volunteers discussed the issue of deportations, i.e. the forced return of rejected asylum seekers to their countries of origin or, as in the case of Dublin III deportations, to the EU member state responsible for processing the asylum case. Deportations were a subject that regularly eschewed controversial discussions among the volunteers, for instance, at the conferences of the Refugee Council of Baden-Württemberg. In a nutshell, these debates revolved around the question of whether governmental decisions to reject and deport certain groups of migrants were acceptable or whether volunteers should oppose such decisions and call for a right to stay for the affected.

For instance, in November 2014, I attended the workshop "Staying Here – Successful Protests and Concepts against Deportations" at a Refugee Council conference. This workshop aimed to discuss possible ways to contest deportations of rejected asylum seekers. To this end, the Refugee Council had invited two "experts" who had travelled all the way from Osnabrück, a city in northern Germany, to Stuttgart in order to recount their experiences in blocking deportations. One was a student in his early twenties called Michael, the other was Aman, a refugee from Eritrea, who was slightly older and spoke German with a heavy accent. Both introduced themselves as members of the group "No Lager Osnabrück"[9], which had a long history of success in preventing deportations. Several years ago, the group had started blocking deportations of rejected asylum seekers to their countries of origin or, in the case of Dublin deportations, to other European member states. Michael and Aman introduced No Lager as an "anti-racist supporter group" (Field notes: 22/11/2014) that, at the time of the workshop, consisted of around 50 active members. In the course of their talk, the two shared their experiences and gave practical hints on how to (peacefully) block deportations on the ground. The audience seemed quite interested and was particularly attentive when it came to the practical details of these blockings. Many participants in the audience also voiced their respect and admiration for the successful actions of No Lager.

When the workshop leaders finally opened the floor for discussion, a lively and heated debate developed among workshop participants. This debate revolved mainly around two issues: Firstly, many voiced dissent towards the workings of governmental authorities in the context of deportations and accused them of the inhumane treatment of asylum seekers. For instance, they denounced the authorities for not informing asylum seekers before their deportation, but simply showing up with police presence in the middle of the night. Secondly, people discussed whether and how deportations could also be blocked successfully in the respective local context of their citizens' initiatives across Baden-Württemberg. For instance, an elderly woman with a heavy Swabian dialect asserted that:

---

9   The group name "No Lager" literally translates as "No Camp", mirroring how self-depicted political activists took a stand against the accommodation of asylum seekers in centralized and large-scale centres, which they called "camps" in order to highlight their problematic and discriminating consequences for their inhabitants.

"People's behaviour in Upper Swabia is not the same as in Osnabrück. It is really difficult to do blocking in places such as Wurzach or other rural towns where we don't have any students."[10] (Field notes: 22/11/2014)

Following the woman's statement, various participants of the workshop shared their experiences of how they themselves had already successfully blocked deportations in their local communities. It turned out that many had opposed deportations through legal means, organized church asylum or even hidden asylum seekers in their houses.

These observations illustrate how people supporting refugees in the area of my field research often did not simply accept governmental deportation orders. Instead, they discussed deportations in critical terms and elaborated ways of opposing orders deemed unjust. By doing so, they demanded a right to stay for the affected. At this early stage of my fieldwork, it came as something of a surprise that the blocking of deportations was not only being conducted by those who openly identified themselves as political activists but also by those who sought to help refugees for ostensibly humanitarian reasons, such as retired pastors or the elderly Swabian woman from Wurzach. In the course of my field research, however, I discovered that many volunteers took a critical stance in relation to the topic of deportations and, in doing so, engaged in a *politics of presence*.

Scholars in the field of critical migration studies have outlined how deportations function as a key moment in which the state exercises and affirms sovereign power (see De Genova 2010). According to Peter Nyers (2010a), the issue of deportations is thus fundamentally a political one:

"In the case of asylum seekers, the decision about who will and who will not be provided with protection is not just a humanitarian determination but a moment when the sovereign state (re)founds its claim to monopolize the political. Anti-deportation activists can therefore be read in terms of contemporary disputes over who has the authority to protect, and under what terms and conditions. Such activism can reveal new problematizations as well as new ways of thinking and acting politically." (Nyers 2010a: 415)

In line with Nyers, I would suggest that volunteers who actively take a stand against deportations directly challenge the authority of the nation-state in

---

10 Translation by LF. German original: "Das Verhalten in Osnabrück ist anders als in Oberschwaben. Es ist schwierig das Blocking in Orten wie Wurzach oder anderen ländlich geprägten Gegenden durchzuführen, da wir hier keine Studenten haben.".

the governance of migration. In doing so, they open up political possibilities that emphasize *presence* and enact alternative visions of society and belonging revolving around the rejected asylum seekers' rights to stay. Yet, Kalir and Wissink (2016) caution against distinguishing neatly between those who attempt to enforce deportations and those who contest them, a distinction that obscures how such positions are, in fact, much more debated and heterogeneous. They thus speak of a "deportation continuum" in order to make room for these differing views (ibid.). In line with their argument, I would suggest that the Refugee Council conferences served as an important "arena", to borrow a term from Hilhorst and Jansen (2010), in which those supporting refugees could articulate and negotiate positions in relation to a 'deportation continuum'.

This arena, which was opened up by the Refugee Council, brought together groups and individuals who embedded their practices of refugee support in quite diverse social imaginaries. Via my regular participation in these conferences, I soon learned that many participants neither took an explicitly left-wing political stance nor did they regard themselves as political activists. Instead, the conferences brought together a broad range of volunteers, including retired teachers, pastors, lawyers or stay-at-home mothers, who often embedded their actions in humanitarian or religious imaginaries. Aman and Michael, the two workshop leaders from the group "No Lager Osnabrück", however, probably did regard themselves as left-wing political activists, although they did not openly identify themselves as such during the workshop. When I studied the group's website in the wake of the workshop, I discovered that it formed part of a network of antifascist activists. Various links connected the website with other explicitly left-wing activist groups, such as "Rote Hilfe e.V." or a left-wing student association at the University of Osnabrück. Moreover, the information on the website revealed that the group had organized various public protests and demonstrations that made explicitly political demands while voicing dissent towards existing asylum and migration policies. Most strikingly, it had previously organized a demonstration demanding an "unconditional right to stay" for all asylum seekers.

Despite their differing self-understandings and motivations, however, the participants of the "Staying Here" workshop had a common denominator: they elaborated ways of blocking deportations and were thus determined to oppose governmental decisions. Yet, while the political activists of the "No Lager Osnabrück" group would probably reject *any* deportation in favour of an unconditional right to stay, this was not the case for many of those who supported refugees for ostensibly humanitarian reasons. As I discovered in the course of my field research, the latter were often much more reluctant and ambivalent in this regards.

Such disputed standpoints became apparent in relation to the deportations of Sinti and Roma and those originating from Eastern European countries[11] such as Serbia, Kosovo and Albania. On the one hand, I came across numerous moments when volunteers openly denounced such asylum seekers for claiming asylum on false pretences and even called for their deportation. On the other hand, several initiatives organized campaigns or talks criticizing the problematic conditions in Eastern European countries, and raising awareness for the systematic discrimination against Sinti and Roma. For instance, the group "Freiburger Forum aktiv gegen Ausgrenzung" launched a campaign on behalf of a local Roma family demanding an "immediate right to return" (see Open Petition: 2015)[12]. Its online petition received more than 8,000 signatures and widespread regional and national media attention (see Focus: 17/2/2015)[13]. In another town, a group supporting refugees handed over a petition entitled "No deportations of Roma!" to the local mayor (see Aktion Bleiberecht: 20/7/2014)[14].

More widespread dissent formed around the deportations of asylum seekers from Gambia. Due to a national distribution formula, Baden-Württemberg accommodated a majority of the migrants originating from the small country in western Africa, and processed their asylum cases. During the time of my field research, however, most asylum claims by Gambians were rejected (cf. Flüchtlingsrat Niedersachsen: 2016)[15]. These decisions were denounced by many volunteers who criticized how Gambian asylum seekers were being sent back to a brutal dictatorship with an intolerable political

---

11 Throughout 2014 and in the first months of 2015, Serbia, Kosovo and Albania were among the top countries of origin among those who claimed asylum in Germany. However, recognition rates for asylum seekers from these countries were approximately zero. See: https://www.proasyl.de/hintergrund/zahlen-und-fakten-2015 (last accessed 1/8/2020).
12 See: https://www.openpetition.de/petition/online/sofortiges-wiedereinreise-und-rueckkehrrecht-von-frau-ametovic-und-ihren-kindern-nach-freiburg (last accessed 1/8/2020).
13 See: http://www.focus.de/regional/freiburg/fluechtlinge-fall-ametovic-jugendhelfer-wollen-serbien-reise-mit-gall_id_4481827.html (last accessed 1/8/2020).
14 See: https://www.aktionbleiberecht.de/?p=6271 (last accessed 1/8/2020).
15 See: https://www.nds-fluerat.org/19551/aktuelles/bereinigte-schutzquoten-fuer-ausgewaehlte-herkunftslaender-von-fluechtlingen/ (last accessed 1/8/2020).

situation. Several citizens' initiatives thus organized campaigns demanding a right to stay for Gambians. For instance, in mid-2016, the group "Arbeitskreis Asyl Donaueschingen" ("Asylum Working Circle Donaueschingen") published an open letter to the German minister of the interior, calling for an end to all deportations to Gambia (Arbeistkreis Asyl DS: 2016)[16]. Another initiative, the "Helferkreis Breisach" (literally "Helping Circle Breisach"), launched an online petition against the deportation of Gambians that gained more than 5,000 signatures. In December 2016, when presidential elections in the African country were scheduled, the Refugee Council of Baden-Württemberg organized a "state-wide Gambia week" in order to call attention to the situation of asylum seekers originating from the country (see Flüchtlingsrat BW: 2016)[17]. According to the official website of the campaign, more than 50 volunteers' initiatives across Baden-Württemberg participated, organizing numerous local actions and events that received widespread media attention (see Abschiebestopp Gambia: 2016)[18].

These instances, I would argue, clearly illustrate how some of the volunteers did not hesitate to systematically oppose deportation orders, demanding a right to stay for certain groups of asylum seekers. Although they did not directly demand an unconditional right to stay, their aim was nonetheless to change the status quo towards a more inclusive alternative. Rosenberger and Winkler (2014) argue that the opposition to deportations in local communities often depends on the individual case or on personal ties to the affected asylum seeker. Based on the observations of my field research, however, I would argue that it was often also the national and ethnic background of the affected asylum seekers that determined whether volunteers perceived deportations as unjust and took a stand against them.

Summing up, those who sought to help refugees for humanitarian reasons often elaborated where, when, for whom and under what circumstances a deportation was inappropriate and, in doing so, took up more conditional and ambivalent positions in relation to a right to stay. An issue, however,

---

16 See: http://www.ak-asyl-ds.de/wp-content/uploads/2014/06/Offener-Brief-Gambia.pdf (last accessed 1/8/2020).
17 See: http://fluechtlingsrat-bw.de/files/Dateien/Dokumente/INFOS%20-%20Fluechtlingsarbeit%20BW/2016%20landesweit/Aufruf%20Gambia-Woche%203-.12.%20Dezember%202016.pdf (last accessed 1/8/2020).
18 See: https://abschiebestoppgambia.wordpress.com/tag/presse/ (last accessed 1/8/2020).

that triggered more unanimous views among the volunteers were so-called "Dublin cases", as I will illustrate in more detail in the following subsection.

4.4.2. Counteracting the European Union

Volunteers in the area of my field research quite often demanded an unconditional, albeit temporary right to stay in the context of "Dublin cases". These deportation orders fell under the Dublin III Regulation, an EU act stipulating that responsibility for processing an asylum case lies with the member state through which an asylum seeker first enters the European Union (for more information on the Dublin Regulation see Kasparek & Matheis 2016; Picozza 2017). Often this meant that countries at the margins of the European Union, such as Greece and Bulgaria, had to assume responsibility. If registered asylum seekers moved on to Central European countries, for instance to Germany, the authorities could then deport them to the first-entry state. Campaigning against the Dublin Regulation became one of the central aspects of the work of the Refugee Council of Baden-Württemberg in the first half of 2015. Around the same time, such tendencies also occurred on a national level: the Refugee Councils of different German states joint forces with the non-governmental organization "Pro Asyl" in order to implement campaigns with the aim to abolish this regulation.

Thus, the Dublin Regulation and related deportation orders became a major source of criticism among people supporting refugees even before the events of the long summer of migration. For instance, during an introductory speech to a Refugee Council conference in March 2015, the chairperson called the Dublin Regulation a "bureaucratic monstrosity" (Field notes: 7/3/2015). Later that day, I participated in a workshop entitled "Campaigns against the Dublin Regulation", which was moderated by two employees of the Council. During their presentation, the two moderators asserted that "Fortress Europe had two components" (Field notes: 7/3/2015): first, the fortification of European borders and second, the Dublin Regulation. In the subsequent discussion, a heated debate developed in which audience members elaborated potential ways of protesting against and circumventing this EU regulation, for instance by blocking Dublin deportations. In this context, the moderators also recommended a brochure by the social welfare organization "Diakonisches Werk Kassel" to the workshop participants. Available online, this brochure provided a step-by-step guide on how to legally intervene against a Dublin deportation. The workshop moderators thus encouraged volunteers to legally contest such deportation orders in their local communities, explaining that these interventions often proved successful if they were justified in terms of the "sovereignty clause" (literally "Selbsteintrittsrecht"): if the asylum seeker had faced human rights violations in the EU member state to which he or she was to be deported, then volunteers should call on the German state to apply this clause and not enforce the Dublin Regulation. Other volunteers in the audience recalled how they had successfully hidden an asylum seeker threatened with a Dublin deportation in their house for several days, so that the time limit for implementing the deportation expired and the German state became responsible for processing the relevant asylum case. Together with the participants, the moderators also discussed possibilities of "lobbying against" the Dublin Regulation at a local level (Field notes: 7/3/2015). For instance, several volunteers in the audience emphasized that it was important to "spread the word" in their local communities and to influence political representatives via conversations on the ground.

These observations resonate with something I encountered repeatedly in the course of my field research: committed volunteers considered the Dublin Regulation unjust and discriminatory and viewed it as a wider symbol of the ineffectiveness and inhumanity of the European Union. For instance, a volunteer strikingly remarked that the Dublin Regulation was responsible for "sending asylum seekers back and forth as if they were goods, not humans" (Field notes: 7/3/2015). My interlocutors also often condemned the terrible conditions asylum seekers faced in the member states to which they were returned – in Hungary and Greece for instance – and criticized those countries' inhumane treatment of asylum seekers. Others considered the Dublin regulation to be a direct result of the lack of cohesion among European member states, who were denounced for washing their hands of the responsibility to receive asylum seekers. In this context, volunteers also often criticized the EU for being heartless, ineffective and over-bureaucratic.

These criticisms, I would argue, offer a striking example of the emotional disconnect many of my interlocutors felt in relation to the European Union, something that has been acknowledged in academic works on the European identity (see for instance Balibar 2004). This antipathy towards the European Union appeared to be a common denominator among many of the volunteers I encountered in the area of my field research. Some even told me that they were mobilized into refugee support in response to the European Union's inhumane treatment of asylum seekers. For many of my interlocutors, especially those who became involved *before* the long summer of migration, their practices of refugee support also served as a means to enact an alternative to the heartless European asylum and border policies and thus to challenge the European Union 'from below'. Quite connectedly, Monforte (2020) argues that pro-migrants' protest movements mobilize alternative visions and counter-stories of Europe and its borders. I would argue that my field research clearly revealed how those who supported refugees for ostensibly 'apolitical' humanitarian reasons were often also driven by such an impulse to enact alternative visions of Europe and challenge dominant ones.

Summing up, many groups in the area of my field research did not hesitate to radically oppose the Dublin regulation and related deportation orders in their local communities. Kirchhoff (2020) observed a similar tendency in the northern German city of Osnabrück. These critical voices highlighted the deficiencies of the Dublin system months prior to what became known as the "refugee crisis", when it eventually collapsed and asylum seekers could more or less travel freely to and claim asylum in Central European member states (cf. Kasparek 2016). Many volunteers also regarded their attempts to subvert Dublin deportations as a means to contest the EU asylum policies in general. They emphasized the *presence* of asylum seekers on the ground over the policies of the European Union and, by so doing, demanded a right to stay, at least for the duration of the asylum process.

4.5. Contestations around a Right to Migrate

The *politics of presence* that formed among those who supported refugees around the long summer of migration not only revolved around demands for equal rights and a right to stay, but also around a demand for a right to migrate. In the course of my field research, I came across numerous instances when my interlocutors discussed the possibility of global freedom of movement. By doing so, they elaborated alternatives that would enable the free global circulation of people, alternatives that often went hand in hand with criticisms of fortified borders. However, this demand for a right to migrate was met with diverse and, at times, ambivalent positions among those supporting refugees. They ranged from a call to abolish all territorial borders to more circumspect and sceptical views.

Those who openly identified themselves as "political activists" often called for a universal right to free global movement. This was particularly evident when I attended a conference in Berlin organized by the "International Coalition of Sans-Papiers Migrants and Refugees" in February 2015. This conference brought together around 200 participants from various European countries, including politically active migrants and their supporters. Topics that were discussed during this two-day workshop included the European border and asylum policies, forms of legal and social exclusion, discrimination and racism, and the situation of asylum seekers on the ground. Although these topics resembled those discussed at the regular conferences of the Refugee Council of Baden-Württemberg, not only were the participants at the Berlin conference younger on average, the tone of criticism was also much harsher. For instance, European border policies were compared to a "war on migrants" and national asylum policies were described as "persecution" (Field notes: 7/2/2015; see also CISPM: 2015)[19]. What appeared to be a common denominator among conference participants was the demand for an unconditional and universal right to free movement for all and the opposition to any policy restricting such a right (Field notes: 7/2/2015). For instance, the conference organizers instigated a protest march entitled "Stop War on Migrants", for which they prepared around twenty cardboard coffins that protesters carried on their shoulders as they marched through the streets of central Berlin. These cardboard coffins, as the organizers told me, represented the thousands of dead migrants who had drowned in their attempt to cross the Mediterranean Sea. Through such means, they drew attention to the violent and deadly consequences of border protection. Other protesters carried banners calling for freedom of movement. During this "funeral march", as the event organizers described it, protesters also chanted their demands out loud: "No borders, no nation, stop deportation!" or "Brick by brick, wall by wall, make the Fortress Europe fall!" (Field notes: 6/2/2015).

The positions I encountered at the workshop in Berlin resembled what scholars have discussed as 'No Border Network', a loose, Europe-wide network of groups opposing territorial borders (see Hayter 2004; Walters 2006; Rigby & Schlembach 2013; Bauder 2015). As Walters (2006: 22) puts it, such groups "imagine a democratized mobility that encompasses autonomous movements of flight, circulation, settlement and unsettlement". Rigby and Schlembach (2013: 159) argue that actions revolving around a demand for no borders "develop a politics of equality autonomously from the categories of citizenship, sovereignty and the state". In a similar vein, many of those who supported

---

19 See: https://cispmberlin.wordpress.com/deutsch/samstag-7-februar-2015/ (last accessed 1/8/2020).

refugees for decidedly political reasons often strived for an alternative that established mobility as a democratic right and, in doing so, subverted territorial borders.

Volunteers who supported refugees through 'hands-on' interventions, by contrast, were often more reluctant when it came to demanding the abolition of territorial borders. Nonetheless, the possibility of global freedom of movement appeared to be something many volunteers in the area of my field research considered. I came across numerous instances when they positioned themselves in favour of a right to migrate. Such positions frequently arose out of their immediate practices of refugee support, which confronted them with questions of whether and under what conditions migrants should have a right to come. Many of my interlocutors told me that, through their personal interactions with asylum seekers, they had heard dreadful stories of flight and escape and were often quite shocked by the eyewitness reports of the asylum seekers' perilous illegalized journeys across the Mediterranean. Others told me that they struggled with the fact that the families of many asylum seekers were separated or stuck in war-torn countries due to rigid European border policies (Field notes: 6/3/2016). These personal stories often evoked critical positions in relation to the fortification of territorial borders among volunteers. Quite connectedly, in her study on practices of refugee support in Milan, Sinatti (2019) found that volunteers were often deeply affected by migrant stories, an experience that led them to take up more political and dissenting standpoints. She puts this as follows:

> "Exposed to the suffering of otherwise distant others [...] they [the volunteers] read the human and social situations of migrants within an international geo-political vision, became sceptical about institutional responses, and nurtured the ambition to do more than help people in distress" (Sinatti 2019: 144)

Indeed, the situation at the external borders of the European Union often preoccupied those who were mobilized to help in the area of my field research. For instance, this was illustrated during an informal conversation with two elderly women actively supporting asylum seekers in a small town in Baden-Württemberg. As we discussed possible alternatives to the Dublin Regulation, I asked them how they felt about a situation that would allow asylum seekers to move freely to Germany without any restrictions. One of the women simply replied: "We need them!" (Field notes: 7/3/2015). She asserted that, due to the recent demographic change, Germany needed an additional 400,000 migrants per year in order to sustain its economic workforce, but was only having around 200,000. Thus, the woman put forward quite a positive attitude towards the possibility of free movement, which, to her, might even improve the country's economic situation. The second woman held a more sceptical or ambivalent view in this regards. She remarked that she was really unsure about the question of whether it would be beneficial to open all borders and worried that there might simply be too many wanting to come in. However, she asserted, the primary focus for dealing with the growing global migration flows should not be the fortification of borders but rather the implementation of measures to tackle global inequalities: "If we produce our t-shirts cheaply in India, then we should not be surprised about the rising numbers of irregular migrants from these countries" (Field notes: 7/3/2015).

This points to something I encountered repeatedly in the course of my field research: many volunteers discussed the reasons of flight in critical terms and articulated possible ways of tackling them. Although they claimed to act for ostensibly 'apolitical' humanitarian reasons, many would nonetheless embed their actions in wider questions concerning global inequalities and injustices, while adopting critical political positions towards them. In this context, some would even voice favourable attitudes towards the possibility of global freedom of movement.

Other volunteers, however, told me that they struggled to picture a world without territorial borders as a realistic alternative. For instance, Klaus Böhlen, a volunteer I interviewed in a medium-sized town in Baden-Württemberg, emphasized the moral conflict he felt in this regard:

> "So that means that it is only reasonable to take people in, other than just to drag them out of an emergency situation [...] but there has to be a possibility that you might actually be able to integrate them and, to do that, many conditions have to be met. That's why – however difficult such images are for me, such as those from the border in Macedonia – I'm not able to come up with a good alternative. We won't be able to integrate one million here within four years [...] We don't have the people for language classes, we don't have the housing ... so many things are lacking." (Interview with Klaus Böhlen: 25/4/2016)[20]

---

20 Translation by LF. German original: "Das heißt es macht nur dann Sinn Leute aufzunehmen, außer sie aus seiner Notlage rauszuziehen, aber dann mit der Perspektive [...] dass man sie tatsächlich auch integrieren kann und dazu gehören eben viele Voraussetzungen. Also von daher, so schwer mir selbst auch Bilder fallen, also von der

The volunteer thus admitted that he struggled with the injustices relating to the external borders of the European Union, while being unsure about possible alternatives. On the one hand, my interlocutor, who described himself as part of the generation of '68[21], problematized the situation of asylum seekers who were stuck in Idomeni, a border post between Macedonia and Greece, when the so-called Balkan route was blocked in the wake of the long summer of migration in late 2015 (see also Santer & Wriedt 2017). On the other hand, he argued that the capacity to integrate migrants was constrained by local circumstances and conditions. In other words, the right to come had certain limits. To him, it was the consideration of local circumstances and practicalities that took priority over the possibility of a global freedom of movement. This position, I would argue, epitomizes the significance of the local for many who supported refugees around the long summer of migration.

By contrast, my interlocutor Markus Bayer explained the significance of a utopian dimension for his practices of refugee support. Markus was a member of "Bündnis Abschiebestopp Konstanz" ("Konstanz Anti-Deportation Alliance"), a group opposing deportations and challenging asylum policies in Konstanz, a medium-sized town in southern Baden-Württemberg. In early 2015, the group consisted of around ten members with a variety of backgrounds and motivations, some of whom did not necessarily identify themselves as "political activists". When I asked Markus if the name of the group implied that its members opposed deportations of all kinds and if this, in consequence, meant they were in favour of freedom of movement and the abolition of borders, he replied as follows:

> "I wouldn't necessarily put my signature to such a statement. But I think that, sometimes, you have to be utopian in order to take small steps towards those aims." (Conversation with Markus Bayer, Field notes: 8/3/2015)

While my interlocutor Klaus Böhlen thus gave priority to practical matters, Markus Bayer stressed the importance of being "utopian" in order to change

---

mazedonischen Grenze oder so, ich habe keine gute Alternative anzubieten. Wir werden nicht nach vier Jahren eine Million hier integrieren können [...] wir haben nicht die Leute für den Sprachunterricht, wir haben nicht die Wohnungen ... es mangelt an verschiedenen Dingen.".

21   He claimed that he was "politically socialised" in 1968, a time when left-wing student protests spread across Germany and many lasting changes to the social and political landscape were triggered, including denazification and the sexual revolution.

the status quo in favour of a different alternative. In his essay on urban possibilities, Bauder (2016) argues that 'utopia' always contains a certain impossibility of practical implementation. However, he suggests that a key function of utopian imaginaries is their criticisms of existing social relations and orders. This chimes with how my interlocutor Markus Bayer expressed support for the utopian ideal of free movement, knowing full well that it might not be practicable yet still seeing it as a means to achieve a 'better' alternative.

4.6. Concluding Remarks: Emerging Meanings of Political Action in Migration Societies

In the course of this chapter, I analysed the political meanings and effects emanating from the practices of refugee support that emerged around the German 'summer of welcome'. Scrutinizing my concept of a *politics of presence*, I argued that many of those supporting refugees were striving for social and political transformation within their local communities, while they did not necessarily describe their actions as 'political'. Even though many were mobilized by an ostensibly 'apolitical' humanitarian imperative, they did often not hesitate to contest exclusions and inequalities on the ground, denounce governmental deportation orders and take a critical stance towards the fortification of borders. Volunteers also *enacted* alternatives that challenged the nation-state 'from below' or counteracted the inhumane policies of the EU. In consequence, their practices of refugee support became *political*.

The alternatives that were formulated and enacted around the long summer of migration revolved around the criterion of *co-presence*. They often emphasized the material act of being there, of an imagined personal immediacy, over national origin or cultural belonging. 'The local', in this context, played an important role for the volunteers; it was *their* neighbourhood, town or village that appeared most likely to be shaped or transformed through their immediate practices of refugee support. I would thus argue that 'the local' became an important means of political claims-making around the long summer of migration.

The question of how these envisaged alternatives should look like in practice, however, triggered differing understandings among those acting in support of refugees. On the one hand, I encountered individuals and groups demanding the unconditional and universal implementation of a right to equal rights, a right to stay and a right to migrate and thus calling for a radically egalitarian society. They included, for instance, the moderator at the Welcome2Stay conference, the Solidarity City network in Freiburg, the members of No Lager Osnabrück and the activists at the "Stop War on Migrants!" conference in Berlin. On the other hand, many of the volunteers in the area of my field research were much more hesitant and ambivalent in relation to such demands. They placed limitations, restrictions and conditions on their strive towards a more egalitarian society and adapted them to local practicalities.

Taken together, these insights illustrate how those who support refugees for ostensibly 'apolitical' humanitarian reasons cannot be reduced to mere accomplices in the governance of migration. Nevertheless, I would caution against an overly optimistic and romanticized perspective on the practices of refugee support that emerged around the long summer of migration. As outlined elsewhere, there is also a dark side to practices of refugee support (see Chapter 2 and Chapter 3). Despite these caveats, however, the contested solidarities that emerged around the long summer of migration introduced new visions of society and enacted alternatives that might be better equipped to cope with intensified global mobilities and an increasingly heterogeneous migration society.

5. RECASTING SOLIDARITY: The Political Agency of Asylum Seekers in Relationships of Solidarity

5.1. Insubordinate Recipients: Asylum Seekers' Interventions in Relationships of Solidarity

On a weekday in February 2016, something out of the ordinary occurred in Bad Waldsee, a small rural town in southern Germany. A group of around 60 asylum seekers marched through the streets of the town centre to protest publicly against the conditions of their reception. Eventually, they gathered at the town hall and demanded to speak to a representative of the local council who could address the reasons for their protest. Most of the protesters had fled from Syria or Afghanistan and, since late summer 2015, had been accommodated at the emergency reception centre ("Notunterkunft") in Bad Waldsee. This interim facility for 170 asylum seekers was established at the local community centre when existing reception schemes proved insufficient. After several months of waiting for their asylum cases to be processed, the refugees became increasingly discontent and aimed to publicly call attention to various issues surrounding the situation they found themselves in. Their reasons for protesting ranged from demands for their asylum cases to be processed to anger at incompetent management staff at the facility to discontent with the intolerable living conditions they faced. Following their protest march, the asylum seekers continued their actions with what they termed a "hunger strike" at the reception centre: for several days, a majority of the inhabitants collectively refused the food served in the canteen in order to draw attention to their grievances. With these protests, the asylum seekers in Bad Waldsee clearly showed that they were not prepared to silently accept the terms and conditions of their reception, choosing instead to make themselves visible as insubordinate recipients.

These protests were not an isolated case in the area of my field research. From early to mid-2016, in the wake of the long summer of migration, similar incidents occurred at several interim reception centres across southern Germany. For instance, in April 2016, asylum seekers protested against their transferral to a container village in Offenburg, where they were no longer allowed to cook for themselves. They organized a protest march and collectively refused the food served at the canteen. In early February 2016, the inhabitants of an emergency reception centre in a neighbourhood of Stuttgart protested against the intolerable hygiene at the facility by means of a collective "hunger strike". Just a few days later, there was a public protest at another interim facility in Stuttgart, at which asylum seekers demanded that their asylum cases finally be processed. These are just a few of the examples that gained media coverage during my field research. There may, however, have been many more examples of protests within emergency reception centres that went unnoticed by the public or were strategically covered up by the governmental actors responsible for the facilities.

Conditions at emergency reception centres had been quite tough from the outset, but, during the first half of 2016, they became increasingly intolerable for their inhabitants. When regular initial reception centres proved to be insufficient and overcrowded during the long summer of migration, additional interim facilities were hurriedly set up across Germany, thereby averting a situation where asylum seekers had to sleep on the streets (cf. Hinger, Schäfer & Pott 2016). In some places, public sports or assembly halls were turned into reception centres; in others, large tents or "container villages" were established in improvised locations such as car parks. In many cases, more than one hundred asylum seekers with different backgrounds and nationalities were squeezed into a single space that, if they were lucky, had been divided up into smaller compartments via thin partition walls; in Bad Waldsee, for instance, four asylum seekers had to share a compartment of nine square metres. At these interim facilities, asylum seekers often had to contend with a lack of privacy, insufficient sanitation, contagious illnesses, an absence of cooking facilities meaning external service providers catered for them, and a shortage of competent employees able to address their concerns. Moreover, due to the sharp increase in the numbers of asylum seekers, the Federal Office for Migration and Refugees (BAMF) was unable to process and manage all the accumulating asylum cases. Asylum seekers thus routinely spent months waiting under such conditions for their asylum cases to be heard.

In critical migration studies, scholars have discussed such situations of waiting and 'being stuck' as a central technology in the management and governance of asylum seekers (Rotter 2016; Turnbull 2016; Fontanari 2017; Tazzioli 2018). Yet, they have also pointed to the agency of asylum seekers and their ability to resist and challenge these static conditions (Griffiths 2014; Ramsay 2017; Eule et al. 2019). For instance, Kallio, Meier and Häkli (2020: 3) argue that "waiting does not equal staying still, indifferent, or unchanged [...] spaces of waiting are thus also spaces of struggle, action and political possibility". The protests at emergency reception facilities in the area of my field research illustrated strikingly how asylum seekers also challenged and resisted the conditions of their reception around the long summer of migration.

So far, the voices of asylum seekers have played a marginal role throughout this book. The practices of refugee support that I investigated during the long summer of migration often served quite diverse interests and did not necessarily empower asylum seekers to voice their own demands. This tendency echoes academic works outlining how asylum seekers become "mute victims" (Rajaram 2002) or "speechless emissaries" (Malkki 1996) in the context of their humanitarian reception. In consequence of humanitarian imaginaries, asylum seekers would become 'bare life' that is reduced to its basic needs and deprived of political agency (Agamben 1998; Vaughan-Williams 2009; Darling 2014; Schindel 2016; Vandevoordt 2020). And still, scholars working on refugee and migrant activism have pointed to the need to take into account the political agency of asylum seekers (see Nyers 2011; Squire 2011a; Tyler & Marciniak 2013; Ataç et al. 2015). For instance, Moulin and Nyers (2007: 357) emphasize that "refugees are problematizing [...] regimes of power/knowledge and making their own interventions in the governmentality of care and mobility". Agier (2010: 40) illustrates how asylum seekers' protests repoliticize their ascribed identity as 'silent victims', challenging the parameters of a humanitarian imaginary.

This chapter contributes to this body of work by illustrating how asylum seekers' expressions of political agency are *intermediated* through relationships of solidarity. In what follows, I investigate how actors involved in the humanitarian reception of asylum seekers make sense of and respond to their insubordinate acts. On the one hand, I take a closer look at how such moments of interruption intervene in and contest the 'right' conduct of solidarity. On the other hand, I investigate how asylum seekers' protests lead to a reconsideration of practices of refugee support, how they provoke the parameters of helping to be disputed and how they subsequently *recast* the contested solidarities that developed around the long summer of migration. In the protests that I witnessed during my field research, the issue of food took on important political meanings. It served as a political platform that brought to the fore differing and competing interventions in the parameters of a humanitarian reception. The issue of food also provided a clear illustration of how different actors intermediated the asylum seekers' scope for political agency. Throughout this chapter, I thus conceptualize asylum seekers' political agency as the intermediated capacity to alter and contest the conditions of their reception in favour of a different alternative.

I draw on field research during and shortly after several protests that occurred in southern Germany in the first half of 2016. I focus on two intriguing incidents that were particularly revealing for the purpose of this chapter: firstly, the aforementioned acts of protest in Bad Waldsee, and, secondly, an incident in Offenburg, a medium-sized town at the southwestern edge of Germany. I refer to interviews with protesting asylum seekers; with representatives of the local government; with volunteers; and with reception centre staff such as managers, security guards and social workers. In addition, I draw on my own observations at the respective reception facilities during and after the acts of protest. I also consider the media coverage by analysing local newspaper articles that reported on the incidents. My aim is to provide multiple perspectives on the insubordinate acts of the protesting asylum seekers.

This chapter consists of four parts. In section two, I scrutinize my analytical perspective on *intermediated agencies*. I then take a closer look at the storying of the protests in Bad Waldsee via different actors involved in the reception of asylum seekers. In section four, I provide insights into another case study from the medium-sized town of Offenburg. In this context, local governmental actors (re)defined the protesting asylum seekers as economic migrants who should be excluded from humanitarian protection, a conception that was, however, highly contested by volunteers in the town. I close off with concluding remarks on the role of asylum seekers in the recasting of solidarity.

5.2. The Intermediated Agency of Asylum Seekers

Academic works on migrant activism offer useful starting points for a conceptualization of asylum seekers' interventions in relationships of solidarity. Such studies point to the need to take into account the agency of asylum seekers and irregular migrants, underlining the political significance of those moments when non-citizens make claims on a nation-state to which they technically do not belong (Nyers 2006b; Rigby & Schlembach 2013; Ataç et al. 2015). For instance, Johnson (2014: 204) argues that a migrant is "a transgressive and disruptive figure in world politics who challenges the ways in which we understand political subjectivity and agency". Others have outlined that, in moments when they raise their own voice, migrants challenge the primacy of citizens as legitimate political subjects within the nation-state (McNevin 2011; Ilcan 2014). In doing so, they are said to blur the dividing line between citizens and non-citizens, thus questioning the central premises of sovereign power (Nyers 2006b). McNevin (2011: 2) therefore regards acts of protest by asylum seekers as "contestations of citizenship" that undermine the raison d'être of the nation-state.

Such reflections on the political agency of asylum seekers often build on the works of the French philosopher Jacques Rancière (Rancière 1998, 2001, 2009). Rancière argues that the limits of the political are contested when those who are not represented in the dominant order make claims to be counted. From such a perspective, moments of disagreement and interruption constitute the essence of the political, something he expresses as follows: "Politics exists when the natural order of domination is interrupted by the institution of a part of those who have no part" (Rancière 1998: 11). Building on Rancière's writings, scholars writing on migrant activism often tend to ascribe a naturally destabilizing quality to those moments when asylum seekers make claims and constitute themselves as rights-bearing subjects. For instance, this is illustrated in a special issue of the journal *Citizenship Studies* on migrant activism, in which the editors proclaim that, in remaking citizenship "from the margins", migrant struggles exhibit "transformative potential" (Ataç, Rygiel & Stierl 2016: 530). Such works are also inspired by an 'autonomy of migration' perspective that refuses to see migrants as objects of governmental control and, instead, stresses their transformative power (see for instance Papastergiadis 2000; Papadopoulos, Stephenson & Tsianos 2008; Mezzadra 2011). This line of thought regards unauthorized migration flows themselves as a social movement that continuously resists and challenges governmental attempts at regulation. However, I would echo the thoughts of Walters (2008), who cautions against romanticizing and overestimating the agency of irregular migrants in staging resistance and disruption.

So far, works on migrant activism have only rarely investigated how acts of protest alter and recast relationships of solidarity in migration societies. Yet, a number of works point to the relational qualities of the political agency of asylum seekers. For instance, Topak (2016), based on his findings on protests and hunger strikes by asylum seekers in Greece, argues that: "It is one thing to demonstrate political agency, quite another to have that agency recognized" (ibid.: 8). According to Topak, few works take into account that protests and resistances often do not have the consequences the asylum seekers intended and generally enjoy limited success. In a similar vein, Johnson (2014: 192) suggests that migrant protests require the interventions of citizens in order to be regarded as meaningful political action, writing: "The citizen becomes a necessary partner – indeed, a central partner – in effective change, and is the translator of action into political agency on behalf of the non-citizen". Huysmans (2006) argues that migrant protest is only of political significance if it is mediated by public media and human rights organizations.

In line with these works, my field research in southern Germany showed that protests in emergency reception centres only provoked discussion and action from actors involved in their reception if they became visible to the public eye. For this reason, governmental actors often tried to prevent asylum seeker protests from coming to public attention. The head of the city administration of Stuttgart, for instance, turned down my requests for an interview on the protest at a local emergency reception centre with the excuse that it would mean entering a 'secure area' to which there was no public access. In another case in Stuttgart, I witnessed how representatives of the Greens, the main governing party in the state government of Baden-Württemberg, directly intervened in order to stop asylum seekers from staging a public protest march shortly before state elections were scheduled to be held.

In this chapter, I thus explore asylum seekers' political agency as their *intermediated capacity* to bring about change that transforms the dominant order in favour of a different alternative. With this conceptualization, I emphasize that agency is always relational, that it only comes into being in relationships of solidarity with those deemed legitimate citizens. Through the intermediation and translation by other actors involved in their humanitarian reception, actions of protesting asylum seekers are either cast as meaningful political action or deemed illegitimate. In other words, asylum seekers' protest actions only offer political possibilities to transform the status quo and to enact a more inclusive alternative if they are mediated as meaningful political action.

Such an analytical perspective puts emphasis on the *storying* of protests through actors participating in the contestation of solidarity, for instance volunteers, governmental representatives or social welfare organizations. This connects to an apt observation by Tyler (2013: 12f, emphasis in original), who writes: "It is often not events of protest [...] but rather the *storying* of revolts [...] which *matters* most". Building on Tyler, I argue that the storying of migrant protests is of crucial importance not only to develop a more nuanced picture of how asylum seekers recast the terms of their reception but also to illustrate how humanitarian action might become a site of political possibilities. As I will illustrate in the following sections, the responses mediating the political agency of asylum seekers in the area of my field research ranged from *depoliticizing* to *politicizing* storyings; storyings that were contested among different actors. They either circumscribed the asylum seekers' scope of agency and stripped their protests of political content or they translated them into meaningful political action. In the following sections, I investigate how different actors in Bad Waldsee (Section 3) and Offenburg (Section 4) made sense of and responded to moments when asylum seekers raised their own voice and made claims.

5.3. (De)politicizing the Meanings of Food: The Intermediation of Migrant Protest in Bad Waldsee

Food took on important political meanings during the protest in the small southern German town of Bad Waldsee. As part of their protests, the asylum seekers not only staged a march in the town centre and demanded to speak to local governmental representatives, they also engaged in a subsequent "hunger strike". Almost all of the 170 inhabitants of the emergency reception centre collectively refused their food, which was supplied by an external service provider three times per day, in order to draw attention to the reasons for their protest. The collective refusal of food appeared to be a central means for asylum seekers in the area of my field research to voice discontent and to call attention to their problems. Many of the instances of protest in the first half of 2016 involved similar 'hunger strikes', although some of my interlocutors claimed that they were not 'real' hunger strikes since the asylum seekers continued eating food from elsewhere. In what follows, I provide insights into the storying of the protests in Bad Waldsee via different actors involved in the reception of asylum seekers. I show how the refusal of food provided at their reception facility served as a means for asylum seekers to demonstrate political agency. Actors involved in the reception of asylum seekers, however, used it as a means to *depoliticize* the protests and to reduce them to mere dissatisfaction with the food provided. To begin with, I outline how the asylum seekers took a public stand as claims-making subjects by submitting a written appeal, albeit their requests were largely ignored in the wake of the protests.

5.3.1. The Unheard Requests of the Protesting Asylum Seekers

"Here is our request: we are the refugees here in the city hall in Bad Waldsee and we want you to look after these requests and to help us if you can do this and to solve our problems and reveal us from our suffering and we ask you for mercy and humanity as a human with consciousness. We thank you very much with our love and our respect. And at the end we write our complaint which we want to explain and this complaint is against the officers, that are responsible directly for the refugees in this city hall and their names are Simone Fischer, Michael König, Annette Braun[1] and other names … By the way, these officers which have their names written, they give us no help, they do not do their duties and they spend the time smoking, drinking café and tea, they make private phone calls during the job time and by the way, when we ask them about anything, they give us no answers and they answer us with unclear answers and they don't help us and they say to us, they are busy and say we don't really know. And maybe they would say we are not responsible about this or that and that they cannot help us and they give us false excuses and if we ask them about anything, their answer would be: they don't know. And they treat us badly and they do not care or take our needs seriously. We are always looking for somebody to hear us, to solve our problems, but unfortunately, we found nobody. They treat us in a bad way, as if we are prisoners and when they ask us to do something, they do it impolite and they just give us orders to do or not to do and they say to us bad words and unrespectable words that hurt our feelings." (Appeal by protesting asylum seekers in Bad Waldsee: March 2016; English original)

My interlocutor Malik Hamdan read the above from a small, hand-written sheet of paper. It was the appeal protesting asylum seekers in Bad Waldsee handed over to local governmental representatives in the hope they would address their reasons for protesting. I interviewed Malik Hamdan and two other protesting asylum seekers in March 2016, shortly after they had staged

---

[1] The names mentioned in the appeal have been changed.

their protests in the town. Clearly, they were unwilling to accept the conditions of their reception and instead sought to alter them by making various complaints. The primary reason for the asylum seekers to protest appeared to be a discontent with the management staff at the emergency reception centre. They were thoroughly unhappy with the behaviour of those they considered "responsible directly" for their reception, namely the management staff employed by the social welfare organization Die Johanniter. As was often the case, the district council, which was officially in charge of the facility, had outsourced its management to a social welfare organization. The asylum seekers accused these employees of not doing their job properly, of not caring and of not taking the asylum seekers' needs seriously. Instead of solving the problems of the asylum seekers, they refused "to help" and spent their time procrastinating.

This appeal, I would argue, illustrates how the asylum seekers in Bad Waldsee cast themselves as suffering victims and recipients of humanitarian help in the course of their protests. This is most obvious in the following phrase at the beginning of their appeal: "We want you to look after these requests and to help us if you can do this and to solve our problems and reveal us from our suffering and we ask you for mercy and humanity as a human with consciousness". They thus ask the reader for "help", while emphasizing their "suffering" and identifying themselves as subjects of care and compassion. Ticktin (2011) argues that an emphasis on the suffering body relegates asylum seekers to a non-political space. She puts this as follows:

> "When sans-papiers [undocumented migrants in France] make claims based on their suffering bodies, they appeal not to a nation-state but to an understanding of humanity as a biological species, where suffering finds its universal measure in medical science." (Ticktin 2011: 12)

This self-identification as suffering bodies is echoed by the appeal of the protesters in Bad Waldsee, asking for "humanity" and calling on the reader's "consciousness". The repeated expressions of gratitude in the appeal further reproduced the asylum seekers' subjectivity as suffering victims and recipients of help. This also came across in my interview with three of the protesting asylum seekers, who recalled how they had adorned the banners they carried at the march to the town hall with printed photographs of Angela Merkel and expressions of gratitude. They explained this as follows:

LF: And what was on the posters? What did you write there?
Mohammed Gabri: Vielen Dank for Deutsch people (Ismail Abbas: for the Deutsche Regierung) and Vielen Dank for Gastfreundschaft.
LF: So you printed the picture of Angela Merkel in the library?
Mohammed Gabri: Yes, three. Two big and one small and we write 'Vielen Dank'.
Ismail Abbas: Ja.
LF: And why did you do this, write Vielen Dank?
Mohammed Gabri: It is Vielen Dank for the people here in Bad Waldsee, in Deutschland, for keeping us safe and Vielen Dank for being in Deutschland [giggles].
Ismail Abbas: To show the world that it is a peaceful protest, not protest with violence, not with bad things ... (Interview with Ismail Abbas, Mohammed Gabri and Malik Hamdan: 5/3/2016, English original)

My interlocutors thus felt a need to say "thank you" to German citizens and to the German government in order to demonstrate that it was a "peaceful protest". This echoes something works on humanitarianism have often outlined, namely that the ostensible beneficiaries of humanitarian action are expected to show gratitude in return for the help (see for instance Barnett 2016).

With their storying of the protests, the asylum seekers thus reproduced the humanitarian imaginary that characterized the discourses and practices of solidarity that emerged around the long summer of migration (see Chapter 2). Scholars have argued that such a humanitarian imaginary relegates asylum seekers to a space of exclusion and marginalization, reinforces dominant inequalities and power asymmetries and is thus complicit in the governance of migration (Ticktin 2006, 2011; Fassin 2012). As a result, refugees are said to become passive beneficiaries of humanitarian practices, 'bare life' that is stripped of political rights, and thus consigned to the non-political realm (cf. Schindel 2016).

A humanitarian imaginary, however, might also offer its beneficiaries potentials for making political claims and voicing discontent. As Vandevoordt (2020) observed in the city of Brussels: 'bare life' can also present a political subject category, one that can be resisted and challenged. This connects to Jabri's (2006) thoughts on agency in relationships of protection. She argues that "the dissenting voice, in other words, is only meaningful in terms of the grammar against which that voice is aimed" (ibid.: 145). The asylum seekers in Bad Waldsee also embedded their protest in a humanitarian grammar and (re)defined themselves as suffering victims and recipients of help in order to voice their requests. Their acts of protest, I would suggest, should therefore be read as interventions in the practices of solidarity that emerged around the long summer of migration and an attempt to recast the terms and conditions of their humanitarian reception.

With their appeal, the asylum seekers not only voiced demands from the position of suffering victims, they also constituted themselves as 'clients' of service providers. They framed their appeal as a complaint against management staff at the facility, who were not doing their "duties" properly and instead spent their work time drinking coffee or making private phone calls. Rather than as rights-bearing subjects within the nation-state in which they reside, they cast themselves as recipients of services from the social welfare organization responsible for the management of the facility. Since these services were not being carried out to the satisfaction of the 'clients', asylum seekers complained to a higher authority. This connects to something outlined elsewhere in this book: social welfare organizations played an important role in the reception of asylum seekers in the course of the long summer of migration (see Chapter 2). Around this time, governmental actors outsourced various duties to social welfare organizations, which appeared to act as service providers for the government (see also Muehlebach 2012). These organizations increasingly fulfilled pivotal tasks in the reception and management of asylum seekers. It is this important role, I would argue, that became apparent in the asylum seekers' complaints about the managing staff at their reception centre.

The asylum seekers' requests and complaints, however, went virtually unheard in the wake of their protests. Although the protesters handed their appeal over to both local governmental actors and management staff at their reception centre, their reasons for protesting were lost amidst the various responses from actors involved in their reception. I will examine these depoliticizing responses to the asylum seekers' protests in more detail in the following section.

5.3.2. Depoliticizing Responses to the Protests

The actors involved in the reception of asylum seekers in Bad Waldsee responded in manifold ways to the protests, thereby intermediating the protesters' scope of political agency. Despite expressions of seeming understanding, many stripped the protests of political meanings and relegated the asylum seekers to a non-political space with limited agency. In consequence, the asylum seekers were recast as suffering victims in need of help while their concrete requests remained unaddressed, their protest eventually being reduced to mere dissatisfaction with the food served at the reception centre's canteen.

I interviewed Regina Bayer, a senior official on the town council, two weeks after the asylum seekers' protests in Bad Waldsee. As head of social services, it was she who assumed responsibility for dealing with and responding to the group of 60 asylum seekers protesting at the town hall and demanding to speak with a governmental representative. When I asked her for her view of these protests, she replied: "These are justifiable questions or worries. I always say, we need to put ourselves in their shoes. Maybe we would react in a similar way"[2] (Interview with Regina Bayer: 2/3/2016). In the course of our interview, she repeatedly expressed her sympathy for the protesting asylum seekers and voiced compassion regarding their discontent. She admitted the tough conditions at the emergency reception centre, where the asylum seekers struggled with a lack of privacy and an unknown future, and depicted them as understandable reasons for such discontent. My interlocutor thus ascribed the protests to the various struggles the asylum seekers faced at the reception facility. This sympathetic view was also reflected in her legal assessment of the protest march as a lawful "spontaneous assembly". She explained this as follows:

> "LF: What conclusions did you reach from the city council's perspective? Was the gathering lawful or unlawful? Did anything happen that was not by the book?
> RB: Yes, a spontaneous assembly is permissible, it's permissible according to the Basic Law. Usually, assemblies need to be registered at least 48 hours beforehand ... that wasn't the case here and wouldn't have been possible. Like I said, because it arose spontaneously, as the name says, so at short notice, and because they just said "Hey, we are going to march up there", that's why, for me, it was a lawful form of assembly, one that initially caused a bit of turmoil, let's say, on the council, because you cannot plan for this. [...]
> LF: And so the same law applies as to German citizens? Are the refugees allowed to assemble spontaneously and protest just as German citizens are?

---

2   Translation by LF. German original: "Das sind ja auch berechtigte Fragen oder Sorgen. Ich sag immer, wir müssen uns mal in die Lage von denjenigen versetzen. Wir würden ja vielleicht gleich reagieren.".

RB: For me, it was first and foremost an assembly. My thought process is not: "What kind of people are they?" For me, it is about the thing itself; it is a spontaneous assembly and that is fundamentally permissible."[3]
(Interview with Regina Bayer: 2/3/2016)

Citing Germany's constitution or Basic Law, my interlocutor did not call the protest's legitimacy into question. She claimed that she judged protests not primarily by considering the actors responsible for the protest but rather the act of protesting itself. Works on migrant activism, however, have often argued that governmental actors regard protesting non-citizens as threats to sovereign power and therefore criminalize and illegalize their activities (Nyers 2010a; Johnson 2014). Rigby and Schlembach (2013), for instance, argue that protests by non-status migrants present de jure "impossible" forms of protests. By contrast, however, my interlocutor in Bad Waldsee seemingly recognized the protesting asylum seekers as legitimate rights-bearing subjects within the nation-state.

Despite these expressions of sympathy and empathy, however, governmental actors stripped the protests of political meanings and circumscribed the protesters' political agency. Although my interlocutor Regina Bayer asserted that it was important to listen to the demands of the protesters and to take them seriously, she admitted that the protests had not translated into concrete outcomes or solutions. She explained this by claiming that the asylum seekers had not been able to communicate their specific requests clearly

---

3   Translation by LF. German original: "LF: Und zu welchem Schluss sind Sie denn dann gekommen von städtischer Seite, also war die Spontanversammlung rechtens oder ist da irgendwas nicht ganz ordnungsgemäß verlaufen? RB: Ja, eine Spontanversammlung ist ja zulässig. Das ist ja grundgesetzrechtlich zulässig. Normalerweise müssen die Versammlungen ja rechtzeitig vorher, also 48 Stunden sind das vorher, angemeldet werden ähm ... war hier nicht der Fall, auch nicht möglich, wie gesagt, weil es denke ich mal spontan, wie der Name schon sagt, kurzfristig entstanden ist und die gesagt haben ‚Mensch, jetzt laufen wir halt mal da vor'. Deshalb ist das auch für mich eine zulässige Versammlungsart gewesen, die sag ich jetzt mal kurzfristig erst einmal ein wenig Hektik in der Verwaltung verursacht, wenn man das nicht planen kann [...] LF: Und da gilt dann gleiches Recht, wie für deutsche Bürger dann. Also die Flüchtlinge dürfen sich genau so spontan versammeln und demonstrieren, wie auch deutsche Staatsbürger? RB: Erst mal ist es für mich eine Versammlung gewesen. Also ich argumentiere jetzt nicht: was für eine Art von Person ist das, sondern für mich ist es die Sache, es ist eine spontane Versammlung und die ist grundsätzlich zulässig.".

and that they had voiced their discontent to the wrong governmental authority. Since it was the district council that was legally responsible for the emergency reception centre, the protesters' requests lay outside of her "sphere of responsibility". Therefore, she told me, she had passed on their appeal to those responsible at the district council. In the course of my field research on similar instances of protest across southern Germany, I repeatedly encountered such a shifting of blame and responsibility among governmental representatives. A town council would transfer responsibility to the relevant district council, while the district council would, in turn, put the blame on the Federal Office for Migration and Refugees or other authorities. Through such responses, local governmental actors deferred the responsibility for addressing the protesters' requests and thus limited their political agency to affect the conditions of reception.

Yet, when the asylum seekers organized a 'hunger strike' in order to call attention to the reasons for their protest, the district council eventually felt the need to respond to their actions. It staged what it called a "food test" at the emergency reception centre: several high-ranking representatives, including the district's chief administrative officer, visited the facility and had lunch together with the asylum seekers in order to "test" the food provided. The district council also invited representatives of the local press and several photographers, turning it into a publicity-generating event that would bring the council's conciliatory approach to a wider audience. The local newspaper *Schwäbische Zeitung*, for instance, published an article on the "food test" and concluded that all concerned found the food served at the facility to be tasty and varied (Schwäbische Zeitung: 18/2/2016)[4].

Through this 'food test', I would argue, the asylum seekers' collective refusal of the food served in the canteen was reduced to mere dissatisfaction with its taste. It is thus a striking illustration of how the district council *depoliticized* the asylum seekers' demands and limited their agency to affect the conditions of their reception. Instead of considering the asylum seekers' requests, it stripped their protests of political content, refusing to acknowledge the governmental handling of asylum seekers as the cause of the protests and instead reducing them to a matter of differing cultural tastes in food. This was even more apparent in the solution with which the district council sought to

---

4 See: http://www.schwaebische.de/region_artikel,-Nach-Demo-SZ-testet-Essen-in-Not unterkunft-_arid,10395682_toid,86.html (last accessed 1/8/2020).

reconcile the protesters: members of staff provided additional spices considered typical of Arabic cuisine. During my interview with the three protesters, however, they repeatedly emphasized that their protests did not have anything to do with the taste of the food. Instead, the collective refusal of food functioned as a means to pressure governmental actors into responding to their problems and requests. It is no surprise, then, that my interlocutors appeared seemingly upset by this staged 'food test' since neither the local press nor the representatives of the district council took the time to talk to them about their "real" reasons for protesting. Through such means, I would argue, the protesters were recast as bare life, becoming stripped of political rights and reduced to basic biological needs such as food and shelter (Agamben 1998). This clearly shows how food took on political meanings in the course of the protests in Bad Waldsee, serving, on the one hand, as a means for asylum seekers to demonstrate their political agency and, on the other, as a means for governmental actors to depoliticize their protests.

Local residents who volunteered with refugees in Bad Waldsee often embedded the reasons for protesting in a more nuanced and contextualized account. And yet, by pathologizing their insubordinate behaviour, they likewise depoliticized the asylum seekers' protests. This became particularly clear when I talked to a group of volunteers involved in the local citizens' initiative supporting refugees in Bad Waldsee. They recalled how they had struggled with the fact that the asylum seekers had, as part of their protest, also boycotted the daily language classes they offered. After joint discussions, however, they had arrived at the conclusion that they had sympathy for the protesting asylum seekers. The asylum seekers were "traumatized" due to their displacement and would thus need time to adapt to their new surroundings, they noted.

Through such a storying, I would argue, the volunteers pathologized the asylum seekers' acts of protest. Instead of recognizing the protests as legitimate instances of political claims-making, they reduced them to the asylum seekers' ostensibly traumatized condition. This connects strikingly to Malkki's (1995) writings on the condition of the refugee. She outlines how displacement is commonly understood as an "anomaly in life" that results in a vulnerable psychological condition for those who are displaced. Refugees, in consequence, are often portrayed as suffering from disorders, mental illnesses and trauma, which relegates them to a vulnerable place (ibid.: 510). Similarly, the volunteers in Bad Waldsee stripped the asylum seekers' protests of political content and reduced them to symptoms of their traumatized psychological condition.

The storyings of events by volunteers also substantially limited the agency of asylum seekers by recasting the protesters as *mute* victims and *passive* recipients of help and support. This is encapsulated by an article published in the regional newspaper *Schwäbische Zeitung* entitled "The residents of the reception centre are frustrated". It included a short interview with Gerd Wagner, the official spokesperson of the local citizens' initiative supporting refugees. When asked for his assessment of the protests, he responded as follows:

> "And now they have publicly expressed their frustration for the first time. It's something that has been germinating for a while. And you can understand it all the more if you know their stories and experiences. Every day, on the internet or in the media, they read how their home towns are still being bombed to bits and hope that their families are okay."[5] (Schwäbische Zeitung: 18/2/2016)

The article thus depicted the protesters as suffering victims of atrocities in their home countries, while their reasons to protest remained hazy, with not a single reference to their specific requests; instead, it talked merely of a vague "frustration" leading the asylum seekers to protest. Elsewhere in the interview, Gerd Wagner also blamed human traffickers for the protests in Bad Waldsee; they had "raised false expectations among the asylum seekers, promising them money, cars and a house in Germany" (Schwäbische Zeitung: 18/2/2016). These expectations then collided with the "reality" of the reception centre in Bad Waldsee, which eventually led to their protests, Gerd Wagner explained. In this storying, thus, the protests were simply due to 'false expectations'.

Through such depoliticizing responses, both governmental actors and volunteers relegated the asylum seekers to the role of passive and mute recipients in relationships of solidarity. In doing so, they substantially limited the asylum seekers' agency to affect the conditions and terms of their own reception. And yet, I would argue, the asylum seekers' insubordinate acts were not

---

5   Translation by LF. German original: "Und nun haben sie ihren Ärger erstmals öffentlich geäußert, das keimt schon eine Weile in ihnen. Und man kann es umso mehr nachvollziehen, wenn man deren Geschichten und Erlebnisse kennt. Täglich verfolgen sie im Internet und über die Medien, wie ihre Heimatstädte weiter zerbombt werden und hoffen, dass es ihren Familien gut geht.".

without impact. In what follows, I illustrate how they opened up discussions on the terms of refugee support and the 'proper' conduct in relationships of solidarity.

5.3.3. Recasting Relationships of Solidarity

The asylum seekers' protests in Bad Waldsee contested the relationships of solidarity that had been forged between newcomers and established residents during the long summer of migration. The storyings of the protests brought to light different perspectives on the 'proper' way to support refugees and to receive support in return.

During my research stay in Bad Waldsee in March 2016, I scheduled an interview with one of the volunteers in the small town, Jana Brühl, a leading member of the local citizens' initiative. We talked at length about her view of the protests that had occurred some days previously. In this context, she problematized the behaviour of certain volunteers who reacted "over-emotionally" and thus stirred discontent among the asylum seekers at the emergency reception centre, something she described as follows:

> "I always think that whenever you have such groups of helpers, you get people who react, let's say, *over-emotionally* and who think they have to do everything for *their* refugees and to remove every obstacle from their path. It's just the way it is and it is difficult, this situation with 150 people in too little space. And then we have some in our initiative who believe that they need to pursue everything. So there was one time when a woman went all the way to a higher authority and complained that people were not being cared for properly. But it turned out that she was just ill-informed [...] She didn't know anything but just wanted to rough up the situation"[6] (Interview with Jana Brühl: 5/3/2016; emphasis added)

---

6   Translation by LF. German original: "Ich glaube immer, dass wenn man solche Helferkreise hat, dass da so Leute sind, die sagen wir mal überemotional reagieren und die dann immer glauben, sie müssen alles für ihre Flüchtlinge tun und ihnen alle Steine aus dem Weg zu räumen. Es ist nun einfach mal so, es ist schwierig, eine Situation mit 150 Leuten auf so engem Raum. Und dann haben wir natürlich in unserem Helferkreis auch Leute, die glauben sie müssen allem hinterherrennen. Also da gab es auch eine Geschichte, da ist eine wirklich an höhere Stellen geklettert und hat sich beschwert, man würde sich nicht richtig um die Leute kümmern und da war sie dann aber einfach schlecht informiert. [...] Also das wusste sie dann gar nicht, aber sie mischt ordentlich auf".

My interlocutor thus partly blamed 'improper' relationships of solidarity for the protests. She accused fellow volunteers for trying to "remove every obstacle from the asylum seekers' path" and to "rough up" the situation, generating false expectations among them. This reflects a storying that I encountered repeatedly in the course of my field research, with volunteers ascribing the ostensibly insubordinate behaviour of certain asylum seekers to a pathological "recipient mentality" (literally "Nehmer-Mentalität"). They claimed that such exploitative behaviour would develop among asylum seekers, when volunteers responded unconditionally to their requests and wishes. As the interview progressed, my interlocutor took her argument even further, surmising that the asylum seekers could not have acted independently, but were probably instigated to protest by volunteers. As she put it:

> "At this demonstration, there were printed posters that could not practically have been produced by the people at the reception centre. So there was a suspicion that somebody in the background must have spurred them on [...] So, they probably didn't organize it themselves, it bears the stamp, I would say, of somebody else being involved."[7] (Interview with Jana Brühl: 5/3/2016)

In the eyes of the volunteer Jana Brühl, the asylum seekers at the emergency reception centre were incapable of organizing such a protest on their own, which meant someone "in the background" had "spurred them on". With this explanation, she portrayed the protesting asylum seekers not as self-determined actors capable of acting on their own behalf but as passive victims who were instrumentalized by trouble-making volunteers. Yet, when I asked the three protesters I interviewed if they had any outside support in organizing the protest and printing the pictures, they insisted that they were the sole initiators and organizers of the protests. In my interlocutors' storying of events, both asylum seekers and volunteers might instrumentalize relationships of solidarity for their own ends.

The Volunteer Coordinator at the emergency reception centre likewise problematized relationships of solidarity when I talked to her about the

---

7   Translation by LF. German original: "Auch bei dieser Demonstration, die es gab, gab es einfach ausgedruckte Plakate, die praktisch von Leuten aus der Stadthalle so gar nicht hergestellt werden können. Deshalb war auch schon der Verdacht, dass es jemanden aus dem Hintergrund gibt, der die Leute da losgeschickt hat [...] Also das haben die garantiert nicht von alleine, also die Handschrift, würde ich mal sagen, dass da jemand mit dabei war.".

protests. She told me that she and her colleagues, employees of the social welfare organization Die Johanniter, advised volunteers not to form overly personal relationships with the asylum seekers. Still, some would get "too involved on an affective level". Strong emotional ties, the Volunteer Coordinator claimed, would enable asylum seekers to exert "moral pressure" on the volunteers and to thus gain control over relationships of solidarity. My interlocutor further suggested that some volunteers "don't know what's good for the refugees" and that they "fuel negative sentiments instead of quelling them". Thus, she also blamed volunteers who were 'too involved' for fuelling the asylum seekers' protests. What such a reading implicitly asserts, I would argue, is that the 'proper' relationship between supporters and their beneficiaries would be one that irons out discontent rather than responding to it.

Furthermore, the storying of the protests in Bad Waldsee recast the volunteers as a necessary mouthpiece that enables asylum seekers' problems to be heard. This became apparent when I talked to Regina Bayer, the local council's head of social services. During our interview, I asked her if and how she usually communicated with asylum seekers about their problems. She replied as follows:

> "We communicate a lot via the helpers. The helpers bring us the problems because they are there on the ground almost every day. They pass problems on to us and then we have to see how we can deal with this or that problem."[8]
> (Interview with Regina Bayer: 2/3/2016)

My interlocutor thus recast the volunteers as crucial mediating agents in relationships of solidarity. A similar tendency is apparent in the newspaper articles on the protests in Bad Waldsee, none of which directly quoted the asylum seekers in order to inform readers about their reasons for protesting. This was particularly well illustrated by an account of the incidents in the local newspaper *Schwäbische Zeitung* (17/2/2016)[9]. Instead of quoting the protesters themselves, the article drew on a conversation with Simone Fischer, the head of the management staff at the emergency reception centre, who problematized the

---

8   Translation by LF. German original: "Wir kommunizieren sehr viel über die Helfer. Die Helfer bringen die Probleme, weil die sind ja bei denen vor Ort, die tragen die Probleme weiter zu uns her und dann müssen wir gucken, wie wir da das ein oder andere Problem abarbeiten.".
9   See: http://www.schwaebische.de/region_artikel,-Fluechtlinge-demonstrieren-vor-dem-Rathaus-_arid,10395021_toid,86.html (last accessed 1/8/2020).

asylum seekers' insubordinate behaviour. Yet, the report neglected to mention that Fischer and her colleagues at the facility were the primary focus of the asylum seekers' complaints, as their appeal clearly illustrated. Accompanying the article was an interview with Gerd Wagner, the spokesperson of the local citizens' initiative. In it, the volunteer, who is described as "very close" to the asylum seekers and "in daily contact" with them, is asked for his views on the protests. The newspaper depicted the volunteer as a trustworthy person to explain the protests while not consulting any of the asylum seekers themselves. In a study on refugee protests in Turkey, Erensu (2016: 672) identifies a similar pattern, arguing that civil society groups became necessary partners who "speak on behalf" of refugees. From this perspective, it is the volunteer who determines how a situation is interpreted and whether the asylum seekers' protests are recast as legitimate political action or not.

Moreover, in response to the protests, the 'proper' conduct of asylum seekers in relationships of solidarity was recast as one that silently accepts the conditions and terms of the support offered. This was clearly evident in various angry comments under the online version of the article reporting on the protests in *Schwäbische Zeitung*. For instance, one reader posted the following:

> "The refugees protest and don't know why? What's that about? Are they hoping that, if they demonstrate, another German idiot will blow even more smoke up their backsides? This is just arbitrary and an exploitation of German democracy. Simply intolerable behaviour by our guests. I don't like to say it, but it makes you lose the will to help."[10] (Schwäbische Zeitung: 17/2/2016)

The commenter thus regarded the incidents as grounds for ending any relationships of solidarity with the protesters. He or she presented their actions as "arbitrary", "exploitation" and "intolerable", while those who continued offering their help to the protesters were "idiots". The asylum seekers, on the other hand, were constituted as "guests" who should uncritically accept the terms and conditions of their reception. Other posts in the online comments

---

10   Translation by LF. German original: "Die Flüchtlinge demonstrieren und wissen nicht warum? Was soll den (sic) das? Besteht die Hoffnung, dass wenn man demonstriert irgend ein deutscher Idiot denen noch zusätzlich Zucker in den Hintern bläst? Das ist doch wirklich Willkür und das Ausnutzen der deutschen Demokratie. Echt eine Unverschämtheit von unseren Gästen. Ich sage es ungern: Da verliert man die Lust am Helfen."

section even called for the protesting asylum seekers to be deported because of their insubordinate acts. This connects to what Topak (2016: 10) describes as "conditional hospitality": "the other, the newcomer or the guest is obliged to follow some specific routes to enter and remain in the host state; otherwise his existence would be deemed illegal and she would be treated as criminal" (ibid.). In this storying the protesting asylum seekers are recast not as legitimate claims-making subjects but as mute and thankful recipients.

Nevertheless, the protests in Bad Waldsee also triggered politicizing responses that opened up possibilities for the asylum seekers to make political claims and to effect changes in the conditions of their reception – although they remained comparatively marginalized. Such responses recast relationships of solidarities as, what Johnson (2014: 202) calls, "transgressive solidarities". According to Johnson, such forms of solidarity imply not "a legitimate voice speaking for an illegitimate/vulnerable/less out-spoken one, but a multitude of voices speaking together in the same message, demand or refusal" (ibid.: 197). This came out clearly in my conversations with the volunteer Jana Brühl. During our preliminary phone call, my interlocutor told me that a "friend" of hers was there to answer my questions first-hand. That friend turned out to be Malik Hamdan, a member of the group of protesting asylum seekers. Soon after we had started our conversation, she handed the phone to the asylum seeker, letting him speak while occasionally complementing his accounts of the protests with her own views. The volunteer thus clearly chose not to speak on behalf of the asylum seekers but instead empowered Malik Hamdan to put forward his own storying of the protests.

To sum up, in this section, I analysed the multiple storyings of the protests at an emergency reception centre in Bad Waldsee. I outlined how various actors involved in the reception of asylum seekers responded to these protests by *depoliticizing* the asylum seekers' scope for political agency. As a result, the protesting asylum seekers were predominantly recast as mute victims and passive recipients in relationships of solidarity. In what follows, I will turn to another striking example of protest I came across in Offenburg, a medium-sized town in southern Germany. The storying of events I found, however, turned out to be highly contested among different actors involved in the asylum seekers' reception, while opening up possibilities for politicizing relationships of solidarity.

5.4. Deterring 'Economic Migrants': The Intermediation of Migrant Protest in Offenburg

In April 2016, a group of asylum seekers collectively refused the food served at their new interim accommodation centre in Offenburg for several weeks. I found out about their protest via an article in the regional newspaper *Mittelbadische Presse* (9/4/2016)[11]. According to the article, the asylum seekers were collectively refusing food because they were discontent with their transferral from one of the emergency reception facilities to a new interim accommodation centre, a so-called "container village" on the outskirts of town, set up to accommodate the asylum seekers for up to two years. While the asylum seekers had been able to cook for themselves at their previous reception centre, the new one offered no such facilities. Instead, an external caterer provided food to the asylum seekers three times per day. At first glance, this protest resembled what I had witnessed at the emergency reception centre in Bad Waldsee. In both cases, food served as an important means for asylum seekers to make themselves visible as claims-making subjects. The storying of events in Offenburg, however, turned out to differ strongly from the one in Bad Waldsee. While, in the latter, the protesters were recast as mute victims and passive recipients of help and support in the wake of their protests, this was clearly not the case in Offenburg, where the local district council recast the protesting asylum seekers as "bogus" asylum seekers or "economic migrants" who should be excluded from humanitarian protection, whose presence was deemed illegitimate and who were rendered deportable. And yet, this storying was highly contested by volunteers supporting refugees in town. In what follows, I scrutinize this contested storying by outlining how different actors responded to and made sense of the protests at the Offenburg container village. To start off, I illustrate how the district council deemed the protests illegitimate and stripped them of political meanings.

5.4.1. Depoliticizing Responses to the Protests

The article in the regional newspaper *Mittelbadische Presse* (9/4/2016) reporting on the incidents at the container village in Offenburg termed the asylum seekers' insubordinate acts not an instance of protest but a "food boycott". The

---

11   See: http://www.bo.de/lokales/offenburg/fluechtlinge-boykottieren-essen-im-containerdorf (last accessed 1/8/2020).

group of around 60 protesters had refused the food at the facility, the article claimed, because they "wanted to receive more money". Having meals provided affected the financial allowances asylum seekers received from the German state. Asylum seekers received 176 euros per month if they were catered for and, if they cooked for themselves, an additional amount of 144 euros. The article thus rated the protest as being 'all about the money'. It built its estimation largely on comments by the spokesperson of the district council, who had denounced the protests as "incomprehensible" and "disappointing" and described the asylum seekers as "riding roughshod over others' hospitality" (literally "Gastfreundschaft mit Füßen getreten"). Both the district council and the newspaper thus depicted the protests not as legitimate political action but as an illegitimate attempt to 'extract' more money from the German state. In consequence to their protests, the protesters thus became "ungrateful subjects" (Moulin 2012) who refused to silently accept whatever support is offered and not showing the gratitude expected of them.

No surprise then, the article on the Offenburg 'food boycott' caused an extraordinary wave of public resentment. Two days after the article was published, a second article entitled "Outrage on Facebook about Refugees' Food Boycott" appeared. It asserted that:

> "The report on the food boycott [...] has caused heated debate on the Facebook page of the *Mittelbadische Presse*. On Saturday morning, the online editors posted a summary and a link to the article. Reaction came thick and fast. As of Monday afternoon, the post had reached more than 37,000 Facebook users and triggered around 980 comments [...] Most voiced their outrage over the asylum seekers' behaviour and expressed incomprehension."[12] (Mittelbadische Presse: 11/4/2016)[13]

When I scanned the nearly 1,000 comments on the Facebook page, I was deeply shocked by the hatred I found, including various racist and xenopho-

---

12   Translation by LF. German original: "Der Bericht über den Essensboykott [...] hat auf der Facebook-Seite der Mittelbadischen Presse für heftige Debatten gesorgt. Die Onlineredaktion postete am Samstagvormittag einen Vorspann sowie einen Link zum Artikel. Die Reaktionen ließen nicht lang auf sich warten. Der Beitrag erreichte – Stand Montagnachmittag – mehr als 37 000 Facebook-Nutzer. Das Posting wurde rund 980 Mal kommentiert [...] Auf Facebook zeigte sich die Mehrheit der User empört über das Verhalten der Asylbewerber und äußerte Unverständnis.".

13   See: http://www.bo.de/lokales/offenburg/empoerung-auf-facebook-ueber-essensboykott-der-fluechtlinge (last accessed 1/8/2020).

bic attacks on the protesting asylum seekers. Almost all of the commenters deemed the acts of protests illegitimate and voiced neither sympathy for nor compassion with the protesting asylum seekers. Various posters even called for the asylum seekers' immediate deportation. Although most of the newspaper accounts on protesting asylum seekers in the area of my field research were met with similarly negative comments online, the extent of public outrage in Offenburg was extraordinary. The district council's storying, I would suggest, contributed significantly to this lack of public understanding.

Indeed, the district council seemed to have no understanding whatsoever for the actions of the protesters. Shortly before I travelled to Offenburg, I scheduled a telephone interview with Beate Gerber, the head of the local migration department, in order to find out about her take on the protests. She also emphasized that the collective refusal of the food provided was "all about money" and should be seen in light of the fact that the protesters were 'bogus' asylum seekers. This clearly came across in the following lines from our interview:

> LF: So you believe that the reason for the asylum seekers' protest was not a demand to cook for themselves but rather financial reasons?
> BG: Both. The financial aspect is definitely the main reason. We have a lot of young single men, especially in these bigger facilities. These young men are from countries that mean they have basically no chance of recognition, such as Gambia. We have many Gambians and the protection rate lies at 0.9%. So these are clearly ... and they also say this to our social workers, these are economic migrants who come here, who are under pressure from their families at home, from the people smugglers who want their money and if the neighbour's son sends home more money than him, the family is under pressure, he is under pressure. But this is clearly not what our asylum system is for.[14] (Interview with Beate Gerber: 14/4/2016)

---

14 Translation by LF. German original: "LF: Also Sie meinen, es geht den Flüchtlingen jetzt auch gar nicht mal darum, dass die selber kochen wollen, sondern es ist wirklich einfach der finanzielle Aspekt, der da im Vordergrund steht? BG: Sowohl als auch. Der finanzielle Aspekt steht auf jeden Fall im Vordergrund. Wir haben gerade in diesen größeren Anlagen viele alleinstehende junge Männer. Diese jungen Männer kommen aus Ländern aus denen sie so gut wie gar keine Anerkennungschancen haben, wie zum Beispiel Gambia haben wir sehr viele und da liegt die Schutzquote bei 0,9%. Also sind ganz klar ... also das sagen die auch unseren Sozialarbeitern gegenüber, das sind ganz klar Wirtschaftsflüchtlinge, die hierherkommen, die unter Druck stehen natürlich von den Familien zu Hause, von den Schleppern, die ihr Geld haben möchten und wenn

She thus explained the asylum seekers' protests mainly in terms of financial reasons. They protested not because they wanted to be able to cook their own food, but because they were "single young men" from Gambia, a country in western Africa with little chance of being accepted as refugees. These 'bogus' asylum seekers were protesting in order to pressure the district council into dispensing with the outside catering and, in turn, increasing their monthly financial allowances. In this storying, the protest thus became a symbol of the asylum seekers' illegitimate presence on German soil and their exploitation of the German asylum system. This contrasts sharply with the storying of events in Bad Waldsee, where local governmental actors embedded the collective refusal of food in a humanitarian imaginary that reconstituted the protesters as suffering victims and recipients of help.

Despite these differing storyings, governmental representatives in Offenburg, like their Bad Waldsee counterparts, also used food as a means to depoliticize the protests and strip them of political meanings. This is clear from my interlocutor's description of the district council's response to the protests:

> "The day before yesterday, our chief administrative officer was there, we all were there, we had lunch there, together with the press, in order to show that the food is okay, and it actually tasted great. Nothing like our own canteen here [giggles]. We were also able to persuade one or two of them to eat with us [...] But we made it clear to them that nothing was going to change. The system in this facility is that there is catering, and that's not going to change."[15] (Interview with Beate Gerber: 14/4/2016)

As in Bad Waldsee, the district council thus staged a 'food test' by sending several representatives to the interim reception centre to have lunch with the asylum seekers and invited members of the local press. According to my interlocutor, who tried the food herself, the food "tasted wonderful", better than

---

dann der Nachbarssohn mehr Geld nach Hause schickt, wie er, dann bekommt die Familie Druck, er bekommt Druck. Aber das ist natürlich nicht Sinn und Zweck unseres Asylsystems.".

15 Translation by LF. German original: "Also vorgestern war unser Landrat dann eben dort, wir waren alle dort, haben mitsamt der Presse dort gegessen, um eben auch zu zeigen, dass das essen in Ordnung ist, hat auch wunderbar geschmeckt. Also das ist wirklich kein Vergleich zu unserer eigenen Kantine im Haus [kichert] Wir konnten auch den ein oder anderen überreden bzw. überzeugen, dass er halt mitisst. [...] Aber ihnen halt eben auch nochmal klargemacht, dass sich da nichts ändern wird. Also das System in dieser Anlage ist so, da gibt es Catering und da wird es auch keine Änderung geben.".

in the canteen of her own workplace. A newspaper article on the 'food test' further underlined the notion that the food served was tasty, thus claiming that the protest was "inappropriate" and "incomprehensible" (see Mittelbadische Presse: 13/4/2016)[16]. With this response, the district council discredited the asylum seekers' collective refusal of food while legitimizing an uncompromising stance in relation to the facility's catering. In the remainder of our interview, my interlocutor added that a tough position was necessary in order to demonstrate that local authorities could not be "blackmailed" by asylum seekers.

Through such means, I would argue, the district council presented itself as the legitimate authority in charge of the conditions of reception while depoliticizing the asylum seekers' demonstrations of agency. This connects strikingly to what Nyers (2010a) outlines in his writings on instances of protest by non-citizens. He argues that such protests challenge the governmental prerogative to decide upon inclusion and exclusion in the nation-state. In response, governmental actors seek to regain control and power by delegitimizing the protesters. I would suggest that the district council in Offenburg also discredited the protesting asylum seekers and disputed their reasons for protesting in order to regain control over the terms of their reception. Through their delegitimizing responses, local actors relegated the asylum seekers to a non-political space while substantially limiting their scope of political agency.

In the following subsection, I illustrate how this depoliticizing storying of the Offenburg protests served wider aims in the local governance of migration. It presented a means for governmental actors to demonstrate sovereign power by reinforcing the distinction between those who should be offered protection and those who should not.

5.4.2. Food Provision as a "Strategy of Deterrence"

The asylum seekers' protest was still ongoing when I travelled to Offenburg in mid-April 2016. My aim was to visit the protest site myself in order to secure an interview with one of the protesting asylum seekers. Their protests occurred in one of the two newly established 'container villages' on the southern outskirts of the town. These interim facilities were designed to host the

---

16 See: http://www.bo.de/lokales/offenburg/landrat-scherer-besuchte-streikende-fluechtlinge (last accessed 1/8/2020).

increased number of asylum seekers and consisted of small, stacked containers of the kind conventionally used as site huts in construction. As I walked around the southern outskirts of Offenburg expecting to find the container village of the protesting asylum seekers, I caught sight of dozens of stacked containers on a disused airfield. I approached them, confident of having reached the place I was looking for. I entered the compound of the facility unchecked and found a group of men chatting outside a container block. I approached them and asked about the protests that had occurred during the past days. The men, though, looked puzzled and exchanged some words in Arabic. Eventually, they turned to me again and informed me in English that this was not the place I was looking for. In their "camp", they were allowed to cook for themselves in kitchen facilities set up in separate containers. Apparently, I had mistakenly entered the wrong container village. The asylum seekers thus gave me directions to the second container village, which was located just a few hundred metres down the road. When I eventually arrived at the place where the asylum seekers were protesting, I was struck by the sense that this interim reception centre was clearly different from the one I had just visited, having the appearance of a high-security complex. An intimating fence surrounded the site, which was monitored by several surveillance cameras. There was only one entrance, at which several security guards checked those entering and leaving the facility. While observing the scene, I noticed another striking difference between the two container villages: the first appeared to host mainly people from Arabic countries, whereas a majority of these inhabitants were people of colour. When I arrived at the gate, I addressed the two guards and asked them whether I could enter the facilities in order to speak to one of the protesting asylum seekers. They flatly refused and explained that they were not allowed to let anyone pass without permission from the district council. They did, though, offer to call Jens Riess, the head of the facility's management staff. Some minutes later, a middle-aged man approached the gate and introduced himself as an employee of a private company. This company was subcontracted by the district council to manage the facility and supply food to the asylum seekers. Although Jens Riess refused to allow me in, he chatted quite openly about his perspective on the ongoing acts of protest. He asserted that the residents in this facility were nothing but "economic refugees" with little chances of being recognized as refugees and a poor "perspective of staying" ("schlechte Bleibeperspektive") (Field notes: 25/4/2016). The container village I had entered earlier, on the other hand, hosted "genuine" asylum seekers from Syria or Iraq who had good chances of being recognized as refugees, he explained. The protesting asylum seekers at this facility had not fled war and persecution, he told me, they were simply out to send as much money as possible back to their families in Africa while they were in Germany. However, he explained, their relocation from the emergency reception centre to the container village a few days ago had entailed a major drop in their cash allowances. According to my interlocutor, this change from self-catering to outside catering formed part of a deliberate *"strategy of deterrence"* with which the district council aimed to prevent further "economic migrants" from coming and to break the "vicious cycle of people smuggling" (ibid.).

My observations and conversations at the two container villages clearly illustrate how the district council deliberately denied the asylum seekers the ability to cook for themselves as part of a wider "strategy of deterrence" directed at those depicted as economic migrants. Through a subsequent reduction in their monthly allowances, governmental actors sought to prevent "economic migrants" from saving money and sending remittances back home, as the manager of the facility told me. The contrasting designs of the container villages also reflected strikingly how the district council established a clear segregation between those deemed 'genuine' refugees and those deemed 'illegitimate economic migrants' based on their nationality and skin colour and even before their asylum case had been processed. While those with good chances of staying were accommodated in a container village where they could cook for themselves and thus received higher cash allowances, asylum seekers from sub-Saharan African countries were put up in a similar container village that did not feature kitchen facilities. Moreover, while the first facility I visited allowed the asylum seekers to move around freely, the second resembled a high-security complex and thus contributed to the criminalization and stigmatization of its inhabitants. This connects to what Welander (2019: no page number) calls "politics of exhaustion", understood as "a complex deterrence approach with the objective of exhausting asylum seekers, mentally and physically, with the ultimate goal of deterring them from [...] European asylum systems". In a similar vein, Ambrosini (2020: 198) observes the implementation of "local policies of exclusion", which he defines as "those measures, adopted by local authorities, that aim to exclude migrants, to separate them from the native component of the population by establishing specific, albeit implicit, prohibitions against them and which may be indirect or hidden". Ambrosini witnesses a sharp increase in such 'local policies of exclusion' since the so-called 'refugee crisis'. And yet, he also acknowledges that they do not go unchallenged (ibid.).

With their protests, I would suggest, the asylum seekers in Offenburg were thus actively challenging their local exclusions, demanding nothing more than equal conditions of reception – a possible explanation that, however, went largely unheard in the wake of the protests. The protesting asylum seekers were probably well aware of their discriminating treatment since they most likely knew about the cooking facilities at the other container village up the road. Governmental actors in Offenburg, however, constituted the protesters as illegitimate asylum seekers even before they began protesting against their transferral. The protests then served as a welcome means for local governmental actors to recast this discrimination between 'genuine' and 'bogus' refugees and, thus, to reinforce sovereign power over the management of asylum seekers.

This connects with academic works in the field of critical migration studies that have outlined how processes of abjection exclude certain groups of migrants from the realm of humanitarian protection and render them vulnerable to the arbitrary operations of government (see Papastergiadis 2006; Nyers 2010a; Tyler 2013; Laziridis 2015). Migrants thus become "human waste" (Bauman 2003) or "abject bodies" (Kristeva 1982; Butler 1993), beings that are stripped of any rights and to be discharged to the exterior. Others have argued that the distinction between those who are included and those who are excluded from governmental protection forms the essence of sovereign power. For instance, Nyers (2006b: 48) asserts that sovereign power "gets played out through the state's decision to provide protection – or not", while Scheel and Ratfisch (2014) argue that the distinction between "villains and victims" forms a central technique in the governance and management of migration movements.

A similar tendency is illustrated in the case of Offenburg. The local government recast the protesters as abject beings and thus reproduced its power over the governance of migration. And yet, this dominant storying of the protests in Offenburg was highly contested. In the course of my field research, I realized that volunteers who supported refugees in town *(re)politicized* the asylum seekers' scope of political agency by putting forward a rather different albeit marginalized storying of events.

5.4.3. Politicizing Responses to the Protests

During my field stay in Offenburg, I scheduled interviews with two leading members of local citizens' initiatives supporting refugees. Their storying of events clearly differed from the district council's depiction of the protests as being "all about the money". Both took a clear stand against the district councils' portrayal of the protesters as illegitimate economic migrants who should be excluded from humanitarian protection. With their storying and reactions, the volunteers thus recast the protesting asylum seekers as subjects in relationships of solidarity, while blurring the dividing line between 'genuine' and 'bogus' asylum seekers.

When I visited Offenburg in April 2016, I met Angelika Berg, a Protestant pastor and head of the "Ökumenischer Arbeitskreis Asyl e.V." ("Ecumenical Working Circle on Asylum") for an interview. As we talked, I could clearly sense that she was thoroughly upset about the council's reactions. She repeatedly denounced its tough stance while voicing her sympathy and empathy with the protesting asylum seekers. She told me that it was a "false insinuation" to assert, as the district council had, that the asylum seekers were protesting in order to illegitimately extract as much money as possible from the German welfare state. From the additional allowance of 144 euros per month provided to self-caterers, she claimed, there would not be much left to send back home to their poor families in Africa. And even if the asylum seekers did send money home, she couldn't really understand why that constituted a problem. After all, the private companies providing food to the asylum seekers were also trying to make a profit and often charged the German government prohibitive fees for their services. Moreover, Angelika Berg acknowledged that cooking had important social meanings for the asylum seekers. Being provided with food for a prospective duration of two years, in contrast, represented a significant diminution of human dignity and self-determination for the asylum seekers. These reasons for protesting, my interlocutor complained, went unacknowledged in the district council's responses. She therefore criticized the council for being "two-faced" and questioned its credibility in the following terms:

> "You can't treat people like that. Behind closed doors they talk about economic refugees and making their lives uncomfortable and, in public, they claim they are providing for them and demonstrating great hospitality and

the asylum seekers are rejecting it. I find that really two-faced."[17] (Interview with Angelika Berg: 14/4/2016)

This clearly shows my interlocutor's critical view of the district council's inhumane treatment of those termed 'bogus' asylum seekers. She claimed that the local authority was deliberately trying to make their lives more uncomfortable while publicly putting the blame on the asylum seekers.

During our interview, the pastor not only voiced her dissent towards local governmental actors but also emphasized that she was not prepared to silently accept their discrimination of those deemed 'bogus' asylum seekers. This was particularly evident when she compared the situation to her experiences at another interim accommodation centre in Lahr, a town close to Offenburg, which she recounted as follows:

"On the first of February, when it became clear that the asylum seekers were going to be relocated to Lahr, I talked to the head of the migration department, Mister Heinz [...] and he said to me on the phone that it's also about making things more uncomfortable for the asylum seekers who have no chance of staying and mentioned the centralized catering at the camp in Lahr. That's when it became clear to me that, for the authorities, centralized catering means we make it more uncomfortable for the refugees. That was a very tense situation because we then obstructed the relocation."[18] (Interview with Angelika Berg: 14/4/2016)

Angelika Berg thus perceived the district council's course of action as discriminatory and unacceptable. Therefore, she and the fellow volunteers in her initiative had directly intervened in order to obstruct the relocation of asylum

---

17   Translation by LF. German original: "[...] dass man so nicht mit Menschen umgeht. Also hinter den Kulissen wird über Wirtschaftsflüchtlinge und wir machen denen das Leben ungemütlich gesprochen und vorne herum heißt es dann, wir machen denen Angebote und unsere Gastfreundschaft ist ja so groß und das nehmen die nicht an. Also, ich empfinde das wirklich als doppel-züngig.".

18   Translation by LF. German original: "Ich hatte am ersten Februar, als das war, dass die nach Lahr verlegt wurden, noch mit dem Migrationsdezernenten gesprochen, Herr Heinz heißt der hier. [...] dann hat er mir am Telefon gesagt, es geht jetzt auch darum, dass es jetzt für die Flüchtlinge ohne Bleibeperspektive ungemütlicher wird und das halt eben auch mit der Zentralversorgung im Lager in Lahr dann ... also da war für mich klar, für die Behörden heißt Zentralversorgung, wir machen es den Flüchtlingen ungemütlicher. Das war eine angespannte Situation, weil wir diesen Transport aufgehalten haben.".

seekers to another facility with "centralized catering". My interlocutor also recalled how the citizens' initiative generally struggled with such discrimination between 'genuine' and 'bogus' asylum seekers in the governance of migration, declaring:

> "I would say that refugees, in general, have long since been treated not first class but second class people. But then there are also people who are third and fourth class. And we really struggle with this".[19] (Interview with Angelika Berg: 14/4/2016)

I would argue that this is a clear example of how volunteers challenged the district council's "strategy of deterrence" while recasting those deemed 'bogus' asylum seekers as subjects of relationships of solidarity. Another came in my interview with Klaus Böhlen, the head of a citizens' initiative supporting refugees in a suburb of Offenburg. Like Angelika Berg, he repeatedly criticized the district council for its inadequate response. In his eyes, the council did not take the asylum seekers' requests seriously and, instead, treated the protesters as "public scapegoats". This behaviour "poured oil" on the flames of right-wing attitudes in society, he complained. He thus criticized the district council for stirring up hatred and resentment among the public instead of encouraging understanding of the protesting asylum seekers. During our conversation, he also linked the protests directly to the question of whether those deemed economic migrants constituted rightful recipients of help and support. He acknowledged that, for the members of his citizens' initiative, it was a question to which there was no easy or straightforward answer. He explained this as follows:

> "This also relates to the question of whether we, as a refugee help initiative, should get involved at this container village. We discussed this last time [...] It was interesting because there were totally different opinions. As a businessman, I would say, I want to work where it will be efficient [...] So there was that one line of argument and there was this other line of argument that said 'hey hey hey, these are human beings and they have their ... that's their right as human beings and we should not see them as refugees who will probably be deported but as human beings who also have the right to

---

19 Translation by LF. German original: "Also ich meine die Flüchtlinge sind ja sowieso schon lange nicht erste Klasse, sondern zweite, aber da gibt es dann auch noch welche dritte und vierte Klasse. Und das hat uns hier richtig zugesetzt.".

be taken seriously and to receive what is possible,'"[20] (Interview with Klaus Böhlen: 25/4/2016)

Maestri and Monforte (2020) argue that volunteers supporting refugees are often guided by notions of deservingness. Yet, they observe that the boundaries between 'deserving' and 'undeserving' refugees are challenged when volunteers experience the effects of governmental processes of exclusion. As they go on to argue, "in these situations, volunteers are faced with moral and emotional dilemmas related to how lines are being drawn between who is included or excluded, accepted or not, deserving of their compassion or undeserving" (ibid.: 2). In a similar vein, the question of whether ostensibly 'bogus' asylum seekers with 'little chance of staying' should also benefit from their help and intervention caused dilemmas among the volunteers in my interlocutors' initiative. While Klaus Böhlen suggested he would not offer support to those who were likely to be deported due to considerations of "efficiency", he highlighted another line of argument that recast those deemed economic migrants as equal human beings and deserving recipients of help. My interlocutor recalled how the volunteers found a compromise that was deemed acceptable to all: if they had spare capacity, the volunteers would include asylum seekers with little chance of staying in their practices of solidarity. Rather than uncritically accepting the distinction between 'genuine' and 'bogus' asylum seekers, a central component in the governance of migration, the initiative's members thus recast and contested this dividing line in response to the asylum seekers' protests.

The two volunteers I interviewed not only contested the storying of protests put forward by the district council but also intervened in order to actively demonstrate their dissent with the council's responses to the protests. Both Angelika Berg and Klaus Böhlen recalled that the council had invited them to join the "food test" and have lunch together with the press

---

20 Translation by LF. German original: "Das betrifft jetzt auch die Frage, ob wir als Flüchtlingshilfe Rebland jetzt in diesem Containerdorf was machen. Das haben wir beim letzten Mal diskutiert [...] Das war interessant, weil es da ganz unterschiedliche Meinungen gab. Als Kaufmann sage ich da, ich möchte gern dort arbeiten, wo es effizient ist [...] Also es gab diese eine Linie und es gab die andere Linie, die gesagt hat: ‚Hey Hey Hey, das sind Menschen und die haben ihr ... das ist ganz legitim als Mensch und wir müssen nicht den Flüchtling drin sehen, der wahrscheinlich abgeschoben wird, sondern ein Mensch, der auch Anspruch drauf hat, dass er ernst genommen wird und dass man ihm das zukommen lässt, was möglich ist.'".

and the asylum seekers. However, they had deliberately boycotted the event. I could sense that they were both deeply upset about the council responding to the protests in this way. As Klaus Böhlen put it:

> "I think the impression that we were needed so that the head of the district council wouldn't be there on his own, so he'd have others with him, is right, or at least hasn't been refuted. It's always very useful when people helping the refugees support the position of the head of the district council and say: 'Yes, we as helpers also believe that it was an inappropriate reaction on their part' [...] Basically, there was a danger – and the newspaper coverage reflects this – that we would be used as material for press photos. And when the head of the district council then says: 'Yes, but this is a good meal' ... that doesn't completely do justice to the problem situation."[21] (Interview with Klaus Böhlen: 25/4/2016)

According to Klaus Böhlen, the district council invited the volunteers to bolster the council's position in relation to the protests and concentrate blame on the protesters. He therefore refused to take part in what he termed an "image event". Similarly, Angelika Berg phoned those responsible in the council in order to voice her dissent towards this 'food test' and to explicitly decline to take part, thus deliberately refusing to side with the council and to legitimize its responses to the protests. Through these means, I would argue, the volunteers contested the government's actions and (re)politicized the asylum seekers' demonstrations of political agency.

As a result, the staged 'food test' intensified an already conflictive relationship between the local authority and the two citizens' initiatives in town. Both volunteers told me that governmental representatives had repeatedly tried to exploit volunteers for their own ends. Drawing parallels to other experiences with the district council, they voiced their deep frustration and dissatisfaction with this attitude towards volunteers. Angelika Berg, for example, apologized

---

21   Translation by LF. German original: "Also ich glaube, der Eindruck stimmt, zumindest ist er nicht widerlegt, dass wir eigentlich gebraucht wurden, damit der Landrat da nicht alleine steht, sondern auch andere. Und das ist immer sehr gut, wenn die Leute, die den Flüchtlingen helfen dann die Position des Landrats unterstützen und sagen, ja also wir als Flüchtlingshelfer finden auch, dass das unangemessen ist als Reaktion von den Leuten dort [...] Im Prinzip bestand die Gefahr, und die Zeitungsartikel geben das eigentlich auch wieder, dass wir als Fotomaterial für die Pressebilder da benutzt werden, und wenn der Landrat dann sagt, ja, aber das ist doch eigentlich ein gutes Essen ... aber es wird halt der Problemlage insgesamt nicht zu hundert Prozent gerecht.".

for her angry tone, saying that I had caught her in a week in which "people like her" were "really frustrated" with the district council, while Klaus Böhlen explained his dissent towards the council as follows:

> "They say: 'As the district council, we decide. All those volunteers, that's great and we can also invite them to events and shower them with praise, but we're not letting them influence us in our decisions. Where would that lead?'"[22] (Interview with Klaus Böhlen: 25/4/2016)

My interlocutor thus felt that the district council did not take them seriously and would not include them in their decision-making processes. Our conversations also shed light on a longer history of conflict between volunteers and the local authority. Keen to voice their increasing discontent with this situation, my interlocutors told me, their initiatives had recently joined forces to request a meeting with council representatives in order to discuss their conflictive relationship.

Summing up, I would argue that the acts of protest in Offenburg did indeed come with political outcomes. Although the asylum seekers' request to cook for themselves went unaddressed, their protests nevertheless contested the conditions of reception and recast the relationships of solidarity in the town. They brought about contrasting storyings and intensified already existing conflicts between volunteers and governmental actors. In response to the protests, the volunteers challenged the governments' prerogative to decide upon those included and those excluded from humanitarian protection. This is another clear example of how relationships of solidarity that build on a humanitarian imaginary can come with political meanings and effects.

5.5. Concluding Remarks: The Agency of Asylum Seekers in the Contestation of Solidarity

This chapter investigated how actors involved in the reception of asylum seekers made sense of and responded to protests in emergency reception facilities in the wake of the long summer of migration. I illustrated that the political

---

22 Translation by LF. German original: "[...] sie sagen: wir entscheiden, wir als Landratsamt entscheiden. Das mit den Ehrenamtlichen ist super und die kann man dann auch zu den Empfängen einladen und so und vielfältig loben, aber wir lassen uns doch in unserer Entscheidung nicht reinreden, wo kommen wir denn da hin?".

agency of asylum seekers, i.e. their capacity to change the conditions of their reception, was *intermediated* in various ways in response to their protests. The storying of events by actors involved in the reception of asylum seekers was central for determining whether the protests were considered meaningful political action or stripped of political content. The two case studies that were discussed in more detail in the course of this chapter suggest that it was the latter of these two possibilities that prevailed.

In both cases, the issue of food took on important political meanings. It presented a way for asylum seekers to draw attention to their grievances and to pressure local governmental actors into addressing their demands. Nevertheless, actors involved in their reception employed it as a means to *depoliticize* their reasons for protesting. Through publicly staged 'food tests', local governmental actors distilled the protests to mere dissatisfaction with the food provided and, almost sarcastically, offered additional spices to season the meals. In doing so, they (re)constituted the asylum seekers as 'bare life', beings reduced to their basic needs, while (re)affirming their power to decide upon the conditions of reception. These depoliticizing responses substantially limited the asylum seekers' scope for political agency.

The storying of the protests also recast a key tenet of the governance of migration, the discrimination between 'genuine' and 'bogus' asylum seekers. On the one hand, the asylum seekers in Bad Waldsee were relegated to the role of suffering victims and passive recipients of humanitarian help. This was most apparent when volunteers explained the asylum seekers' acts of protests in terms of their vulnerable and traumatized condition. On the other hand, the protesters in Offenburg were recast as 'bogus' refugees or economic migrants whose presence was deemed illegitimate and whose actions were explained as being 'all about money'.

Despite these *depoliticizing* responses, however, the asylum seekers' protests came with transformative effects and opened up political possibilities. They brought about storyings that *recast* the 'right' subjects and terms of solidarity. In the wake of the protests in Bad Waldsee, volunteers problematized how relationships of solidarity became instrumentalized by either the givers or receivers of help. In Offenburg, volunteers recast those deemed economic migrants as 'rightful' recipients of help and support while voicing dissent towards the governmental discrimination between 'genuine' and 'bogus' asylum seekers. In the latter case, the protests also led volunteers to intervene in their increasingly conflictive relationship with governmental authorities, demanding to be included in local decision-making processes.

This illustrates, I would suggest, how asylum seekers actively shaped and contested the solidarities that emerged around the long summer of migration, however limited and intermediated their agency may be.

6. BREAKING SOLIDARITY: Refugee Activism as a Conflicting Imaginary of Solidarity and Community

6.1. At the Frontlines of Solidarity and Community

"Never before has the district court witnessed such a hearing: on Monday, amidst intense security checks and police protection, the trial in a case of criminal coercion got underway, accompanied during the day by a group of refugees from Africa demonstrating noisily on the streets of Schwäbisch Gmünd and finally in front of the court building itself."[1] (Remszeitung: 11/5/2015)[2]

Shortly before the migration summer reached its climax in 2015, this story from a local newspaper came to my attention. It reported on a trial that marked the culmination of a long-running series of conflicts between a group of around twelve "refugee activists", as they called themselves, and several local actors involved in the reception of asylum seekers. The site of conflict was Schwäbisch Gmünd, a small town in the area of my field research. According to the newspaper article, the man facing charges was a Nigerian refugee, apparently the group's leader, who was accused of "yelling at people through

---

1 Translation by LF. German original: "Eine solche Gerichtsverhandlung hat das Amtsgericht noch nicht gesehen: Mit äußerst strengen Sicherheitskontrollen der Justiz und unter Polizeischutz ging dort am Montag eine Verhandlung wegen des Vorwurfs gemeinschaftlicher Nötigung über die Bühne. Tagsüber begleitet von lautstarken Protestzügen einer Gruppe von Flüchtlingen aus Afrika durch Gmünd und schließlich auch vor dem Amtsgerichtsgebäude.".
2 See: https://remszeitung.de/2015/5/11/streit-um-noetigung-durch-einen-fluechtling-aus-afrika-und-um-muell-kamera-vor-dem-gmuender-amtsgericht/ (last accessed 1/8/2020).

a megaphone" and "appearing very aggressive and unresponsive to attempts to engage in conversation" (Remszeitung: 11/5/2015). This violent and escalating behaviour, the article asserted, led to "disturbances" at the local refugee accommodation centre in March 2014, incidents that included the forceful blocking of the facility's entrance and the harassment of social workers. After several hours of proceedings, during which various witnesses testified, the district court found the accused guilty of criminal coercion and assault and ordered him to pay a fine of 25 daily rates of five Euros, a total of 125 euros, to the court. In comparison to the costly legal action, this relatively insignificant sum points to the symbolic function of the trial, serving to condemn the entire activist group and signifying the breaking of all relationships of solidarity between local actors and protesters; something that I will investigate in more detail in the course of this chapter.

While the court proceedings were still ongoing, the remaining members of the "Refugees Initiative Schwäbisch Gmünd", as the activists called their group, staged another protest in order to call attention to their version of the story (see The Voice Refugee Forum: 18/6/2015)[3]. They accused the district council, which was responsible for their accommodation centre, the local press and the local citizens' initiative supporting refugees of false accusations and denounced their complicity in the repression and discrimination of refugees in the town. What local actors wrongly depicted as instances of criminal coercion and assault, they claimed, were actually peaceful protests calling for the immediate removal of a camera monitoring the entrance to their accommodation centre. According to the refugee activists, the district council had installed this camera in order to bully and control the refugees. The group thus regarded the trial as a symbol of the injustices it had been enduring in Schwäbisch Gmünd, as just one of many moments illustrating the discriminating behaviour of local actors, including volunteers supporting refugees.

The contrasting interpretations of the trial in May 2015 are emblematic of the conflicting notions of solidarity and community that unfolded between the refugee activists and local actors in Schwäbisch Gmünd from 2012 onwards. These steadily intensifying conflicts that ultimately resulted in the court trial strikingly illustrate the possibility for relationships of solidarity to eventually break down and dissolve. When the refugee activists started

---

3   See: http://www.thevoiceforum.org/node/3949 (last accessed 1/8/2020).

protesting in late 2012, roughly three years prior to the court trial, they received support and understanding from several local actors, including the left-wing youth centre Esperanza, the citizens' initiative supporting refugees and the media. During their first protests, the activists also entered into dialogue with local governmental actors, something that resulted in a "Memorandum of Understanding" signed by the local mayor and the activists. As the protests continued, however, the relationships between them became increasingly conflictive. The citizens' initiative withdrew its offers of support and publicly voiced its unsympathetic stance towards the protest actions. The refugee activists, on the other hand, denounced the "deceptive solidarity" of local actors, including the citizens' initiative (Refugees Initiative Schwäbisch Gmünd: 12/6/2014)[4]. These disagreements, I would suggest, illustrate in a striking way how claims made in the name of solidarity are embedded into differing social imaginaries and are thus highly contested among different actors. As Agustín and Jørgensen (2019: 28) put it: "solidarity is itself a battlefield, concerning which type of solidarity should prevail and how, constituting the possibility of articulating and imagining alternatives".

This chapter investigates the conflicting imaginaries of solidarity and community in Schwäbisch Gmünd. While I scrutinized how actors mobilized and forged solidarities with refugees in the second chapter of this book, my aim in this final chapter is to take into consideration how the *breaking of solidarities* occurred. This outline of the book attests to the elusive nature of solidarity with refugees, which I interpret not as a static condition but as a volatile social relationship. As Bauder (2019: 3) argues: "solidarity is a never-finished practice that prevents political closure and preserves plurality, while acknowledging the complex, fragmented and multifaceted relations between people and groups in different circumstances". The 'proper' conduct of solidarity and refugee support is thus open for interpretation and embedded in varying social imaginaries that respond to the needs and interests of different actors involved. As the case of Schwäbisch Gmünd illustrates strikingly, these social imaginaries can be so contrasting and conflicting that it becomes impossible to find a common denominator. While academic works on solidarity have intensively discussed how individuals are mobilized to act and drawn into supportive relationships (see for instance Featherstone

---

4 All citations of "Refugees Initiative Schwäbisch Gmünd" throughout this chapter refer to posts in the activists' Facebook group, which can be accessed at https://www.facebook.com/refugeesinitiative/ (last accessed 1/8/2020).

2012; Johnson 2012; Karakayali 2017; Agustín & Jørgensen 2019), less attention has been paid to the processes that lead such relationships to disintegrate or be deliberately broken. In what follows, I thus investigate how relationships of solidarity can also materialize in contrasting claims, practices, discourses and, ultimately, in conflicts. This highlights the conflicting understandings of and demands on collectivity and togetherness in migration societies.

In contrast to the asylum seeker protests I investigated in Chapter 5, the actions of the Refugees Initiative Schwäbisch Gmünd were more long-term and organized. Over a period of roughly three years, its members repeatedly took a public stand, organizing several protests in the town and in other localities across Germany. Most of the activists were rejected asylum seekers from Sub-Saharan African countries who remained in Germany due to "obstacles to deportation". They often had to cope with years of "Kettenduldungen" (literally "chains of toleration"), an insecure and precarious residence status in which the right to remain is renewed every few months and no work permit is granted. These activists were well organized, with a Facebook group that had more than 500 members and functioned as a platform for sharing information on their protests and demands. Form the very beginning, their actions were embedded in a German-wide network of left-wing activists campaigning for refugee rights (see Ataç et al. 2015; Bhimji 2016). From late summer 2012 on, similar, loosely connected protests occurred in several German cities, such as Berlin, Hannover and Munich, the most emblematic of which was the 'protest camp' at Oranienplatz in Berlin, a public square that was squatted from October 2012 until April 2014 by a group of around 100 refugee activists and their German supporters (see Landry 2015; Wilcke & Lambert 2015). The following investigation will shed light on how this German-wide movement for the rights of refugees materialized in a small town in the area of my field research.

This chapter builds on field research in Schwäbisch Gmünd, to which I travelled several times in order to talk to various parties involved in the conflicts. I held interviews with the refugee activists themselves, with two leading members of a local citizens' initiative supporting refugees and with a representative of the district council. I also draw on statements and declarations published by the refugee activists in their Facebook group as well as on newspaper articles reporting on their protests. I should note, however, that it is not my intention to offer a complete and objective account of the complex history of these protests. I myself was not present at the refugee activists' protests, which means that I draw on second-hand interpretations and fragmentary reconstructions in order to make sense of the events.

The following chapter consists of four parts. To start with, I briefly sketch out the history of the protests in Schwäbisch Gmünd, arguing that the so-called "camera conflict" presented an important turning point that substantially altered the relationships of solidarity between the refugee activists and various local actors. In section three, I then examine the reasoning that led both the refugee activists and members of the local citizens' initiative supporting refugees to end all relationships of solidarity with the other side. In section four, I investigate the contrasting imaginaries of 'local community' that came to light in the course of these conflicts. Finally, I conclude by looking at the intimate relationship between solidarity and community.

6.2. A Short History of Refugee Activism in Schwäbisch Gmünd

The story of the Refugees Initiative Schwäbisch Gmünd began in summer 2012 when the refugees returned from the "Break Isolation camp" in Jena (see The Voice Refugee Forum: 29/3/2012)[5]. This workshop gathered refugees, their supporters and left-wing activist groups from across the country. Together, they discussed the discrimination and exclusion refugees faced on the ground and elaborated ways of taking a stand against them. Back at their accommodation centre, the asylum seekers in Schwäbisch Gmünd translated words into action. Supported by the local left-wing youth centre Esperanza, they squatted the central market square of town and erected a protest camp for several days in order to raise awareness of the unacceptable conditions at their accommodation centre. Over the following three years, they repeatedly took a public stand in the town in order to voice their discontent over various issues. In these protests, they directed complaints against local authorities, the police department, the employees at their accommodation centre, the local population, the local media and members of the local citizens' initiative supporting refugees. Their accusations included *"police brutality"* (Refugees Initiative Schwäbisch Gmünd: 15/4/2014), *"criminalization* and *persecution* of refugees"* (ibid. 8/5/2015), *"repression* from the Ostalb district authorities" (ibid. 11/6/2014), *"violation* of refugees right" (ibid. 10/3/2014) and *"colonial injustice"* (ibid. 17/4/2013), to name just a few. Local actors in Schwäbisch

---

5   See: http://www.thevoiceforum.org/node/2488 (last accessed 1/8/2020).

Gmünd, in turn, repeatedly criticized the group for its violent and "radical" behaviour, the inappropriateness of their protest actions and their unreceptiveness to de-escalating dialogue and compromise. Eventually, the situation became increasingly tense resulting in the court trial sketched out above, while the issues remained unresolved, and all relationships of solidarity with local actors broke down.

When the refugee activists of Schwäbisch Gmünd first took a public stand in late summer 2012, their actions elicited support from the local citizens' initiative and the left-wing youth centre Esperanza as well as understanding and empathy in local press coverage. With their protest camp on the market square, the activists called attention to the tough conditions at their accommodation centre, their "camp" as they called it, and demanded that "the asylum centre has to be closed immediately" (Refugees Initiative Schwäbisch Gmünd: 21/11/2012). Located at a former barracks complex built by the Nazi regime during the Second World War, the facility hosted around 200 asylum seekers, with five refugees having to share one room. Even before the protests, the accommodation centre's run-down state was well known. More than a year earlier, the citizens' initiative supporting refugees had called on the local authority to refurbish the facility (see Remszeitung: 7/6/2011)[6]. Yet, it was only in response to the refugee activists' protest camp that the council agreed to take action.

While their protest at the market square was still ongoing, the local mayor invited the protesters and representatives of the local citizens' initiative to a joint meeting that would discuss possible solutions to the situation at the facility. The outcome was a "Memorandum of Understanding" that was signed by the mayor, the council's chief administrative officer and the refugee activists. It consisted of a twelve-point action plan that defined various steps to be implemented by the local authorities in order to improve the conditions of reception in Schwäbisch Gmünd. For instance, they agreed to work towards the long-term goal of closing the accommodation centre and replacing it with a decentralized housing scheme that would host asylum seekers in smaller units dispersed across the town. Another immediate step agreed to was the abolition of the discriminating voucher system in favour of monthly cash allowances paid directly to the asylum seekers. These agreements clearly illustrate how the refugee activists' protests initially met with understanding

---

6   See: https://remszeitung.de/2011/7/6/mittelfristig-ist-eine-neue-loesung-fuer-das-asylbewerber-wohnheim-noetig/ (last accessed 1/8/2020).

and dialogue from various parties involved in the reception of asylum seekers in Schwäbisch Gmünd. As I write this chapter six years later, the accommodation centre under dispute is still in place. Nevertheless, this action plan illustrates that the local authority was willing to make concessions and enter into dialogue in response to the activists' protest camp. I would suggest that it also laid the ground for what became known as the *"Gmünder Weg"* ("the Gmünd way"), the town's seemingly successful approach to the local integration of refugees. From 2014 on, this narrative put Schwäbisch Gmünd in the national spotlight and made it a role model for the implementation of a local 'welcome culture', something I will illustrate in more detail later in this chapter.

In the months following the protest camp, the Refugees Initiative refrained from further protest actions in Schwäbisch Gmünd. However, from its Facebook group, it was evident that the initiative had not disbanded but was continuing its activities in other parts of the region. In March 2013, the refugee activists joined forces with asylum seekers in the nearby town of Nördlingen in order to raise awareness of the tough conditions at the local accommodation centre. From April to June 2013, the refugee activists organized what they called a "Refugee Liberation Bus Tour", making stops in several towns and villages across the state of Baden-Württemberg. In each place, they visited the local refugee accommodation centre, raised awareness of the problematic conditions on the ground, and mobilized the centre's residents to participate in local protest actions. Their Facebook group featured extensive coverage of the tour, including numerous posts and photos.

In March 2014, around one and a half years after their first protest action, the refugee activists made a reappearance in their town of residence, Schwäbisch Gmünd. This time, their protests were of unprecedented intensity and lasted several weeks. They staged several protest actions at different locations including their accommodation centre, the town centre, the premises of the district council, and the state parliament in Stuttgart. What came to be known as the "camera conflict" assumed particular significance in all of the interviews I conducted and critically altered relationships in the town. I would thus argue that this conflict marked an important turning point in the relationships between the refugee activists and local actors in Schwäbisch Gmünd; relationships that were up until then embedded in mutual understanding and solidarity.

The camera conflict broke out when the district council installed a surveillance camera at the entrance to the central accommodation centre in early

March 2014. Immediately after its installation, the refugee activists complained about the camera and denounced it as another means of surveillance and control. To them, it constituted a symbol for the intolerable "Guantanamo methods" of the district council in the handling of asylum seekers (Refugees Initiative Schwäbisch Gmünd: 8/3/2014). They thus demanded the immediate removal of the camera. The council, however, refused to comply and offered a different explanation of the need for a camera: it was not their intention to keep track of the accommodation centre's inhabitants but, in fact, to monitor the nearby bins, where unknown outsiders had repeatedly dumped their rubbish illegally (Interview with Karl Kurz: 9/3/2016). The refugee activists, in turn, denounced this interpretation as a lie and insisted on the removal of the camera, a demand that resulted in numerous protest actions over the course of several weeks.

In the first days after the installation of the camera, the refugee activists' anger was directed towards employees at the reception facility, such as the head of its management staff, the social workers and the caretaker. The activists blocked the entrance gate so that staff members were unable to leave the building and go home from work for hours. They insulted and threatened social workers to such an extent that some of them quit their jobs and subsequently needed psychological support, as a dedicated volunteer with the local citizens' initiative told me (Interview with Jens Küffner: 12/3/2015). Roughly one week later, the refugee activists redirected their anger to the responsible deputy at the district council. They entered the building and staged a sit-in at his office. Back at their accommodation centre, the activists covered the surveillance camera with a banner on which they had written in large letters: "Camera must be removed. We do not want Guantanamo and no surveillance".

When the district council had still not taken down the camera a month after its installation, the refugee activists staged further protests at the facility and held a protest march through the town, in the course of which they blocked the traffic at a central intersection. This time, their protests were met by a large-scale police operation involving special units from surrounding areas, what the refugee activists later denounced as "police brutality". In the local press, the events also received increasingly negative publicity and were depicted as "refugee riots" (Remszeitung: 13/4/2014)[7] or "disturbances

---

[7]   See: https://remszeitung.de/2014/4/13/landrat-und-ob-sehr-besorgt-wegen-fluechtlings-krawallen/ (last accessed 1/8/2020).

at the accommodation centre" (Schwäbische Zeitung: 11/4/2014)[8]. According to a newspaper article, the local mayor and the council's chief administrative officer were "extremely upset" by the incidents and concerned about the "good cooperation and togetherness" in the town (Remszeitung: 13/4/2014). In response to these articles in the local press, the refugee activists set up an "info tent" on the town's market square and handed out leaflets to passing pedestrians explaining their version of the story, which, they claimed, differed significantly from the press' false accusations.

Eventually, the object of dispute – the camera – was stolen by unknown offenders. Neither the refugee activists nor the district council ever mentioned this incident in public nor claimed responsibility for it. According to a volunteer I spoke to, this apparent solution also went unnoticed by the local media, which had previously reported extensively on the camera conflict. Nevertheless, the sides remained unreconciled and conflicts only reached a symbolic ending in the court trial in May 2015.

6.3. The Breaking of Relationships of Solidarity

The camera conflict substantially altered the relationships between refugee activists and local actors, including the citizens' initiative supporting refugees, the local media and the district council. Over the course of the dispute, these relationships became steadily more conflictive and, ultimately, remained irreconcilable. On the one hand, the refugee activists deliberately refused all support offered to them by local actors, whom they accused of "deceptive solidarity". On the other hand, citizens acting in support of refugees withdrew help and support and broke off all ties to the protesters. In the following section, I investigate in more detail how, as a result of the conflict, relationships of solidarity were broken by both refugee activists (first subsection) and volunteers supporting refugees in town (second subsection). In the third subsection, I then illustrate how the refugee activists, from the very beginning of their struggle, reached out in order to forge alternative relationships of solidarity that went beyond the boundaries of Schwäbisch Gmünd.

---

8   See: https://www.schwaebische.de/landkreis/ostalbkreis/schwaebisch-gmuend_artikel,-tumult-in-der-asylbewerberunterkunft-_arid,5625635.html (last accessed 1/8/2020).

6.3.1. Breaking with "Deceptive Solidarity"

Three months after the district council had installed the camera at the accommodation centre in Schwäbisch Gmünd, the refugee activists staged a protest at the state parliament of Baden-Württemberg in Stuttgart, demanding to speak to representatives of the state government. As they explained in their Facebook group, they aimed to raise awareness of the "repeated acts of repression" they had been facing in Schwäbisch Gmünd (Refugees Initiative Schwäbisch Gmünd: 11/6/2014). Their anger had been exacerbated by a letter from a representative of the district council addressed to the Federal Office for Migration and Refugees (BAMF). This document listed the activists' full names and asked for their "inappropriate behaviour" in Schwäbisch Gmünd to be taken into account when deciding on the renewal of their residence permit. For unknown reasons, the letter was leaked to the activists, who published it in their Facebook group.

It was in this context that the activists accused local actors of "deceptive solidarity" and broke off all ties with them. This is illustrated strikingly in a post in their Facebook group informing on their protests at the state parliament. In it, they criticized various actors in the town and accused them of complicity in their stigmatization and discrimination, as stated in the following quote:

> "We denounce the continuous act of stigmatisation and splitting of refugees with the dubious justification of compromises to further isolate and persecute refugees in the district. This form of institutionalised discrimination and stereotyping engineered by the district Authorities through the local conservative press "Rems Zeitung" and the local initiative "Bürger Innitiative" both element that project the repression of the State with *deceptive solidarity*" (Refugees Initiative Schwäbisch Gmünd: 11/6/14; English original, emphasis added)

The activists thus blamed local actors for their perceived "stigmatization", "isolation" and "persecution" in Schwäbisch Gmünd. They directed their dissent towards the district council, the local press and the citizens' initiative ("Bürger Innitiative") supporting refugees and denounced them collectively for collaborating in the "repression of the state". In the eyes of the activists, the relationships with these actors were characterized by "deceptive solidarity". This is added by the activists' recurring accusations against the citizens' initiative over its "false credibility" in the remainder of the Facebook post (ibid.). They claimed that the initiative was "not in solidarity with" their struggle since its members had "obviously distanced themselves" from the activists' demands and protests. Instead, all the volunteers did was "negotiate compromises" with the district council at the expense of the refugees.

This quote clearly illustrates how the activists regarded the solidarity offered to them as a deceptive façade that ultimately contributed to their very repression and stigmatization. To them, the citizens' initiative and the district council represented two sides of the same coin, both of which were complicit in their discrimination. In consequence, they deliberately rejected all relationships of solidarity with local actors.

In his writings on community, Bauman acknowledges the possibility for solidarity to 'dissolve':

> "Ghetto experience dissolves solidarity and destroys mutual trust before they have been given a chance to take roots. A ghetto is not a greenhouse of community feelings. It is on the contrary a laboratory of social disintegration, atomization and anomie." (Bauman 2001: 122)

Instead of producing "community feelings" or fostering social bonds, Bauman argues, experiences of isolation lead to social disintegration and atomization. Quite connectedly, the refugee activists in Schwäbisch Gmünd experienced the camera and the responses to their protests as symbols of their isolation, discrimination and repression, what eventually led to the dissolving of solidarities with local actors.

It was Jens Küffner, a leading member of the local citizens' initiative supporting refugees, who became the symbol for the refugee activists' accusations of "deceptive solidarity". The activists published various Facebook posts that explicitly denounced the long-term volunteer. For instance, they depicted him as a "refugee spy" who had been installed by the district council in order to monitor refugees in the town (Refugees Initiative Schwäbisch Gmünd: 25/3/2015). During my interview with the refugee activists in March 2015, I was personally struck by the great anger the activists felt towards this volunteer. In the course of our conversation, I asked them about their relationship with the local citizens' initiative and mentioned that I had scheduled an interview with Jens Küffner. This remark triggered an unexpected reaction and a sudden change of mood among the activists. They were extremely upset that I was going to meet the volunteer in order to talk about their protests and repeatedly let me know that they considered him to be a "traitor" who "blackmails" refugees and "always comes in between" (Interview with refugee activists: 11/3/2015). When I asked them about the reasons for these accusations, they told me that Jens Küffner had publicly criticized their protests in the local press. He had thus clearly sided with the district council instead of supporting their struggles. In the remainder of our interview, the conversation repeatedly came back to my scheduled meeting with Jens Küffner. I had the impression that, with my intention to talk to the volunteer, I myself became complicit in the very oppression they were fighting against. Moreover, the activists let me know that they regarded him as a "symbol" of the patronizing help and support that charitable volunteers offered to refugees (ibid.). Such help did nothing more than keep refugees in a marginalized and powerless place, my interlocutors asserted. This illustrates how the refugee activists clearly rejected to be receivers of help and instead emphasized the importance of self-organization and self-representation in their protests.

These insights suggest that, to my interlocutors, 'genuine' solidarity consisted of the unrestricted support of *their* specific demands and ways of protesting. Criticism, in turn, signalled an attempt to patronize and infiltrate their activities via "deceptive solidarity". In the following subsection, I will outline in more detail how the citizens' initiative, in response to the activists' accusations, withdrew all help and support, while clearly distancing itself from the group's behaviour.

6.3.2. Refusing to Help

I met Jens Küffner for an interview as scheduled. We had arranged to meet at the premises of the accommodation centre in Schwäbisch Gmünd, the site where the object under dispute, the camera, had been installed in 2014. I was greeted by a friendly, smiling middle-aged man. In his day job, he worked as a carer for the elderly and since he had no family, he told me, he dedicated most of his spare time to refugees and asylum seekers in the town. He supported them in legal or administrative matters, gave advice concerning their asylum case and organized joint leisure activities. Jens Küffner was one of the most experienced volunteers I encountered in the course of my entire field research, having been actively supporting refugees in Schwäbisch Gmünd for around 20 years. He was also a leading member of "Arbeitskreis Asyl"[9] ("Asy-

---

9   The local citizens' initiative supporting refugees in Schwäbisch Gmünd was extraordinary in many regards. Most of the groups and initiatives I encountered in the course of my field research were founded no earlier than 2014 or 2015, when the topic of asylum

lum Work Group"), the local citizens' initiative supporting refugees. Due to his long-term commitment, he was known and respected by many in town. For instance, he told me, the mayor of Schwäbisch Gmünd regularly asked him for advice on matters relating to the local reception of refugees and asylum seekers.

In the course of our intense interview, which lasted several hours, my interlocutor shared his personal views on the camera conflict in Schwäbisch Gmünd. From his emotional reactions during our conversation, I could tell that the refugee activists' accusations and insults weighed heavily on him. There were several moments when he appeared close to tears. He repeatedly emphasized that it was hard for him to take that the refugee activists had turned against him, despite his long-standing commitment to improving the situation of asylum seekers in the town.

When I asked the volunteer about his recent relationship with the activists, he pulled out a small letter, unfolded it and read it aloud to me, saying:

"I jotted it down here, just for myself, but I haven't done anything else with it ... So, I could not support the activists of the Refugees Initiative Schwäbisch Gmünd any further, either last year or in the current conflict because, in all past conflicts, their strategy has been based on four strategies. Firstly, verbal attacks on their counterparts. Secondly, intimidation and threats. Thirdly, humiliation of their counterparts. Fourthly, propaganda. And this makes it impossible to find solutions to disagreements, even with manageable problems."[10] (Interview with Jens Küffner: 12/3/2015)

---

attracted rising media attention. Founded in 1991, the initiative in Schwäbisch Gmünd was thus a rare example of an initiative dating back to the early 90s, when the influx of asylum seekers to Germany also increased sharply due to the arrival of large numbers of asylum seekers from the former Yugoslavia and Romania. In the course of the long summer of migration, the initiative experienced major changes, as my interlocutors Jens Küffner and Kristin Böhm told me, with more local residents than ever seeking to help and wanting to join. In consequence, the number of members rose sharply.

10   Translation by LF. German original: "Hier habe ich das mal zusammengeschrieben, also für mich selbst, und habe das jetzt nicht weiter ... Also ich konnte die Aktivisten von der Refugees Initiative Schwäbisch Gmünd nicht unterstützen, im letzten Jahr und auch jetzt im aktuellen Konflikt, weil ihre Strategie bei allen bisherigen Konflikten auf vier Strategien aufgebaut ist. Erstens, Beleidigung des Gegenübers. Zweitens, Einschüchterung und Drohung. Drittens, Demütigung des Gegenübers. Viertens, Propaganda. Und das macht es bei Meinungsverschiedenheiten unmöglich eine Lösung zu erzielen, auch bei überschaubaren Problemen.".

The note that my interlocutor had written to himself clearly illustrates how he refused to support the refugee activists any further. In it, he listed four patterns of behaviour that prevented him from siding with them and, from his perspective, made it impossible to respond with dialogue and constructive solutions to disagreements.

A similar perspective on the refugee activists' actions was offered by Kristin Böhm, another leading member of the citizens' initiative. A self-confident and outgoing woman in her late 20s who had been volunteering with refugees for several years, she agreed to meet me for an interview in Schwäbisch Gmünd in February 2016. In the course of our conversation, she asserted that the camera conflict had altered the relationships between the activists and the initiative substantially: "The breakdown came with the camera protest"[11], she remarked (Interview with Kristin Böhm: 15/2/2016). From that point on, she told me, the activists lost all sympathy with the members of the initiative. She thus distanced herself from their behaviour, as was illustrated in the following remark:

> "Me personally, I share their ideas, I share their attitudes towards the system, really, their political background ... but their methods [...] if they really want to reach people, then they have to use different methods."[12] (Interview with Kristin Böhm: 15/2/2016)

Like Jens Küffner, she denounced the activists "methods" of protest, although she acknowledged that she held sympathy for their "ideas" and "attitudes towards the system".

Jens Küffner and Kristin Böhm were among the rare volunteers I encountered during my field research who had started supporting refugees long before the summer of migration. I met them both several times at the regular Refugee Council conferences that I attended in Stuttgart as part of my field research. Their participation in these events suggests that they were among the more politically informed of the volunteers. However, they explained their practices of refugee support with quite distinct motivations.

---

11   Translation by LF. German original: "Der Einbruch kam mit dem Kameraprotest".
12   Translation by LF. German original: "Ich persönlich teile ihre Ansätze, teile ihre Haltungen gegen das System, wirklich, ihre politischen Hintergründe, aber ihre Wege, um wirklich Menschen damit zu erreichen [...] wenn sie die wirklich erreichen wollen, dann müssen sie andere Wege bestreiten.".

While Jens Küffner told me that it was his Christian faith and a desire to contribute charitably to the public good that inspired him to act, Kristin Böhm claimed it was her critical, left-wing political attitudes that mobilized her to volunteer with refugees. Despite these differing motivations, both eventually withdrew their help and support for the protesting refugees.

My interlocutors also recalled that there had been times when the relationships between the citizens' initiative and the refugee activists were still characterized by mutual understanding and solidarity. They told me about instances when they had worked together with the refugee activists and offered them support. Jens Küffner acknowledged that, when the activists staged their first public protest in 2012, the relationship with the activists had still been "really harmonious" and that "everyone tried to achieve improvements together" (Interview with Jens Küffner: 12/3/2015). They also both told me they had felt "responsible" for the activists when the protests against the camera arose in March 2014 and offered help and support in articulating solutions to the situation. Kristin Böhm recalled that she had formulated a position paper that she handed over to the district council. In this paper, she sided with the protesters, demanding that the camera be removed, and offered to help mediate a solution. As a leading member of the citizens' initiative, Jens Küffner felt a need to be present as "independent observer" at the protests that occurred at the accommodation centre (Interview with Jens Küffner: 12/3/2015). When the district council refused to remove the surveillance camera by arguing that a majority of the accommodation's inhabitants, families in particular, had felt safer since its installation, the citizens' initiative conducted an "independent survey" at the centre. My interlocutors thus asked all inhabitants of the facility whether they felt a need to keep the camera or whether they would like it removed. According to Jens Küffner, the results were very close. I would argue that these examples clearly illustrate how the two volunteers felt a need to engage in relationships of solidarity and offer support to the activists when the camera conflict began to unfold. These support actions ranged from a clear backing of the activists' demands, as is the case in Kristin Böhm's position paper, to a role as "neutral observers" seeking to articulate an acceptable compromise for both sides. The latter, Jens Küffner assured me, would have been easy to achieve.

Yet, the refugee activists deliberately rejected all of their offers of support and solidarity. Jens Küffner recalled with apparent frustration how the citizens' initiative had organized a mediation meeting with an external mediator and representatives of the Refugee Council of Baden-Württemberg. This talk aimed at articulating a compromise between all sides involved in the conflict. The refugee activists, however, withdrew their agreement to participate in the meeting two hours prior to the scheduled start time, which meant that the invited external mediators had travelled to Schwäbisch Gmünd in vain. Kristin Böhm recalled the volunteers' frustration at this uncompromising stance as follows:

> "I told them back then, we, the citizens' initiative will stand by you. Therefore, we offered to start a dialogue and create a platform for them to discuss things sensibly with the district council [...] but they did not want that either. Then we sort of ran out of ideas, with them being so completely uncompromising and saying: 'We don't want anything to do with you. We don't want anything to do with them. And don't want any dialogue.'"[13] (Interview with Kristin Böhm: 15/2/2016)

Kristin Böhm thus described with frustration how the refugee activists had deliberately turned down whatever support and solidarity the citizens' initiative offered.

My two interlocutors also denounced the personal attacks on volunteers during the camera conflict. In spite of their support offers, the citizens' initiative became a central target of the refugee activists' accusations in the course of the conflict. Jens Küffner recalled how he had engaged in a conversation with the protest group and, while offering to help find a joint solution, had criticized their threatening of the social workers during the protest at the accommodation centre. It was this criticism, together with his interview in a local newspaper, my interlocutor told me, which led the refugee activists to turn against him. In consequence, Jens Küffner became one of the primary targets of their dissent and accusations, something I became aware of myself during my interview with the activists. Kristin Böhm criticized the way the activists had personally attacked and threatened Jens Küffner in the course of the camera conflict:

---

13 Translation by LF. German original: "Ich hab ja damals gesagt, wir als Arbeitskreis, wir würden euch auch beistehen, also das haben wir ja angeboten, wir haben ja angeboten den Dialog zu suchen und auch eine Plattform zu schaffen, wo sie sich mit dem Landratsamt auch vernünftig auseinandersetzen können [...] aber auch das wollten sie ja gar nicht. Und da ging uns dann auch so ein bisschen der Ideenreichtum manchmal aus, wenn man so komplett kompromisslos ist und sagt: ‚Wir wollen mit euch nichts zu tun haben, wir wollen mit denen nichts zu tun haben, wir wollen auch keinen Dialog.'".

"They really laid into Jens, really personally laid into him, and, it has to be said, threatened him ... 'We know where you live Mister Küffner' and this and that ... These are threats and, Jens, who is really really sensitive in his manner and has been supporting refugees for years, it hurts him, you know, he doesn't just shrug it off. But even Jens said 'Okay, that is just not on.'"[14] (Interview with Kristin Böhm: 15/2/2016)

As Jens Küffner likewise remarked during our interview, when the activists personally attacked a highly dedicated long-term volunteer, they lost any credibility in the town. Even the left-wing youth centre Esperanza, which had backed the refugee activists from the very beginning, became "very cautious" over supporting further protests (Interview with Jens Küffner: 12/3/2015).

From this point on, my interlocutors broke off all relationships of solidarity with the refugee activists, while the citizens' initiative never again offered help and support to them. This break appeared to be mutual, since the refugee activists had been rejecting all support offers from the volunteers. The camera conflict thus resulted in the breaking of all ties between refugee activists and local actors in Schwäbisch Gmünd. While the activists accused the volunteers of "deceptive solidarity", the citizens' initiative clearly distanced itself from their protests. However, in parallel to this deliberate breaking of "deceptive solidarities" with local actors, the refugee activists reached out beyond the boundaries of the Swabian small town in order to forge alternative relationships of solidarity that might prove more beneficial to their cause, something I will investigate in more detail in the following subsection.

6.3.3. Forging Solidarity beyond the Local

"Solidarity" was one of the most frequently used words in the Facebook group of the Refugees Initiative Schwäbisch Gmünd. A majority of the hundreds of posts, which members of the group had shared between 2012 and 2016, came with a call for solidarity. By doing so, I would argue, the activists sought

---

14 Translation by LF. German original: "Auch Jens, der wirklich hart angegangen wurde, auch persönlich hart angegangen wurde, auch dem dolle gedroht wurde von den Flüchtlingen, dass muss man einfach so sagen, „Wir wissen wo du wohnst Herr Küffner" und dies und jenes ... das sind Drohungen und gerade Jens ist sehr sehr sensibel in seiner Art, der jahrelang für Flüchtlinge dasteht, das tut dem weh, weißte, der steckt das auch nicht so einfach weg, aber das war auch für Jens, der ganz klar gesagt hat, also das geht doch gar nicht.".

to build supportive relationships online, relationships that were neither confined to the local boundaries of Schwäbisch Gmünd nor to the activists' physical presence in the town. At the same time as they deliberately rejected all support offered by local actors, they thus forged supportive networks that promised to be more in line with their imaginaries of solidarity and community.

From the very beginning of their struggle, the refugee activists reached out to other places and areas in order to build supportive networks and alliances. This was illustrated both by their Facebook posts and via concrete actions. For instance, in March and April 2015, roughly one year after the camera conflict, the refugee activists organized a Germany-wide tour entitled "Solidarity Call for Civil Disobedience". The group visited various cities across Germany, including Wuppertal, Erfurt, Hamburg, Berlin and also Konstanz, where I myself attended one of their talks. At these events, they shared insights into their struggles in Schwäbisch Gmünd and aimed to foster alliances with groups in other towns. The activists provided extensive coverage of their tour via their Facebook group, posting updates with photos or films on almost a daily basis. One of these posts strikingly revealed the significance of "solidarity" for the activists. It bore the following title, written in capital letters: "SOLIDARITY IS THE KEY!" (Refugees Initiative Schwäbisch Gmünd: 15/4/2015).

With these repeated calls for solidarity, the group clearly aimed to foster alternative alliances in their fight against discrimination and exclusion in Schwäbisch Gmünd. They identified themselves as part of a wider community of interest that went beyond the boundaries of the Swabian small town. Instead of being determined by their spatial embeddedness, these supportive networks were based on shared interests and shared experiences and thus transcended locality as the defining feature for relationships of solidarity. This connects to Mayo's (2017) work on the "slippery concept of community". In it, she distinguishes three analytical perspectives on community. In addition to an understanding of "community as locality", she identifies two further conceptions: "community as identity" and "community as shared interests". I would suggest that the first of these three understandings of community often played a central role for those who sought to help refugees in the course of the long summer of migration – as illustrated in the previous chapters of this book. Yet, it was the second and the third conception of community that became the focus of the activists' efforts to forge solidarities. This also connects to something identified by Taylor and Wilson (2016 cited in Mayo), tivists to join us at the 'Break Isolation' camp of international solidarity in our communities." [17] (The Voice Refugee Forum: 29/3/2012) [18]

The camp was thus motivated by a desire to foster "international solidarity" and a "Germany-wide network of activists from refugee communities".

Scholars working on refugee protests have scrutinized how, in the run-up to the long summer of migration, a loosely connected (trans)national movement of self-organized refugee groups had been building up across Germany and beyond (Jakob 2016; Steinhilper 2017). For instance, Ataç et al. (2015: 4) provide an overview of the various instances of refugee protest between 2012 and 2014, arguing that they represented "a movement that is a novelty for Germany". The activist group in Schwäbisch Gmünd clearly formed part of this movement. Although this particular case has not been considered by previous studies, relationships of solidarity with a nationwide alliance of refugee groups played a critical role for the Refugees Initiative Schwäbisch Gmünd from the outset.

Summing up, I would suggest that the breaking of solidarities with local actors in the course of the camera conflict was strongly influenced by the activists' self-perception as being part of something 'greater', something that extended beyond the boundaries of the small Swabian town in which they found themselves. The break with all local actors might have even formed a necessary part of their protests, symbolizing a deliberate rejection of a social membership that is centred on spatial embeddedness. As I illustrate in the next section, the protests in Schwäbisch Gmünd are therefore also telling in regard to romanticized imaginaries of 'local community', imaginaries that played an important role in the mobilization of refugee support during the long summer of migration.

---

17   Translation by LF. German original: "Wir wollen eine neue Ära anbrechen lassen, indem wir ein deutschlandweites Netzwerk von Aktivisten von Flüchtlingsgemeinschaften schaffen, um uns über den Kampf von Flüchtlingen in den Isolationslagern hinaus gegenseitig zu informieren. Weiterhin laden wir Aktivisten ein, um am ‚Break Isolation'-Flüchtlings-Camp der internationalen Solidarität in unseren Gemeinschaften teilzunehmen.".
18   See: http://www.thevoiceforum.org/node/2488 (last accessed 1/8/2020).

6.4. The Conflicting Imaginaries of Community

The conflicts between the refugee activists and local actors in Schwäbisch Gmünd are not only telling in regards to differing understandings of the 'right' conduct of solidarity but also shed light on contrasting imaginaries of collectivity and togetherness in migration societies. They were rooted, I would argue, in conflicting notions of *local community* that ultimately proved incompatible. On the one hand, local actors portrayed the community in Schwäbisch Gmünd as a positive antidote to the world 'out there', while focussing on the social integration of asylum seekers *within* the boundaries of the town, thereby often neglecting structural conditions of discrimination (Subsection 1). On the other hand, the activists raised awareness of the structures of discrimination and isolation that reached far beyond the boundaries of the 'local', illustrating how they determined the refugees' experiences on the ground (Section 2 and 3). In what follows, I investigate these differing notions of community in more detail.

6.4.1. Local Community as an Antidote to the World 'Out There'

During my field research on the practices of refugee support around the long summer of migration, I came across the name Schwäbisch Gmünd countless times. From 2014 on, the narrative of the *Gmünder Weg* ("the Gmünd way") painted this small town in Swabia as a particularly successful example of a well-functioning 'welcome culture'. Repeatedly, governmental actors in the area of my field research and numerous national and regional media accounts referred to the town as a role model in regard to an active civil society, favourable local administrations and harmonious cooperation between different actors involved in the reception of asylum seekers. The mayor of Schwäbisch Gmünd, Richard Arnold, became not only the face of the *Gmünder Weg* but also a figurehead for the ostensible German 'welcome culture'. He repeatedly appeared as a keynote speaker at governmentally organized conferences in Baden-Württemberg, while national TV channels and newspapers carried reports on his achievements.

I would suggest that it was not so much the actual handling of asylum seekers that made Schwäbisch Gmünd the success story it seemed to be, but the fact that the town had been particularly successful in promoting an image of local community that had been embraced by the public. The narrative of the *Gmünder Weg* might thus be read as a response to contemporary needs and conceptions of togetherness in migration societies rather than as a model of how to integrate asylum seekers successfully.

The romanticized image of 'the local' that the town has promoted successfully is illustrated on its official website, which contains detailed information on the ostensibly successful integration of asylum seekers and the implementation of a local 'welcome culture' in Schwäbisch Gmünd:

"Schwäbisch Gmünd is a tolerant, open-minded town that welcomes anyone and everyone! Schwäbisch Gmünd epitomizes a welcome culture that not only includes the accommodation but also the reception and integration of refugees. This revolves around individuals and their abilities and talents. The town's mayor and the numerous professionals and volunteers working in Gmündian asylum politics focus first and foremost on interaction and decentrality: from schools and kindergartens to German language classes, volunteering projects and neighbourhood work [...] this is *togetherness*. As a *community of values*, the town can master the challenges of today."[19] (schwaebisch-gmuend.de: 2017; emphasis added)

This extract encapsulates strikingly how the local government of Schwäbisch Gmünd promoted a positive image of local "togetherness" and presented the town as a "community of values" that welcomes "anyone and everyone". With such a harmonious local community, the text suggests, it is possible to "master the challenges of today". This emphasis on local togetherness and harmony also features prominently in the section of the website entitled "Community". It provides detailed information about the "various offers and possibilities" that "facilitate the integration of refugees into the community" (schwaebisch-gmuend.de: 2017).

This imaginary connects with academic works that discuss how the term 'community' generally elicits positive connotations and emotions (see Williams 1981: 76; Amit 2002; Creed 2006b; Mayo 2017). For instance, in

---

19 Translated by LF. German original: "Schwäbisch Gmünd ist eine tolerante, offene Stadt, die jede und jeden Willkommen heißt! In Schwäbisch Gmünd wird eine Willkommenskultur gelebt, die nicht nur die Unterbringung, sondern vor allem die Aufnahme und Integration von Flüchtlingen beinhaltet. Der einzelne Mensch mit seinen Fähigkeiten und Talenten steht dabei im Vordergrund. Das Stadtoberhaupt und die vielen hauptamtlichen und ehrenamtlichen Mitstreiter in der Gmünder Flüchtlingspolitik setzen dabei vor allem auf Begegnung und Dezentralität: von Schulen, Kindergärten, über Deutschkurse, Ehrenamtsprojekte und Quartiersarbeit. [...] Es ist ein Miteinander. Mit dieser Wertegemeinschaft wird die Stadt die aktuellen Herausforderungen meistern."

his monograph *Community*, Bauman (2001) claims that, in an increasingly globalized and insecure world, 'community' evokes a feeling of warmth and safety. He puts this as follows:

> "To start with, community is a 'warm' place, a cosy and comfortable place. It is like a roof under which we shelter in heavy rain, like a fireplace at which we warm our hands on a frosty day [...] To go on: in a community we can count on each other's good will. If we stumble and fall, others will help us to stand on our feet again." (Bauman 2001: 1-2)

According to Bauman, such ideas of 'local community' have become increasingly attractive: in an individualized world characterized by "competition" and "one-upmanship", he argues, people search "safety in an insecure world". The idea of a harmonious and stable local community thus provides a desirable antidote to the perceived reality "out there" (ibid.: 3). As he goes on to argue, such unreservedly positive notions of a local community are, however, much more a reflection of current needs and desires than of the actual situation on the ground. He summarizes these needs as follows:

> "Where the state has failed, perhaps the community, the *local* community, the physically tangible, 'material' community, a community embodied in a *territory* inhabited by its members and no one else (no one who 'does not belong'), will purvey the 'being safe' feeling which the wider world evidently conspires to destroy?" (Bauman 2001: 112-113; emphasis in original)

The success of the *Gmünder Weg*, I would argue, rested to a large extent on the town's enthusiastic promotion of such positive notions of 'local community'. The narrative offered a desirable antidote to the 'challenges' out there and thus responded to a longing for togetherness and dependability in a physically embedded community. To quote Bauman, it depicted this small Swabian town as "a paradise lost" to which "we dearly hope to return", so that we "feverishly seek the roads that may bring us there" (ibid.: 3). The *Gmünder Weg* was particularly successful in presenting itself convincingly as a road that might lead us to membership of a harmonious community.

The narrative of the *Gmünder Weg* epitomizes a recurring feature of the practices of refugee support that I investigated in the course of my field research: those who sought to help often (re)produced an image of a particularly harmonious local community with regard to their own village or town. This positive image of local community is thus emblematic of the social imaginaries pertaining to many of the practices of refugee support that built on humanitarian parameters. Such practices often drew up and reproduced romanticized images of local community based on mutual support and personal immediacy. In the previous chapters of this book, I illustrated how established residents often emphasized their willingness to contribute to the public good in *their* neighbourhood, village or town. The local, in this context, was not only an important mobilizing force but also opened up political possibilities that put an emphasis on presence (see Chapter 4).

The narrative of the *Gmünder Weg* built centrally on the idea that mutual help and support formed a prerequisite for a harmonious local community. This was illustrated by the high public visibility of the local citizens' initiative supporting refugees and the placement of asylum seekers in voluntary community work. According to the town's official website, this voluntary, unpaid work by refugees served as a means to "be part of the social fabric" of the town. In several media articles, the refugees of Schwäbisch Gmünd were depicted as particularly 'helpful' in that they voluntarily contributed to the public good in the town, for instance by collecting litter in green spaces. Volunteers and the local council also placed refugees in work at high-profile public events, such as the "Landesgartenschau 2014", a regional garden show that brought an estimated two million visitors to Schwäbisch Gmünd. Several articles in regional newspapers reported on the refugee volunteers helping to make this huge event happen, by staffing ticket offices, for instance. One of these articles pictured smiling and seemingly happy asylum seekers volunteering at the garden show (Gmünder Tagespost: 21/4/2014)[20]. Through such means, I would argue, the city council promoted an imaginary of local community based on mutual help and support.

An emphasis on personal immediacy and face-to-face interaction further contributed to the success of the *Gmünder Weg*. Various media accounts promoted these facets of local togetherness when reporting on the seemingly successful integration of refugees in the town. This was most evident in the reporting on Schwäbisch Gmünd's decentralized housing scheme. With this approach, the city council aimed to accommodate refugees in smaller units dispersed across the town instead of in one large central facility (cf. Hinger & Schäfer 2019). The high public attention paid to this decentralized accommodation scheme often put a special emphasis on personal immediacy. For instance, a short report on the *Gmünder Weg* that was broadcast on the TV channel '3sat' in January 2016 presented its decentralized housing scheme as

---

20 See: http://www.gmuender-tagespost.de/p/731066/ (last accessed 1/8/2020).

an important factor in the successful local integration of asylum seekers. In an interview that was broadcast as part of the report, the mayor of Schwäbisch Gmünd claimed that such an accommodation scheme reduced local residents' fear of the new arrivals since it meant they could get to know them as "individuals" (3sat: 18/1/2016)[21]. This emphasis on the 'individual' and his or her integration into the harmonious local community, a recurring feature of the *Gmünder Weg*, conveyed a notion of personal immediacy in the town.

Academic works have emphasized the traces of *nostalgia* pertaining to such an image of local community based on personal immediacy and mutual support. Mayo (2017: 130), drawing on Sennett (1976), suggests that the idea of community serves as "nostalgic alternatives to the alienation of contemporary capitalism". Creed (2006a) and Bauman (2001) assert that the emphasis on personal immediacy pertaining to 'local community' paints a romanticized and nostalgic version of 'the local' and functions as an antidote to a world in which people are increasingly atomized and isolated from one another. Creed (2006c) criticizes this "fetishization" of an unreservedly positive image of community since it disregards and silences its problematic features.

In a similar vein, I would argue that the idea of the *Gmünder Weg* painted a one-sided and unreservedly positive picture of 'the local' while ignoring potentially problematic structural aspects and power asymmetries that shaped the living-together on the ground. For instance, the 'voluntary community work' conducted by asylum seekers in the town was romanticized as altruistic contribution to the public good. However, this explanation did not mention the possibility that many asylum seekers may have engaged in this unpaid work because, lacking work permits, they had no other alternative. The asylum seekers may also have engaged in unpaid voluntary work in the hope of influencing their asylum case or improving their chances of getting a 'real' job in the future, as one of my interlocutors suggested. Moreover, none of the positive accounts of the *Gmünder Weg* ever mentioned that the town's ability to provide decentralized accommodation was significantly shaped by a particular local circumstance: after a new initial reception centre opened in Ellwangen in early 2015 (see Chapter 2), the whole of the Ostalbkreis district including Schwäbisch Gmünd became legally exempt from taking in further asylum seekers and did so only on a voluntary basis. This may have reduced the pressure on the town in such a way that it was able to develop alternative housing

---

21   See: https://www.3sat.de/wissen/nano/ein-buergermeister-packt-s-an-100.html (last accessed 1/8/2020).

schemes, as one of my interlocutors suggested. Indeed, Hinger and Schäfer (2019) pointed to a similar tendency to move towards decentralised housing schemes in other cities across Germany in the early 2010s. Yet, they argue that, when the number of arriving asylum seekers increased sharply in 2014 and 2015, most local governments returned to a centralized housing scheme, accommodating the newcomers in mass accommodation centres (ibid.: 64). Due to its specific local context, Schwäbisch Gmünd might thus present a singular example of a town that was able to continue its approach to decentralized accommodation in the course of the long summer of migration.

Summing up, I would argue that this romanticized notion of community that was promoted by many practices of refugee support during the long summer of migration spoke to a void in contemporary society: it conveyed feelings of safety and dependability in a world regarded as increasingly insecure and atomized. The refugee activists, however, embedded their actions of protest in a rather different social imaginary, something I will illustrate in more detail in the following two subsections.

6.4.2. The Spatial Contingencies of Local Community: A Landscape of Unequal Rights

In the course of their protests, the activists of the Refugees Initiative Schwäbisch Gmünd painted a rather different picture of their immediate living situation in the town. In their version of the story, there was little mention of the warm feelings of togetherness, mutual support and personal immediacy that were promoted by the ostensibly so successful *Gmünder Weg*. By contrast, the activists emphasized their experiences of isolation from and discrimination within the 'local community' of Schwäbisch Gmünd. In the eyes of the refugee activists, the structures of discrimination extended far beyond the boundaries of the 'local community', with German and European asylum laws being a key factor in their marginalized position on the ground.

From the beginning, the Refugees Initiative thus called attention to the unjust German asylum laws that critically determined their living situation in Schwäbisch Gmünd. The activists repeatedly blamed such laws for their experiences of exclusion and discrimination on the ground. In doing so, I would argue, the refugee activists linked their immediate situation in Schwäbisch Gmünd to a wider landscape of unequal rights that, from their point of view, prevented them from becoming integrated into society. For instance, they criticized that they were unable to gain work permits, calling for equal access to the labour market and a right to work. In July 2013, they published a post in their Facebook group that clearly expressed this perceived link between their structural exclusion from the labour market and their immediate situation in Schwäbisch Gmünd:

> "Stop every form of exploitation of the oppressed refugees, asylum seekers are not welcome into the labour market in Germany but when it comes to working for 1€ per hour job then asylum seekers are automatically well integrated, even when there is no integration in the so called democracy of refugees [...] Refugees want to contributes to the society and also want to be useful to ourselves, the community we are living, to our own nations and to the whole world in general but not in form of modern day slavery and any form of furthermore exploitation. We demand the right to be accepted in the labour market without compromise" (Refugees Initiative Schwäbisch Gmünd: 25/7/13; English original)

With this post, the refugee activists raised awareness of the discriminating national asylum laws that prevented them from working and called for equal rights. They also related these structures of discrimination to the narrative of the *Gmünder Weg*, which they regarded as a 'bad compromise' and a symbol of their very discrimination. In the post above, for instance, they denounced the placement of asylum seekers in 'voluntary community work' for one euro per hour and criticized it for being not a means of integration but, in fact, a form of "modern day slavery". To the activists, a 'proper' integration into the local community was thus based on having equal rights, a condition that could not be brought about locally, only via change at a national and European level.

The relationship between discriminatory asylum laws and the activists' immediate living situation in Schwäbisch Gmünd was also addressed in their campaigns against the "Residence Obligation" ("Residenzpflicht"), which became a prominent feature of their protests between 2012 and 2016. This "German Apartheid Residence Obligation Law" (Refugees Initiative Schwäbisch Gmünd: 26/6/2014), as the activists often called it, represented a particularly critical example of their perceived legal discrimination and isolation within German society. Described in juridical terminology as "spatial confinement" ("Räumliche Beschränkung"), it forbids asylum seekers whose asylum case is pending, or those who have been granted temporary right to remain ("Duldung"), from leaving the district responsible for them without the local authority's permission[22]. In the eyes of the refugee activists, this law presented a major infringement of their spatial mobility and fundamental human rights. For instance, a post in their Facebook group from March 2013 contained a striking "declaration" against the Residence Obligation. It recalled how, after travelling to a small town around 50 kilometres north of Schwäbisch Gmünd in order to visit friends, the refugee activists were charged with a fine for leaving their district without official permission. The Facebook post denounced this procedure as follows:

> "WE WILL NOT PAY ONE CENT FOR THE RESIDENZPFLICHT! The Residenzpflicht forbids a refugee to leave the Landkreis/Lager where his/her living situation is repression from the administrations and leads to isolation from the society. We do not accept this regulation, because it offends our civil liberties (right of abode, general right of acting/Freizügigkeit, Allgemeine Handlungsfreiheit)" (Refugees Initiative Schwäbisch Gmünd: 23/3/2013, emphasis in English original)

This illustrates how the refugee activists blamed the Residence Obligation for contributing to their perceived "repression" by local authorities and their "isolation" from the local community.

Works in critical migration studies have outlined how the spatial confinement and detention of asylum seekers functions as a central technique to exert sovereign control and power (see for instance Mountz 2011; Fontanari 2015). Through their protests against the Residence Obligation, the activists called attention to how this law subjected them to governmental control and how it contributed to their marginalized position on the ground. Their protests against this law also illustrate how the Refugees Initiative Schwäbisch Gmünd formed part of a wider network of refugee groups across Germany. Several scholars have pointed out how the resistance against the Residence Obligation

---

22 Although the German government announced that it had significantly relaxed the Residence Obligation in December 2014, limiting it to the first three months after an asylum seeker's arrival, this was denounced as a "con" by many commentators (see http://www.residenzpflicht.info/news/geplante-lockerungen-eine-farce; last accessed 9/7/2018). Several non-governmental organizations supporting refugees criticized the Residence Obligation's apparent reform, as did self-organized refugee initiatives such as the Refugees Initiative Schwäbisch Gmünd. Others criticized that the Residence Obligation has simply been repackaged as the "Wohnsitzauflage". Introduced in 2016, this law regulates the place of residence for accepted refugees across Germany and puts even greater constraints on their spatial mobility.

had been a major focus of the actions of a Germany-wide refugee movement since at least 2012 (see Sasse et al. 2014; Kasparek & Schmidt 2016).

The refugee activists in Schwäbisch Gmünd thus remind us that the idea of an isolated and homogenous local community, imagined as an antidote to the world 'out there', can never be more than an illusion. The 'local' always forms part of a wider spatial landscape that is shaped by national and supranational laws and policies. These spatial contingencies, however, were largely ignored by the narrative of the *Gmünder Weg*. It promoted the notion of a homogenous and harmonious 'local community' while silencing how national laws and policies grant its members different rights and possibilities. This connects to what scholars such as Amit (2010) have outlined: a romanticized imaginary of 'local community', depicting all of its members as equals, can never be more than a wishful illusion. Mayo (2017: 126) argues that 'community' is always deeply heterogeneous and characterized by internal power imbalances. Creed proposes to analyse 'community' as a close relationship between inclusion and exclusion:

> "Collectivity and exclusion are two sides of the same coin, and to understand either, we need to look at them together – community is the coinage." (Creed 2006b: 4)

He goes on to argue that 'community' might even function as a source of power for those who are already 'better off'. He explains these ambivalent dimensions of 'community' as follows:

> "In fact, the same positive valence that makes community attractive may provoke discontent and dissatisfaction when such ideals are not realized. The same sentiments that generate community attachments clearly authorize exclusivity on the parts of community [...] The fascination with, and desire for, community may be inadvertently generating disappointment, alienation, fragmentation, and segregation." (Creed 2006b: 13)

The refugee activists in Schwäbisch Gmünd, I would argue, drew attention to these ambivalences of 'community' by pointing to the power relations that determined their situation on the ground. With their protests, they shed light on the national and supranational landscape of unequal rights that critically shaped their marginalized and excluded position in the 'local community' of Schwäbisch Gmünd.

The activists not only highlighted this wider spatial context of unequal rights, they also pointed to the *temporal contingencies* that determined their situation in the Swabian town. In the following subsection, I thus investigate how the activists also called attention to a landscape of (post)colonial injustice in the course of their protests.

6.4.3. The Temporal Contingencies of Local Community: A Landscape of (Post)Colonial Injustice

Out of a sudden, in summer 2013, Schwäbisch Gmünd stood in the spotlight of national media attention. Almost all major daily newspapers and news magazines reported on the situation of asylum seekers in the town, accusing local actors of racism and colonialism. For instance, an article in *Die Tageszeitung* was entitled "Greetings from Colonial Times" (TAZ: 25/7/2013)[23]. The news magazine *Stern* asked the question "Colonialism, Enslavement – or Integration?" (Stern: 25/7/2013)[24] and even the conservative daily *Frankfurter Allgemeine Zeitung* identified "postcolonial times" in the Swabian town (FAZ: 26/7/2013)[25]. Most of these reports featured photographs of a bizarre scene at the station of Schwäbisch Gmünd: black asylum seekers, wearing red shirts printed with the word 'SERVICE' and straw hats to protect against the summer heat, lugged suitcases for rail passengers. To make matters worse, the reports criticized, the asylum seekers were given an allowance of 1.05 euros per hour for their exhausting work.

This employment of asylum seekers as 'voluntary' porters came about when construction work at the train station put the elevator out of service. Subsequently, the mayor and the local citizens' initiative supporting refugees hit upon the idea of using asylum seekers to assist passengers across the bridge to the other side of the tracks. They sold this as another successful example of the 'voluntary community work' with which the town sought to integrate asylum seekers into the local community. Since the asylum seekers did not have work permits, the rail operator could only pay them an allowance of 1.05 euros per hour. According to the newspaper coverage, however, this situation was not a means of integrating asylum seekers but an echo of colonial times.

---

23   See: http://www.taz.de/!5062498/ (last accessed 1/8/2020).
24   See: https://www.stern.de/panorama/gesellschaft/asylbewerber-als-koffertraeger-kol onialismus--sklaverei---oder-integration--3365412.html (last accessed 1/8/2020).
25   See: http://www.faz.net/aktuell/politik/inland/fluechtlinge-als-koffertraeger-arbeitsl os-im-postkolonialismus-12307152.html (last accessed 1/8/2020).

During my interview with the members of the Refugees Initiative Schwäbisch Gmünd, around two years after the newspaper stories of "postcolonial times" in the town, they repeatedly referred to this case of asylum seekers working as voluntary porters in their criticisms of local actors. To them, this incident demonstrated the extent of racism and (post)colonial injustice they had faced in Schwäbisch Gmünd. On the one hand, they accused local actors, including the local citizens' initiative supporting refugees, of racist attitudes towards asylum seekers. On the other hand, they depicted discriminating asylum laws as a continuity of (post)colonial oppression. I had the impression that the refugee activists regarded themselves also as '(post)colonial freedom fighters' calling attention to the ongoing history of colonialism and racial subordination. This echoes a claim long made by scholars in the field of postcolonial studies, namely that colonialism is far from over and, instead, lives on in similar ways (cf. Hall 1996; Gregory 2004).

How the activists embedded their precarious situation in Schwäbisch Gmünd in a wider context of (post)colonial injustices became particularly evident in their protests against the Residence Obligation. In August 2014, the group published a Facebook post entitled "The city of Schwäbisch Gmünd threatens refugee activists with detainment due to the infringement of the Residence Obligation". They explained their dissent towards the Residence Obligation in the following words:

> "With the Residence Obligation in Germany a law of the German colonial history continues – during the German colonialism in Cameroon and Togo, the occupiers had invented this law, which forbid the native population to leave their place of living or district without an application at the colonial white administrations"[26] (Refugees Initiative Schwäbisch Gmünd: 21/8/14)

The refugee activists thus depicted the Residence Obligation as a continuation of the colonial humiliation and subordination of African peoples. In doing so, they called attention to the German colonial history in Africa and illustrated how forms of spatial confinement then and now function as a means

---

26 Translation by LF. German original: "Mit der Residenzpflicht in Deutschland wird ein Gesetz aus der deutschen Kolonialzeit weitergeführt – während der deutschen Kolonialzeit in Kamerun und Togo hatten sich die Besatzer dieses Gesetz ausgedacht, welchem zufolge die einheimische Bevölkerung ihren jeweiligen Lebensort oder festgelegten Distrikt nicht ohne Antrag bei den kolonialen Weißen Gouvernementsverwaltungen verlassen durften.".

of domination and power (cf. Bernault 2003). As the title of the post indicates, they implicitly blamed the town of Schwäbisch Gmünd for being complicit in these (post)colonial injustices through its enforcement of the Residence Obligation. The refugee activists also repeatedly termed the Residence Obligation an "Apartheid law" (see Refugees Initiative Schwäbisch Gmünd: 26/6/2014). By using such a vocabulary, they drew parallels to the South African Apartheid regime, under which the mobility of people of colour was systematically restricted in order to exert control and power. The activists thus highlighted the continuing history of suppression and racism against people of colour.

In the course of their protests, the refugee activists not only highlighted such forms of legal discrimination but also denounced instances of everyday and institutional racism to which they were subjected to in their day-to-day lives. For instance, they published a post in their Facebook group that recalled how they had suffered from "racial profiling", explaining that, on a train journey to a town in eastern Germany, they had their papers checked by police officers, a selective check, they claimed, due to their skin colour. In the eyes of the activists, this check was symbolic of the continuing racial discrimination and suppression they faced on the ground (Refugees Initiative Schwäbisch Gmünd: 26/6/2014).

Summing up, this section showed that the conflictive relationships of solidarity between refugee activists and local actors in Schwäbisch Gmünd are telling in regards to contrasting imaginaries of 'local community'. On the one hand, those who sought to help refugees around the long summer of migration often reproduced romanticized notions of 'the local' and 'local community', with the narrative of the *Gmünder Weg* offering a particularly striking example. On the other hand, the refugee activists embedded their immediate situation in Schwäbisch Gmünd in a wider landscape of unequal rights and (post)colonial injustices. I would thus argue that the refugee activists shed a different light on the romanticized imaginaries of 'local community' that pertained to many of the helping practices I witnessed around the long summer of migration, illustrating how they silenced the unequal power relations at play.

6.5. Concluding Remarks: The Intimate Relationship between *Community* and *Solidarity*

This chapter investigated the breaking of refugee solidarity by focussing on an intriguing case I encountered during my field research: the conflicts between local actors and a group of refugee activists who repeatedly staged protests in order to call attention to the perceived exclusions, discriminations and inequalities that characterized their immediate living situation. Over the course of their protests, the relationships between the activists and local actors, including the citizens' initiative supporting refugees, became ever more conflictive until all ties between the two sides were irrevocably broken.

The findings presented in this chapter demonstrate that solidarity is a highly volatile and elusive relationship. While the previous chapters of this book shed light on how various actors mobilized, governed, politicized and recast the relationships of solidarity that emerged around the long summer of migration, this chapter showed that they might also eventually break down again. Solidarity, in other words, is not a static condition 'out there' waiting to be discovered. Instead, it is subject to constant intervention and contestation, and thus continuously adapting to new circumstances. In the case of Schwäbisch Gmünd, the adverse effects of one small object – a newly installed surveillance camera – substantially and irrevocably altered relationships of solidarity, bringing to the fore conflicting social imaginaries that eventually proved incompatible.

The social imaginaries pertaining to relationships of solidarity can thus be so contrasting and conflicting that it becomes impossible to find a common denominator among the different actors involved. On the one hand, the refugee activists accused local actors, including the citizens' initiative supporting refugees, of "deceptive solidarity" that contributed to the very oppression and discrimination they were fighting against. On the other hand, committed volunteers deliberately withdrew help and support from the activists and collectively distanced themselves from their continuing protests. Although there had previously been times when their relationships were characterized by mutual understanding and compassion, the situation eventually proved irreconcilable.

This breaking of solidarities corresponded with the activists' view of themselves as part of something 'greater', something that extended beyond the small town of Schwäbisch Gmünd. From the very beginning of their protests, the activists positioned themselves within a Germany-wide network of left-wing activists and self-organized refugee groups. In the course of their protests, the refugee activists used their Facebook group to deliberately forge solidarities beyond the boundaries of the town in which they found themselves. In doing so, they established themselves as part of a wider community of interest that was based on similar experiences of exclusion and discrimination and transcended individual situations on the ground. The break with local actors may thus have represented a necessary step in the activists' fight against structures of discrimination, a struggle that went beyond the confines of 'the local'.

This illustrates that *solidarity* and *community* are closely related, that conceptions of solidarity and ideas of collectivity in migration societies are co-produced and interdependent. The conflicts in Schwäbisch Gmünd are therefore also telling in regards to contrasting imaginaries of 'community' pertaining to the practices of refugee support that emerged around the long summer of migration. Helping practices that were embedded in humanitarian parameters often drew on romanticized notions of a spatially embedded local community, an idea that responded to the longing for safety in an uncertain world. The refugee activists, however, remind us that such a notion can never be more than a wishful illusion. Local communities are always embedded in a spatial and temporal context that is determined by a situation of unequal rights and a history of racial discrimination and suppression. Practices of refugee support cannot and should not be dissociated from these more uncomfortable realities regarding the local reception of asylum seekers.

7. WORDS IN CONCLUSION: Lines of Contestation in Contemporary Migration Societies

This book investigated the manifold practices of refugee support that emerged around the German 'summer of welcome' in 2015. Focussing on the perspective of *contested solidarity*, my aim was to step back from the ostensibly clearcut distinctions between 'humanitarianism' and 'political activism', highlighting instead the political ambivalences of refugee support. My empirical investigation thus paid particular attention to the transformative relationships of solidarity that are forged between long-term residents and newcomers, relationships shaped by contested social imaginaries of living-together in an age of intensified migration.

This investigation revealed that refugee support is situated, embedded into differing, contested and at times conflicting imaginaries, subjected to manifold forms of claims-making, and infused with power struggles. Practices of refugee support bring together a wide range of actors who all attempt to shape the 'proper' conduct of solidarity according to their particular interests and world views. What crystallized in the course of this book is that refugee solidarity and questions of power are therefore intertwined in complex and ambivalent ways. There were moments when refugee support inspired *political* action and fostered a more egalitarian social alternative, blurring the line between those deemed legitimate citizens and those deemed non-citizens, and challenging dominant discriminations and exclusions within migration societies. At the same time, however, refugee support also proved capable of inspiring practices that had *antipolitical* effects and meanings, by becoming complicit in the reproduction of governmental discriminations or in the fostering of new forms of exclusion within migration societies.

Taken together, these findings illustrate that migrant solidarity forms a contested intersection at which actors and individuals with different backgrounds and different imaginaries come together in order to elaborate the parameters of contemporary living-together. Refugee support might thus be read as a prism that sheds a new light on current social and political developments in European migration societies. Practices and discourses of migrant solidarity are revealing in terms of how people imagine the world around them, at the same time as they are also world building. They forge new relations among different groups and actors; produce collectivity and enact ideals of a 'better society'. Therefore, practices of refugee support should always be read in relation to the political and social context in which they take place.

The long summer of migration in 2015 epitomized strikingly how intensified global migration movements are profoundly altering European societies. Perhaps more than ever before, this situation led long-term residents to reflect upon their ideals, wishes and needs concerning living-together in an increasingly heterogeneous migration society. The contested solidarities of the migration summer thus responded to a desire to build new forms of collectivity and togetherness amidst migration movements.

In this concluding section, I draw together the findings of this book and discuss how they contribute to our understanding of contemporary migration societies. I suggest that the German 'summer of welcome' might be read as a telling case that sheds a new light on wider challenges, tensions and issues surrounding living-together in contemporary migration societies. In what follows, I conclude this study by highlighting three *lines of contestation* that crystallized in the course of this book. It was along these lines that actors disagreed with each other and struggled with the question of how to position themselves. These lines of contestation, in my view, mirror not only the differing and contested social imaginaries pertaining to migrant solidarity, they also point to the contested question of how an increasingly heterogeneous and diverse society should look like. Over the following pages, I scrutinize these three *lines of contestation* in more detail.

7.1. The Contested Line between Insiders and Outsiders

One issue that repeatedly inspired differing positions among those who participated in the contestation of solidarity was the question of where to draw the line between 'genuine' and 'bogus' asylum seekers; between those to be included and those to be excluded from relationships of solidarity and help; between victims and villains of migration. This categorization of newcomers into unwanted economic migrants, on the one hand, and those who could potentially be integrated as fellow citizens, on the other, was one of the most challenging and controversial issues among those who supported refugees. Some had quite clear preconceptions of who was deserving of their help and support and who was not; they made their help and support contingent on the asylum seekers' nationality, on their assumed reasons for migrating, on their willingness 'to integrate', on their gratitude, or on factors such as family status, gender and skin colour. Others, however, took a more universal approach, claiming to give their support to each and every member of 'humanity' whatever their origin or reason for migrating. In either case, the line between insiders and outsiders clearly transcended the distinction between recognized citizens and non-citizens that, according to some scholars, represents the central pillar of the modern nation-state and the source of sovereign power (cf. Agamben 1998; Papastergiadis 2006). Those who supported refugees built relationships of solidarity that clearly stretched across this divide. I would suggest that this illustrates how residents in contemporary European migration societies are (re)shaping the parameters of inclusion and exclusion, increasingly moving beyond national citizenship as the primary expression of community membership.

At times, the tendency to include certain newcomers as potential co-citizens and exclude others coincided with governmentally institutionalized distinctions between 'genuine' and 'bogus' asylum seekers. For instance, one of my interlocutors – a committed volunteer in a medium-sized town in Baden-Württemberg – told me that, for reasons of "efficiency", he only wanted to help those asylum seekers who had a good "perspective of staying", i.e. a high statistical probability, based on past cases from their country of origin, that their asylum claim would be accepted. Scholars in the field of critical migration studies have long outlined how the production of different categories of migrants is a cornerstone of the governance of migration (Papadopoulos, Stephenson & Tsianos 2008; De Genova 2010; Squire 2011a). During the long summer of migration, asylum seekers originating from Syria were generally depicted as 'rightful' subjects of help and support by those who engaged in refugee solidarity. This might partly be explained by the extensive media coverage of the civil war raging in that country. Whether asylum seekers from eastern European and sub-Saharan African countries were equally 'deserving' of help and support, however, was a more controversial issue among helpers. Recognition rates for asylum seekers from these countries were almost zero, while governmental actors in the area of my field research openly stigmatized them as 'economic migrants' whose presence was deemed illegitimate (see Chapter 5). While some nevertheless offered help and support to these ostensibly 'bogus' asylum seekers, other volunteers openly called for their effective deportation. At times, those who supported refugees thus deliberately excluded certain groups from relationships of solidarity, thereby perpetuating their marginalized status and becoming complicit in the governance of migration. In consequence, such ostensible 'economic migrants' were often relegated to the status of outsiders who should be excluded from 'rightful' membership of migration societies.

However, my findings also illuminated numerous moments when those supporting refugees took a critical stance towards the exclusion and marginalization of those deemed 'bogus' refugees. Critical migration scholars have long pointed out that closer inspection shows migration movements to always be much more complex than distinctions between 'bogus economic migrants' and 'suffering refugees' suggest (cf. Ratfisch 2015). The inconsistencies surrounding this binary categorization of newcomers also became an issue for many of those who were drawn into supportive relationships around the long summer of migration. Indeed, the line between insiders and outsiders appeared to be highly contested among those who engaged in practices of refugee support. This was most apparent around the issue of deportations, which repeatedly sparked heated debates during my field research. I highlighted several instances when committed citizens voiced their dissent towards deportation orders or challenged the exclusion of those deemed 'bogus' asylum seekers in other ways. Often, volunteers did not distinguish between different groups of migrants but instead deliberately offered help and support to each and every one arriving in their town, village or neighbourhood, even if some had little chance of staying. In Chapter 4, I argued that many forged relationships of solidarity with whoever was 'there' on the ground. In doing so, they positioned themselves in relation to a *politics of presence* that articulated new modes of belonging revolving around 'the local', thus clearly eschewing distinctions based on national citizenship and instead emphasizing *co-presence*.

The question of where to draw the line between inclusion and exclusion in contemporary migration societies also became the focus of numerous interventions in the 'right' conduct of solidarity. Those who openly depicted their actions as "left-wing political activism", for example, often called for radical equality and unrestricted openness, demanding an "unconditional right to stay" or "equal rights for all". In the second and fourth chapters, I outlined how such 'activists' built alliances with those who sought to help asylum seekers, using these alliances to promote their political world views and to further their own aims. In stark contrast, governmental actors often drew a clear line between ostensibly 'genuine' and 'bogus' asylum seekers while making committed citizens complicit in the reproduction of this division. As I outlined in the third chapter of this book, the state government of Baden-Württemberg intervened in volunteering with refugees, promoting those practices that it deemed beneficial to its objectives in the governance of migration. For instance, governmental actors portrayed volunteers as being responsible for providing "returnee counselling" to rejected asylum seekers, thus asking them to contribute to the enforcement of deportation orders and expecting them to accept governmental decisions uncritically. Nonetheless, I also identified numerous occasions when volunteers demanded a space for disagreement with governmental actors and refused to recognize the distinction between those deemed insiders of a migration society and those considered deportable.

I would argue that these differing and at times contrasting positions and imaginaries shed light on how the line between insiders and outsiders is increasingly difficult to draw. The line between insiders and outsiders thus presents a highly contested issue in contemporary European migration societies. The ways in which this line is (re)negotiated among different groups and actors involved in relationships of solidarity merits further research. It would be particularly fruitful to learn how this line is contested through relationships of solidarity forged in different geographical areas and temporal contexts.

7.2. The Contested Line between 'the State' and 'Civil Society'

Another issue that provoked different understandings and positions was the relationship between 'the state' and its citizen-subjects. As one of my interlocutors, a representative of the state government of Baden-Württemberg, put it, she struggled with the following question: "How far should the state's sphere of action extend and how useful is it if civil society assumes certain responsibilities?". The unprecedented willingness to support refugees around the long summer of migration indicated that established residents felt a growing responsibility for the 'public good' and perceived an obligation to volunteer on behalf of migrants. These tendencies not only led to new ways of relating among established residents and newcomers in migration societies, they also substantially altered and (re)shaped the relationships between governmental actors and citizens: tasks and responsibilities were (re)ordered between the entities imagined as 'the state' and 'civil society', while the boundary between these entities often became blurred. I would suggest that these findings indicate how the German 'summer of welcome' also served as a laboratory that produced contested understandings of the role and responsibility of the individual vis-à-vis 'the state' in migration societies.

When governmental actors appeared to be underequipped for the growing numbers of asylum seekers arriving in late summer 2015, established residents often felt compelled to 'step in' in order to improve the deteriorating conditions on the ground. In the second chapter, I argued that a feeling of being morally obligated to help in an extraordinary emergency situation mobilized many to take action. However, it was often not only an impulse to alleviate immediate human suffering but also a desire to re-establish 'public order' that drove them to refugee support. With their commitment, they joined in with governmental efforts to ameliorate the perceived 'crisis' and bring order to the tense situation. For instance, one of my interlocutors, a committed volunteer and retired school teacher, told me that he considered his helping practices as "a means to give something back to the welfare state". This example clearly illustrates how many of those supporting refugees felt responsible for the functioning of the 'public good'. One of my interlocutors, a governmental representative whose job was to facilitate citizen engagement across the state, summed this up when he remarked "the state – is that not all of us?". Indeed, my empirical investigation indicated that those who got involved around the long summer of migration often – but not always – acted in concert with 'the state' in order to facilitate the reception of asylum seekers.

This led to a situation where migrants increasingly became governed through extended state-citizen networks wrapped in a cloak of humanitarian care and compassion. In many places, those who sought to help took on responsibilities in the reception of asylum seekers that were formerly carried out by 'the state'. In the course of my field research, I came across numerous instances of volunteers providing for the basic needs of asylum seekers. I argued that they thus acted as "street-level bureaucrats" (Lipsky 2010 [1980]), compensating for the lack of professionally employed social workers and caretakers and bringing relief to underequipped local authorities. In consequence, 'civil society' emerged as a responsible actor in the reception of asylum seekers, while tasks and responsibilities passed from the level of 'the state' to the level of committed citizens (see Chapter 3).

In order to (re)gain control over these developments, the state government of Baden-Württemberg introduced numerous programmes seeking to regulate, coordinate or facilitate citizen engagement across the state. Such programmes were often based on the notion that refugee support needed governmental intervention in order to be "effective". I argued that, through such means, governmental actors aimed to shape the (self-)conduct of committed citizens in a way that was beneficial to wider aims and objectives in the governance of migration, while depoliticizing practices of refugee support. This argument connects with academic works that have pointed to a shift from 'welfare states' to 'active societies', one that outsources responsibilities from 'the state' to 'responsible citizens' and places an emphasis on self-conduct (cf. Walters 1997; Dean 2010; Lessenich 2011). In parallel, scholars in the field of the anthropology of humanitarianism have discussed how humanitarian actors have come to govern in areas abandoned by the state. Such writers have blamed humanitarians for acting in concert with governmental actors, arguing that this situation perpetuates exclusions and fosters new discriminations. For instance, Ticktin (2011) problematizes how, in what she calls "regimes of care", ostensibly non-governmental organizations govern marginalized subjects through an emphasis on human suffering, while Fassin (2016) identifies a shift from "right to favour" that makes the situation of asylum seekers increasingly dependent on the goodwill of benevolent citizens.

Although such works provide valuable insights into the questions of power that pertain to refugee support, my study revealed that the effects and meanings of migrant solidarity are actually much more ambivalent and contested than such a reading suggests. This book highlighted numerous moments when those supporting refugees problematized their part in sustaining flawed asylum and border policies, while making governmental reforms redundant. Many of my interlocutors admitted that they felt generally uncomfortable with the idea of being seen as "unremunerated labour" for 'the state', to be deployed at the whim of governmental actors. Others reflected on the ambivalent effects of having 'stepped in' when local authorities proved underequipped and asylum regimes appeared inadequate. I also explored numerous instances of volunteers openly criticizing governmental interventions over their role and conduct in the reception of asylum seekers, volunteers who insisted on remaining "independent" of governmental actors and their objectives, while demanding space for disagreement. My investigation thus revealed that measures to extend governmental control over committed citizens did not go uncontested, while volunteers proved to remain to a certain extent *ungovernable*. Volunteers did often not hesitate to voice dissent towards governmental actors, to point at shortcomings in the handling of asylum seekers and to demand reforms.

What is more, my investigation illustrated that the shifting of responsibilities from 'the state' to committed citizens not only extended governmental control and power over the sphere of 'civil society' but, at the same time, opened up new possibilities for political action. The enhanced role of committed citizens in the management of asylum seekers might therefore also be read as a greater capacity to exert influence and foster change towards a different alternative on a grassroots level. The (re)ordering of responsibilities around the long summer of migration, I would suggest, redistributed power from formal governmental actors to individual citizens striving to build a 'better society'. Assuming a position that does not stand in opposition to 'the state' but instead puts an emphasis on cooperation can thus provide quite a strong position from which to foster political change. Often, those supporting refugees also demanded a say in local political decision-making processes and in the handling of asylum seekers on the ground. Local authorities that, in their view, did not take volunteers "seriously" or consult them on matters concerning the handling of asylum seekers were a major source of frustration.

I would thus suggest that committed citizens did play an active part in shaping the ways in which asylum seekers were governed and managed on the ground. My findings illustrate that the line between the entities imagined as 'the state' and 'civil society' is opened up for reconsideration and renegotiation in light of increased migration movements. The ways in which intensified migration is causing the relationship between 'the state' and its citizen-subjects to be reshaped is a topic that merits further research and consideration and provides an interesting avenue for future research.

7.3. The Contested Relationship between 'the Local' and 'the World Out There'

Last but not least, my empirical findings illustrate how those supporting refugees (re)considered the relationship between 'the local' and 'the global' in the course of their practices of solidarity. The increased willingness to get involved on behalf of migratory newcomers spoke both to a growing awareness of the transformative effects of intensified *global* migration movements and to a desire to foster *local* alternatives to a world that is increasingly in flux (see Chapter 6). I would therefore suggest that 'the local' and 'the global' can be read as mutually constitutive, entangled frames that crucially shape and structure practices of solidarity in migration societies. Seen from this perspective, my insights into the contested solidarities of the German 'summer of welcome' were also revealing in terms of how 'the local' and 'the global' become related to each other in contemporary migration societies. This chimes with academic works that have investigated the relationship between rootedness and rootlessness (Pailey 2018), mobility and stasis (Glick Schiller & Salazar 2013), and 'nomadic metaphysics' and 'sedentarist metaphysics' (Cresswell 2006) in an age of intensified migration. My analysis in the previous chapters illustrated that the aspirations for local togetherness, on the one hand, and the growing awareness for an increasingly entangled global condition, on the other, brought forth differing, ambivalent and contested social imaginaries. This was most clearly illustrated in Chapter 6, where such imaginaries proved to be so contrasting and conflicting that relationships of solidarity were eventually broken.

On the one hand, those who supported refugees were driven by an impulse to forge alternative forms of social togetherness 'from below' the nation-state, alternatives that they regarded as being 'better' equipped to cope with an increasingly diverse migration society. Over the course of the previous chapters, I outlined how practices of solidarity thus kindled a sense of community that revolved around 'the local' and, to differing degrees, included whoever was present on the ground, regardless of national origin or cultural belonging. In the fourth chapter, I argued that practices of solidarity are inventive of new ways of relating on the local level, while also offering political possibilities to bring about change and enact a different alternative on the ground. However, these imaginaries often went hand in hand with an idealized account of 'the local' that produced romanticized and nostalgic notions of 'local community' as an antidote to the 'world out there' (cf. Bauman 2001). For instance, many of those supporting refugees viewed their actions as a means to enact a local alternative to an ever more divided European Union and its flawed border and asylum policies. In this context, 'the local' was often painted as a safe haven in an increasingly inhumane world. The significance of a romanticized imaginary of 'local community' for practices of refugee support was particularly evident in the narrative of the *Gmünder Weg* (see Chapter 6). This narrative, which depicted the small south German town of Schwäbisch Gmünd as a successful example of the implementation of a local 'welcome culture', conveyed warm feelings of local togetherness and portrayed the 'local community' as being characterized by extraordinary levels of personal immediacy and mutual help. I argued that its great success – the town gained nationwide attention as a model of best practice – spoke to a contemporary longing for a togetherness rooted in 'the local'. These insights point to a more general desire in contemporary migration societies to feel embedded in a tangible 'local community'.

On the other hand, my empirical investigation showed how the extraordinary willingness to support newly arrived migrants spoke to a growing awareness of the increasingly entangled global condition. With their practices, I would suggest, those supporting refugees also embraced that migration forms a constitutive element of living-together in contemporary migration societies. In his seminal book *Distant Suffering*, Boltanski (1999: 23) claims that compassion for 'suffering others' ends when the unfortunates "invade the space of those more fortunate". The humanitarian imaginary at play around the summer of 2015, however, clearly did not end when asylum seekers "invaded" the space of those who were mobilized to support refugees. In fact, I would suggest that the immigration of large numbers of asylum seekers triggered an extraordinary level of humanitarian help and support *because of* their spatial proximity (see Chapter 2). Their arrival illustrated that 'suffering' is no longer something gazed at from a 'safe' distance. It becomes tangible in people's own neighbourhoods and affects the living-together on the ground. In the months preceding what came to be described as the 'refugee crisis', national and international media reported extensively on examples of 'distant suffering', on the atrocities in war-torn Syria, for instance, or migrants dying as they tried to cross the Mediterranean in small vessels. Meanwhile, a growing number of asylum seekers arrived in towns and villages across Germany, leading established residents to recognize that 'the world out there' cannot be shut out. Instead, intensified global migration movements brought the impacts of such 'distant suffering' to their own village, town or neighbourhood. This recognition was apparent from conversations with various volunteers during my field research, in which they told me that they were deeply shocked and affected by the first-hand accounts of violence and the graphic stories of flight they heard from asylum seekers. Often, this led them to reflect on injustices related to increasingly fortified borders, motivating them to take a stand against flawed migration policies (see Chapter 4). At times, those supporting refugees also embedded their immediate practices in a wider sociopolitical and economic context of global inequalities. For instance, the refugee activists in Schwäbisch Gmünd regarded their immediate living situation in the small Swabian town as contingent on a wider landscape of unequal rights and (post)colonial continuities (see Chapter 6).

Practices of refugee support thus lead committed citizens to (re)consider their place in the wider world and to (re)situate themselves both in relation to 'the local' and to the 'world out there'. Put differently, migrant solidarity brings 'the local' and 'the global' together in an ambivalent, contested and at times contradictive relationship, demonstrating that these scales are enmeshed in complex ways. Perhaps, the contested nature of migrant solidarity indicates that people struggle to make sense of their place in an increasingly entangled world. What seems more likely, however, is that the contested forms of migrant solidarity herald new possibilities of bringing 'the global' and 'the local' together in a meaningful relationship, one that fosters a more egalitarian and inclusive way of living-together in contemporary migration societies. After all, migrant solidarity illustrates that the rootedness in a harmonious 'local community' does not necessarily require shutting off the 'world out there', as groups inciting hostile attitudes towards migrants claim. Perhaps migrant solidarity can even provide a template for a future society – one that is rooted in tangible 'local communities' yet remains open to migrating newcomers, accepting the ability of today's intensified global migration movements to shape those communities in profound ways.

References

Abrams, Philip (1988 [1977]): *Notes on the Difficulty of Studying the State.* In: Journal of Historical Sociology, 1(1), pp. 58-89. doi:10.1111/j.1467-6443.1988.tb00004.x

Agamben, Giorgio (1998): *Homo Sacer: Sovereign Power and Bare Life.* Stanford: Stanford University Press.

— (2005): *State of Exception.* Chicago: The University of Chicago Press.

Agier, Michel (2010): *Humanity as an Identity and Its Political Effects (A Note on Camps and Humanitarian Government).* In: Humanity: An International Journal of Human Rights, Humanitarianism, and Development, 1(1), pp. 29-45. doi:10.1353/hum.2010.0005

Agustín, Óscar García; Jørgensen, Martin Bak (2019): *Solidarity and the 'Refugee Crisis' in Europe.* Cham: Springer.

Alexander, Jeffrey C. (2006): *The Civil Sphere.* Oxford: Oxford University Press.

Aliverti, Ana (2012): *Making People Criminal: The Role of the Criminal Law in Immigration Enforcement.* In: Theoretical Criminology, 16(4), pp. 417-434. doi:10.1177/1362480612449779

Allen, John; Massey, Doreen; Cochrane, Allan (1998): *Rethinking the Region: Spaces of Neo-Liberalism.* London: Routledge.

Alvesson, Mats (2009): *At-Home Ethnography: Struggling with Closeness and Closure.* In: Ybema, Sierk; Yanow, Dvora; Wels, Harry; Kamsteeg, Frans (Eds.), Organizational Ethnography: Studying the Complexities of Everyday Life (pp. 156-176). London: Sage Publications.

Ambrosini, Maurizio (2020): *The Local Governance of Immigration and Asylum: Policies of Exclusion as a Battleground.* In: Ambrosini, Maurizio; Cinalli, Manlio; Jacobson, David (Eds.), Migration, Borders and Citizenship: Between Policy and Public Spheres (pp. 195-215). Cham: Springer International Publishing.

Amit, Vered (2002): *Reconceptualizing Community.* In: Amit, Vered (Ed.), Realizing Community: Concepts, Social Relationships and Sentiments (pp. 1-21). London: Routledge.
— (2010): *Community as 'Good to Think With': The Productiveness of Strategic Ambiguities.* In: Anthropologica, 52(2), pp. 357-363.
Anderson, Benedict (1983): *Imagined Communities: Reflections on the Origin and Spread of Nationalism.* London/New York: Verso.
Arendt, Hannah (1966 [1963]): *On Revolution* (3. print ed.). New York: Viking Press.
Armbruster, Heidi (2019): *"It was the Photograph of the Little Boy": Reflections on the Syrian Vulnerable Persons Resettlement Programme in the UK.* In: Ethnic and Racial Studies, 42(15), pp. 2680-2699. doi:10.1080/01419870.2018.1554226
Artero, Maurizio (2019): *Motivations and Effects of Volunteering for Refugees. Spaces of Encounter and Political Influence of the 'New Civic Engagement' in Milan.* In: Partecipazione e Conflitto, 12(1), pp. 142-167. doi:10.1285/i20356609v12i1p142
Asad, Talal (2003): *Formations of the Secular: Christianity, Islam, Modernity.* Stanford: Stanford University Press.
Ataç, Ilker; Kron, Stefanie; Schilliger, Sarah; Schwiertz, Helge; Stierl, Maurice (2015): *Struggles of Migration as In-/Visible Politics. Introduction.* In: Movements. Journal for Critical Migration and Border Regime Studies, 1(2), pp. 1-18.
Ataç, Ilker; Rygiel, Kim; Stierl, Maurice (2016): *Introduction: The Contentious Politics of Refugee and Migrant Protest and Solidarity Movements: Remaking Citizenship from the Margins.* In: Citizenship Studies, 20(5), pp. 527-544. doi:10.1080/13621025.2016.1182681
Austin, Carly; Bauder, Harald (2010): *Jus Domicile: A Pathway to Citizenship for Temporary Foreign Workers?* In: CERIS Working Paper No. 81, pp. i-21.
Bagelman, Jennifer (2013): *Sanctuary: A Politics of Ease?* In: Alternatives: Global, Local, Political, 38(1), pp. 49-62. doi:10.1177/0304375412469314
Bähre, Erik (2007): *Reluctant Solidarity: Death, Urban Poverty and Neighbourly Assistance in South Africa.* In: Ethnography, 8(1), pp. 33-59. doi:10.1177/1466138107076136
Baker-Cristales, Beth (2008): *Magical Pursuits: Legitimacy and Representation in a Transnational Political Field.* In: American Anthropologist, 110(3), pp. 349-359. doi:10.1111/j.1548-1433.2008.00044.x
Balibar, Étienne (2004): *We, the People of Europe? Reflections on Transnational Citizenship.* Princeton: Princeton University Press.

Barnett, Michael N. (2005): *Humanitarianism Transformed*. In: Perspectives on Politics, 3(4), pp. 723-740. doi:10.1017/S1537592705050401
— (2011): *Empire of Humanity: A History of Humanitarianism*. Ithaca: Cornell University Press.
— (2016): *Paternalism beyond Borders*. Cambridge: Cambridge University Press.
Battista, Emiliano (2017): *Dissenting Words: Interviews with Jacques Rancière*. New York: Bloomsbury Publishing.
Bauböck, Rainer (1994): *Transnational Citizenship: Membership and Rights in International Migration*. Aldershot: Edward Elgar Publishing.
— (2003): *Reinventing Urban Citizenship*. In: Citizenship Studies, 7(2), pp. 139-160. doi:10.1080/1362102032000065946
Bauder, Harald (2011): *Immigration Dialectic: Imagining Community, Economy, and Nation*. Toronto: University of Toronto Press.
— (2012): *Jus Domicile: In Pursuit of a Citizenship of Equality and Social Justice*. In: Journal of International Political Theory, 8(1-2), pp. 184-196. doi:10.3366/jipt.2012.0038
— (2013): *Domicile Citizenship, Human Mobility and Territoriality*. In: Progress in Human Geography, 38(1), pp. 91-106. doi:10.1177/0309132513502281
— (2015): *Perspectives of Open Borders and No Border*. In: Geography Compass, 9(7), pp. 395-405. doi:10.1111/gec3.12224
— (2016): *Possibilities of Urban Belonging*. In: Antipode, 48(2), pp. 252-271. doi:10.1111/anti.12174
— (2017): *Sanctuary Cities: Policies and Practices in International Perspective*. In: International Migration, 55(2), pp. 174-187. doi:10.1111/imig.12308
— (2019): *Migrant Solidarities and the Politics of Place*. In: Progress in Human Geography, pp. 1-15. doi:10.1177/0309132519876324
Bauder, Harald; Juffs, Lorelle (2020): *'Solidarity' in the Migration and Refugee Literature: Analysis of a Concept*. In: Journal of Ethnic and Migration Studies, 46(1), pp. 46-65. doi:10.1080/1369183X.2019.1627862
Bauman, Zygmunt (2001): *Community: Seeking Safety in an Insecure World*. Cambridge: Polity Press.
— (2003): *Wasted Lives: Modernity and its Outcasts*. Cambridge: Polity Press.
Bernault, Florence (2003): *A History of Prison and Confinement in Africa*. Portsmouth: Heinemann.
Bhimji, Fazila (2016): *Visibilities and the Politics of Space: Refugee Activism in Berlin*. In: Journal of Immigrant & Refugee Studies, 14(4), pp. 432-450. doi:10.1080/15562948.2016.1145777

Bhuyan, Rupaleem; Smith-Carrier, Tracy (2012): *Constructions of Migrant Rights in Canada: Is Subnational Citizenship Possible?* In: Citizenship Studies, 16(2), pp. 203-221. doi:10.1080/13621025.2012.667613

Bojadžijev, Manuela; Karakayali, Serhat (2010): *Recuperating the Sideshows of Capitalism: The Autonomy of Migration Today*. e-flux, 17.

Boltanski, Luc (1999): *Distant Suffering: Morality, Media, and Politics*. Cambridge: Cambridge University Press.

Bornstein, Erica; Redfield, Peter (2011a): *Forces of Compassion: Humanitarianism between Ethics and Politics*. Santa Fe: School for Advanced Research Press.

— (2011b): *An Introduction to the Anthropology of Humanitarianism*. In: Bornstein, Erica; Redfield, Peter (Eds.), Forces of Compassion: Humanitarianism Between Ethics and Politics (pp. 3-30). Santa Fe: School for Advanced Research Press.

Bosi, Lorenzo; Zamponi, Lorenzo (2015): *Direct Social Actions and Economic Crises. The Relationship Between Forms of Action and Socio-Economic Context in Italy*. In: Partecipazione e Conflitto. The Open Journal of Sociopolitical Studies, 8(2), pp. 367-391. doi:10.1285/i20356609v8i2p367

Brettschneider, Frank; Schuster, Wolfgang (2013): *Stuttgart 21: Ein Großprojekt zwischen Protest und Akzeptanz*. Wiesbaden: Springer.

Brun, Cathrine (2016): *There is no Future in Humanitarianism: Emergency, Temporality and Protracted Displacement*. In: History and Anthropology, 27(4), pp. 393-410. doi:10.1080/02757206.2016.1207637

Burchell, Graham; Gordon, Colin; Miller, Peter (1991): *The Foucault Effect: Studies in Governmentality*. Chicago: The University of Chicago Press.

Burridge, Andrew (2014): *'No Borders' as a Critical Politics of Mobility and Migration*. In: ACME, 13(3), pp. 463-470.

Butler, Judith (1993): *Bodies that Matter: On the Discursive Limits of "Sex"*. New York: Routledge.

— (2011): Bodies in Alliance and the Politics of the Street. *Transversal*. Retrieved from http://www.eipcp.net/transversal/1011/butler/en

— (2015): *Notes Toward a Performative Theory of Assembly*. Cambridge: Harvard University Press.

Cabot, Heath (2016): *'Contagious' Solidarity: Reconfiguring Care and Citizenship in Greece's Social Clinics*. In: Social Anthropology, 24(2), pp. 152-166. doi:10.1111/1469-8676.12297

Calhoun, Craig (2010): *The Idea of Emergency: Humanitarian Action and Global (Dis)Order*. In: Fassin, Didier; Pandolfi, Mariella (Eds.), Contemporary

States of Emergency: The Politics of Military and Humanitarian Interventions (pp. 29-58). New York: Zone Books.

Canepari, Eleonora; Rosa, Elisabetta (2017): *A Quiet Claim to Citizenship: Mobility, Urban Spaces and City Practices over Time*. In: Citizenship Studies, 21(6), pp. 657-674. doi:10.1080/13621025.2017.1341654

Carey, Gemma; Braunack-Mayer, Annette; Barraket, Jo (2009): *Spaces of Care in the Third Sector: Understanding the Effects of Professionalization*. In: Health, 13(6), pp. 629-646. doi:10.1177/1363459308341866

Carstensen, Anna Lisa; Heimeshoff, Lisa-Marie; Jungehülsing, Jenny; Kirchhoff, Maren; Trzeciak, Miriam (2014): *Forschende Aktivist_innen und Aktivistische Forscher_innen: eine Hinleitung*. In: Heimeshoff, Lisa-Marie; Hess, Sabine; Kron, Stefanie; Schwenken, Helen; Trzeciak, Miriam (Eds.), Grenzregime II. Migration - Kontrolle - Wissen. Transnationale Perspektiven (pp. 257-268). Berlin/Hamburg: Assoziation A.

Castelli Gattinara, Pietro (2018): *Europeans, Shut the Borders! Anti-Refugee Mobilisation in Italy and France*. In: della Porta, Donatella (Ed.), Solidarity Mobilizations in the 'Refugee Crisis': Contentious Moves (pp. 271-297). Cham: Springer International Publishing.

Castles, Stephen; Miller, Mark J. (1994): *The Age of Migration: International Population Movements in the Modern World* (Repr. ed.). Basingstoke: Macmillan.

Chouliaraki, Lilie (2012): *The Ironic Spectator: Solidarity in the Age of Post-Humanitarianism*. Malden: Polity Press.

Coleman, Simon (2015): *On Mauss, Masks, and Gifts: Christianities, (In-)Dividualities, Modernities*. In: Journal of Ethnographic Theory, 5(1), pp. 295-315. doi:10.14318/hau5.1.014

Collyer, Michael; King, Russell (2016): *Narrating Europe's Migration and Refugee 'Crisis'*. In: Human Geography, 9(2), pp. 1-12. doi:10.1177/194277861600900201

Comaroff, Jean; Comaroff, John (2003): *Ethnography on an Awkward Scale: Postcolonial Anthropology and the Violence of Abstraction*. In: Ethnography, 4(2), pp. 147-179. doi:10.1177/14661381030042001

Corsten, Michael; Kauppert, Michael; Rosa, Hartmut (2008): *Quellen bürgerschaftlichen Engagements: Die biographische Entwicklung von Wir-Sinn und fokussierten Motiven*. Wiesbaden: Springer VS.

Creed, Gerald W. (2006a): *Community as Modern Pastoral*. In: Creed, Gerald W. (Ed.), The Seductions of Community: Emancipations, Oppressions, Quandaries (pp. 23-48). Santa Fe: School of American Research Press.

— (2006b): *(Re)considering Community*. In: Creed, Gerald W. (Ed.), The Seductions of Community: Emancipations, Oppressions, Quandaries (pp. 3-22). Santa Fe: School of American Research Press.

— (2006c): *The Seductions of Community: Emancipations, Oppressions, Quandaries*. Santa Fe: School of American Research Press.

Cresswell, Tim (2006): *On the Move: Mobility in the Modern Western World*. New York: Routledge.

Cuttitta, Paolo (2018): *Repoliticization through Search and Rescue? Humanitarian NGOs and Migration Management in the Central Mediterranean*. In: Geopolitics, 23(3), pp. 632-660.

Czarniawska, Barbara (1992): *Exploring Complex Organizations: A Cultural Perspective*. Newbury Park: Sage Publications.

Daphi, Priska; Rucht, Dieter; Stuppert, Wolfgang; Teune, Simon; Peter, Ullrich (2014): Occupy Frieden. Eine Befragung von Teilnehmer/innen der 'Mahnwachen für den Frieden'. *ipb working paper series*. Retrieved from https://depositonce.tu-berlin.de/bitstream/11303/5260/3/occupy-frieden.pdf

Darling, Jonathan (2014): *Asylum and the Post-Political: Domopolitics, Depoliticisation and Acts of Citizenship*. In: Antipode, 46(1), pp. 72-91. doi:10.1111/anti.12026

De Genova, Nicholas (2010): *The Deportation Regime: Sovereignty, Space, and the Freedom of Movement*. In: De Genova, Nicholas; Peutz, Nathalie (Eds.), The Deportation Regime. Sovereignty, Space and the Freedom of Movement (pp. 33-68). Durham: Duke University Press.

— (2015): *In the Land of the Setting Sun. Reflections on 'Islamization' and 'Patriotic Europeanism'*. In: Movements. Journal for Critical Migration and Border Regime Studies, 1(2), pp. 1-12.

— (2017): *The Borders of 'Europe': Autonomy of Migration, Tactics of Bordering*. London: Duke University Press.

De Genova, Nicholas; Tazzioli, Martina (2016): Europe/Crisis: New Keywords of 'the Crisis' in and of 'Europe'. *Europe at a Crossroads: Managed Inhospitality*. Retrieved from http://nearfuturesonline.org/europecrisis-new-keywords-of-crisis-in-and-of-europe/

Dean, Mitchell (1996): *Foucault, Government and the Enfolding of Authority*. In: Barry, Andrew; Osborne, Thomas; Rose, Nikolas (Eds.), Foucault and Political Reason. Liberalism, Neo-Liberalism, and Rationalities of Government (pp. 209-230). Chicago: The University of Chicago Press.

— (2010): *Governmentality. Power and Rule in Modern Society*. London: Sage Publications.

della Porta, Donatella (2018): *Solidarity Mobilizations in the 'Refugee Crisis': Contentious Moves*. London, New York: Macmillan Publishers.
Derrida, Jacques; Caputo, John D. (1997): *Deconstruction in a Nutshell: A Conversation with Jacques Derrida*. New York: Fordham University Press.
Derrida, Jacques; Dufourmantelle, Anne (2000): *Of Hospitality. Anne Dufourmantelle Invites Jacques Derrida to Respond*. Stanford: Stanford University Press.
Doidge, Mark; Sandri, Elisa (2019): *'Friends that Last a Lifetime': The Importance of Emotions amongst Volunteers Working with Refugees in Calais*. In: The British Journal of Sociology, 70(2), pp. 463-480. doi:10.1111/1468-4446.12484
Douglas, Mary (1991 [1966]): *Purity and Danger: An Analysis of the Concepts of Pollution and Taboo* (repr. ed.). London: Routledge.
— (2002): *Foreword: No Free Gifts*. In: Mauss, Marcel (Ed.), The Gift - The Form and Reason for Exchange in Archaic Societies (pp. ix-xxiii). London: Routledge Classics.
Durkheim, Émile (1965 [1893]): *The Division of Labor in Society*. New York: Free Press.
Edkins, Jenny (2003): *Humanitarianism, Humanity, Human*. In: Journal of Human Rights, 2(2), pp. 253-258. doi:10.1080/1475483032000078224
Eliasoph, Nina (2013): *The Politics of Volunteering*. Cambridge: Polity Press.
England, Kim V. L. (1994): *Getting Personal: Reflexivity, Positionality and Feminist Research*. In: The Professional Geographer, 46(1), pp. 80-89. doi:10.1111/j.0033-0124.1994.00080.x
Erensu, Asli Ikizoglu (2016): *Notes from a Refugee Protest: Ambivalences of Resisting and Desiring Citizenship*. In: Citizenship Studies, 20(5), pp. 664-677. doi:10.1080/13621025.2016.1182677
Eule, Tobias G; Borrelli, Lisa Marie; Lindberg, Annika; Wyss, Anna (2019): *Time as Waste and Tactic*. In: Eule, Tobias G; Borrelli, Lisa Marie; Lindberg, Annika; Wyss, Anna (Eds.), Migrants Before the Law. Contested Migration Control in Europe (pp. 149-186). Cham: Springer.
Evers, Adalbert; Wintersberger, Helmut (1990): *Shifts in the Welfare Mix. Their Impact on Work, Social Services and Welfare Policies*. Frankfurt/Boulder: Westview Press.
Falzon, Mark-Anthony (2009): *Multi-Sited Ethnography: Theory, Praxis and Locality in Contemporary Research*. Farnham: Ashgate Publishing.
Fassin, Didier (2007): *Humanitarianism as a Politics of Life*. In: Public Culture, 19(3), pp. 499-520. doi:10.1215/08992363-2007-007

— (2009): *Another Politics of Life is Possible*. In: Theory, Culture & Society, 26(5), pp. 44-60. doi:10.1177/0263276409106349

— (2010): *Heart of Humaneness: The Moral Economy of Humanitarian Intervention*. In: Fassin, Didier; Pandolfi, Mariella (Eds.), Contemporary States of Emergency: The Politics of Military and Humanitarian Interventions (pp. 269-294). New York: Zone Books.

— (2012): *Humanitarian Reason: A Moral History of the Present*. Berkeley: University of California Press.

— (2016, 29/06/2018): From Right to Favor. The Refugee Question as Moral Crisis. *The Nation*. Retrieved from https://www.thenation.com/article/from-right-to-favor/

Fassin, Didier; Pandolfi, Mariella (2010): *Introduction: Military and Humanitarian Government in the Age of Intervention*. In: Fassin, Didier; Pandolfi, Mariella (Eds.), Contemporary States of Emergency: The Politics of Military and Humanitarian Interventions (pp. 9-28). New York: Zone Books.

Featherstone, David (2012): *Solidarity: Hidden Histories and Geographies of Internationalism*. London/New York: Zed Books.

Fechter, Anne-Meike; Schwittay, Anke (2019): *Citizen Aid: Grassroots Interventions in Development and Humanitarianism*. In: Third World Quarterly, 40(10), pp. 1769-1780. doi:10.1080/01436597.2019.1656062

Feischmidt, Margit; Zakariás, Ildikó (2019): *Politics of Care and Compassion: Civic Help for Refugees and Its Political Implications in Hungary - A Mixed-Methods Approach*. In: Feischmidt, Margit; Pries, Ludger; Cantat, Celine (Eds.), Refugee Protection and Civil Society in Europe (pp. 59-99). Cham: Palgrave Macmillan.

Feldman, Gregory (2015): *We Are All Migrants: Political Action and the Ubiquitous Condition of Migrant-Hood*. Stanford: Stanford University Press.

Feldman, Ilana; Ticktin, Miriam (2010): *In the Name of Humanity: The Government of Threat and Care*. Durham: Duke University Press.

Ferguson, James (1994): *The Anti-Politics Machine: 'Development', Depoliticization, and Bureaucratic Power in Lesotho*. Minneapolis: University of Minnesota Press.

— (2015): *Give a Man a Fish: Reflections on the New Politics of Distribution*. Durham: Duke University Press.

— (2017): *Presence and Social Obligation: An Essay on the Share*. Paper presented at the Dahrendorf-Lecture, Konstanz.

Ferguson, James; Gupta, Akhil (2002): *Spatializing States: Toward an Ethnography of Neoliberal Governmentality*. In: American Ethnologist, 29(4), pp. 981-1002. doi:10.1525/ae.2002.29.4.981

Fillieule, Olivier (2001): *Dynamics of Commitment in the Sector Known as 'Solidarity': Methodological Reflections Based on the Case of France*. In: Giugni, Marco; Passy, Florence (Eds.), Political Altruism? Solidarity Movements in International Perspective (pp. 51-66). Maryland: Rowman & Littlefield Publishers.

Fleischmann, Larissa (2017): *The Politics of Helping Refugees: Emerging Meanings of Political Action around the German 'Summer of Welcome'*. In: Mondi Migranti, 3(2), pp. 53-73. doi:10.3280/MM2017-003003

— (2019): *Making Volunteering with Refugees Governable: The Contested Role of 'Civil Society' in the German Welcome Culture*. In: Social Inclusion, 7(2), pp. 64-73. doi:http://dx.doi.org/10.17645/si.v7i2.1979

Fleischmann, Larissa; Steinhilper, Elias (2017): *The Myth of Apolitical Volunteering for Refugees: German Welcome Culture and a New Dispositif of Helping*. In: Social Inclusion, 5(3), pp. 17-27. doi:10.17645/si.v5i3.945

Fontanari, Elena (2015): *Confined to the Threshold: The Experiences of Asylum Seekers in Germany*. In: City, 19(5), pp. 714-726. doi:10.1080/13604813.2015.1071112

— (2017): *It's my Life. The Temporalities of Refugees and Asylum-Seekers within the European Border Regime*. In: Etnografia e Ricerca Qualitativa, 10(1), pp. 25-54. doi:10.3240/86886

Fontanari, Elena; Borri, Giulia (2018): *Introduction. Civil Society on the Edge: Actions in Support and against Refugees in Italy and Germany*. In: Mondi Migranti, 3(2), pp. 23-51. doi:10.3280/MM2017-003002

Foucault, Michel (1978): *The History of Sexuality. Volume 1: An Introduction*. New York: Pantheon Books.

— (1982): *The Subject and Power*. In: Dreyfus, Hubert; Rabinow, Paul (Eds.), Michel Foucault: Beyond Structuralism and Hermeneutics (pp. 208-226). Brighton: Harvester.

— (1988): *Technologies of the Self*. In: Martin, Luther H.; Gutman, Huck; Hutton, Patrick H. (Eds.), Technologies of the Self: A Seminar with Michel Foucault (pp. 16-49). Amherst: University of Massachusetts Press.

— (1991): *Governmentality*. In: Burchell, Graham; Gordon, Collin; Miller, Peter (Eds.), The Foucault Effect: Studies in Governmentality (pp. 87-104). Chicago: University of Chicago Press.

Gabriel, Oscar; Schoen, Harald; Faden-Kuhne, Kristina (2014): *Der Volksentscheid über Stuttgart 21: Aufbrauch zu neuen demokratischen Ufern?* Berlin: Verlag Barbara Budrich.

Gauditz, Leslie (2017): *The Noborder Movement: Interpersonal Struggle with Political Ideals.* In: Social Inclusion, 5(3), pp. 49-57. doi:10.17645/si.v5i3.968

Giugni, Marco (2001): *Concluding Remarks: Conceptual Distinctions for the Study of Political Altruism.* In: Giugni, Marco; Passy, Florence (Eds.), Political Altruism? Solidarity Movements in International Perspective (pp. 235-245). Maryland: Rowman & Littlefield Publishers.

Glick Schiller, Nina; Salazar, Noel B. (2013): *Regimes of Mobility Across the Globe.* In: Journal of Ethnic and Migration Studies, 39(2), pp. 183-200. doi:10.1080/1369183X.2013.723253

Goldring, Luin; Landolt, Patricia (2011): *Caught in the Work-Citizenship Matrix: The Lasting Effects of Precarious Legal Status on Work for Toronto Immigrants.* In: Globalizations, 8(3), pp. 325-341. doi:10.1080/14747731.2011.576850

Gomez, Ricardo; Newell, Bryce Clayton; Vannini, Sara (2020): *Empathic Humanitarianism: Understanding the Motivations behind Humanitarian Work with Migrants at the US–Mexico Border.* In: Journal on Migration and Human Security, 8(1), pp. 1-13. doi:10.1177/2331502419900764

Gonzales, Alfonso (2009): *The 2006 Mega Marchas in Greater Los Angeles: Counter-Hegemonic Moment and the Future of El Migrante Struggle.* In: Latino Studies, 7(1), pp. 30-59. doi:10.1057/lst.2009.2

Gramsci, Antonio (1971): *Selections from the Prison Notebooks of Antonio Gramsci.* London: Lawrence & Wishart.

Green, Sarah; Laviolette, Patrick (2016): *Editorial.* In: Social Anthropology, 24(2), pp. 139-141. doi:10.1111/1469-8676.12311

Gregory, Derek (2004): *The Colonial Present: Afghanistan, Palestine, Iraq* (Repr. ed.). Malden: Wiley and Blackwell.

Griffiths, Melanie (2014): *Out of Time: The Temporal Uncertainties of Refused Asylum Seekers and Immigration Detainees.* In: Journal of Ethnic and Migration Studies, 40(12), pp. 1991-2009. doi:10.1080/1369183X.2014.907737

Gudavarthy, Ajay (2013): *Politics of Post-Civil Society: Contemporary History of Political Movements in India.* New Dehli: Sage Publications India.

Hacket, Anne; Mutz, Gerd (2002): *Empirische Befunde zum bürgerschaftlichen Engagement.* In: Aus Politik und Zeitgeschichte, B9, pp. 39-46.

Hall, Stuart (1996): *When was 'the Post-Colonial'? Thinking at the limit.* In: Chambers, Iain; Curti, Lidia (Eds.), The Post-Colonial Question: Common Skies, Divided Horizons (pp. 242-260). London: Routledge.

Hamann, Ulrike; Karakayali, Serhat (2016): *Practicing Willkommenskultur: Migration and Solidarity in Germany*. In: Intersections. East European Journal of Society and Politics, 2(4), pp. 69-86. doi:10.17356/ieejsp.v2i4.29

Hamann, Ulrike; Yurdakul, Gökçe (2018): *The Transformative Forces of Migration: Refugees and the Re-Configuration of Migration Societies*. In: Social Inclusion, 6(1), pp. 110-114. doi:10.17645/si.v6i1.1482

Hammersley, Martyn; Atkinson, Paul (1995): *Ethnography: Principles in Practice*. Abingdon: Routledge.

Hannerz, Ulf (1998): *Other Transnationals: Perspectives Gained from Studying Sideways*. In: Paideuma: Mitteilungen zur Kulturkunde, 44, pp. 109-123.

— (2003): *Being there... and there... and there!: Reflections on Multi-Site Ethnography*. In: Ethnography, 4(2), pp. 201-216. doi:10.1177/14661381030042003

Hansen, Christina (2019): *Solidarity in Diversity: Activism as a Pathway of Migrant Emplacement in Malmö*. Retrieved from https://doi.org/10.24834/isbn.9789178770175

Haraway, Donna (1988): *Situated Knowledges: The Science Question in Feminism and the Privilege of Partial Perspective*. In: Feminist Studies, 14(3), pp. 575-599. doi:10.2307/3178066

Harvey, David (2012): *Rebel Cities: From the Right to the City to the Urban Revolution*. London/New York: Verso.

Haunss, Sebastian; Daphi, Priska; Gauditz, Leslie; Knopp, Philipp; Micus, Matthias; Scharf, Philipp; Schmidt, Stephanie; Sommer, Moritz; Teune, Simon; Thurn, Roman; Ullrich, Peter; Zajak, Sabrina (2017): #NoG20. Ergebnisse der Befragung von Demonstrierenden und der Beobachtung des Polizeieinsatzes. *ipb working papers*. Retrieved from https://protestinstitut.eu/wp-content/uploads/2017/11/NoG20_ipb-working-paper.pdf

Hayter, Teresa (2004): *Open Borders: The Case against Immigration Controls*. London: Pluto Press.

Heins, Volker; Unrau, Christine (2018): *Refugees Welcome: Arrival Gifts, Reciprocity and the Integration of Forced Migrants*. In: Journal of International Political Theory, 14(2), pp. 223-239. doi:10.1177/1755088217753232

Heller, Charles; Pezzani, Lorenzo (2017): *Ebbing and Flowing: The EU's Shifting Practices of (Non-)Assistance and Bordering in a Time of Crisis*. In: Hess, Sabine; Kasparek, Bernd; Kron, Stefanie; Rodatz, Mathias; Schwertl, Maria; Sontowski, Simon (Eds.), Der lange Sommer der Migration. Grenzregime III (pp. 215-235). Berlin/Hamburg: Assoziation A.

Hess, Sabine; Kasparek, Bernd (2017a): *De-and Restabilising Schengen. The European Border Regime after the Summer of Migration.* In: Cuadernos Europeos de Deusto, 56(2017), pp. 47-77. doi:10.18543/ced-56-2017pp47-77

— (2017b): *Under Control? Or Border (as) Conflict: Reflections on the European Border Regime.* In: Social Inclusion, 5(3), pp. 58-68. doi:10.17645/si.v5i3.1004

Hess, Sabine; Kasparek, Bernd; Kron, Stefanie; Rodatz, Mathias; Schwertl, Maria; Sontowski, Simon (2017): *Der lange Sommer der Migration. Grenzregime III.* Berlin: Assoziation A.

Hilhorst, Dorothea; Jansen, Bram J. (2010): *Humanitarian Space as Arena: A Perspective on the Everyday Politics of Aid.* In: Development and Change, 41(6), pp. 1117-1139. doi:10.1111/j.1467-7660.2010.01673.x

Hinger, Sophie (2016): *Asylum in Germany: The Making of the 'Crisis' and the Role of Civil Society.* In: Human Geography, 9(2), pp. 78-88. doi:10.1177/194277861600900208

Hinger, Sophie; Daphi, Priska; Stern, Verena (2019): *Divided Reactions: Pro-and Anti-Migrant Mobilization in Germany.* In: Rea, Andrea; Martiniello, Marco; Mazzola, Alessandro; Meuleman, Bart (Eds.), The Refugee Reception Crisis in Europe: Polarized Opinions and Mobilizations.

Hinger, Sophie; Schäfer, Philipp (2019): *Making a Difference: The Accommodation of Refugees in Leipzig and Osnabrück.* In: Erdkunde, 73(1), pp. 63-76. doi:10.3112/erdkunde.2019.01.06

Hinger, Sophie; Schäfer, Philipp; Pott, Andreas (2016): *The Local Production of Asylum.* In: Journal of Refugee Studies, 29(4), pp. 440-463. doi:10.1093/jrs/few029

Holmes, Seth M.; Castañeda, Heide (2016): *Representing the 'European Refugee Crisis' in Germany and Beyond: Deservingness and Difference, Life and Death.* In: American Ethnologist, 43(1), pp. 12-24. doi:10.1111/amet.12259

Huysmans, Jef (2006): *Agency and the Politics of Protection: Implications for Security Studies.* In: Huysmans, Jef; Dobson, Andrew; Prokhovnik, Raia (Eds.), The Politics of Protection: Sites of Insecurity and Political Agency (pp. 1-18). Abingdon: Routledge.

Ilcan, Suzan (2014): *Activist Citizens and the Politics of Mobility in Osire Refugee Camp.* In: Isin, Engin; Nyers, Peter (Eds.), Routledge Handbook of Global Citizenship Studies (pp. 186-195). Abingdon: Routledge.

Isin, Engin (2002): *Being Political: Genealogies of Citizenship.* Minneapolis: University of Minnesota Press.

— (2008): *Theorizing Acts of Citizenship.* In: Isin, Engin; Nielsen, Greg (Eds.), Acts of Citizenship (pp. 15-43). New York: Zed Books.

— (2011): *Epilogue: The Movement of Politics. Logics, Subjects, Citizenships*. In: Squire, Vicki (Ed.), The Contested Politics of Mobility: Borderzones and Irregularity (pp. 216-231). Abingdon: Routledge.
— (2012): *Citizens Without Frontiers*. London: Bloomsbury.
Isin, Engin; Nielsen, Greg (2008): *Introduction*. In: Isin, Engin; Nielsen, Greg (Eds.), Acts of Citizenship (pp. 1-12). New York: Zed Books.
Isin, Engin; Nyers, Peter; Turner, Bryan (2008): *Citizenship between Past and Future*. London: Routledge.
Jabri, Vivienne (2006): *The Limits of Agency in Times of Emergency*. In: Huysmans, Jef; Dobson, Andrew; Prokhovnik, Raia (Eds.), The Politics of Protection: Sites of Insecurity and Political Agency (pp. 136-153). London: Routledge.
Jäckle, Sebastian; König, Pascal D. (2017): *The Dark Side of the German 'Welcome Culture': Investigating the Causes behind Attacks on Refugees in 2015*. In: West European Politics, 40(2), pp. 223-251. doi:10.1080/01402382.2016.1215614
Jakob, Christian (2016): *Die Bleibenden: Wie Flüchtlinge Deutschland seit 20 Jahren verändern*. Berlin: Christoph Links Verlag.
Jasper, James M. (1998): *The Emotions of Protest: Affective and Reactive Emotions in and around Social Movements*. In: Sociological Forum, 13(3), pp. 397-424. doi:10.1023/A:1022175308081
Johnson, Heather (2012): *Moments of Solidarity, Migrant Activism and (Non)Citizens at Global Borders: Political Agency at Tanzanian Refugee Camps, Australian Detention Centres and European Borders*. In: Nyers, Peter; Rygiel, Kim (Eds.), Citizenship, Migrant Activism and the Politics of Movement (pp. 109-128). Abingdon: Routledge.
— (2014): *Borders, Asylum and Global Non-Citizenship: The Other Side of the Fence*. Cambridge: Cambridge University Press.
Juris, Jeffrey S.; Khasnabish, Alex (2013): *Insurgent Encounters: Transnational Activism, Ethnography, and the Political*. Durham: Duke University Press.
Kalandides, Ares; Vaiou, Dina (2012): *'Ethnic' Neighbourhoods? Practices of Belonging and Claims to the City*. In: European Urban and Regional Studies, 19(3), pp. 254-266. doi:10.1177/0969776412438328
Kalir, Barak; Wissink, Lieke (2016): *The Deportation Continuum: Convergences between State Agents and NGO Workers in the Dutch Deportation Field*. In: Citizenship Studies, 20(1), pp. 1-16. doi:10.1080/13621025.2015.1107025
Kallio, Kirsi Pauliina; Meier, Isabel; Häkli, Jouni (2020): *Radical Hope in Asylum Seeking: Political Agency beyond Linear Temporality*. In: Journal of Ethnic and Migration Studies, pp. 1-17. doi:10.1080/1369183X.2020.1764344

Kallius, Annastiina; Monterescu, Daniel; Rajaram, Prem Kumar (2016): *Immobilizing Mobility: Border Ethnography, Illiberal Democracy, and the Politics of the 'Refugee Crisis' in Hungary*. In: American Ethnologist, 43(1), pp. 25-37. doi:10.1111/amet.12260

Kandylis, George (2017): *Urban Scenes of Citizenship: Inventing the Possibility of Immigrants' Citizenship in Athens*. In: Citizenship Studies, 21(4), pp. 468-482. doi:10.4324/9781351121316-7

Karakayali, Serhat (2014): *Solidarität mit den Anderen. Gesellschaft und Regime der Alterität*. In: Broden, Anne; Mecheril, Paul (Eds.), Solidarität in der Migrationsgesellschaft: Befragung einer normativen Grundlage (pp. 111-126). Bielefeld: transcript Verlag.

— (2017): *Feeling the Scope of Solidarity: The Role of Emotions for Volunteers Supporting Refugees in Germany*. In: Social Inclusion, 5(3), pp. 7-16. doi:10.17645/si.v5i3.1008

— (2019): *The Welcomers: How Volunteers Frame their Commitment for Refugees*. In: Feischmidt, Margit; Pries, Ludger; Cantat, Celine (Eds.), Refugee Protection and Civil Society in Europe (pp. 221-242). Cham: Palgrave Macmillan.

Karakayali, Serhat; Tsianos, Vassilis (2005): *Mapping the Order of New Migration. Undokumentierte Arbeit und die Autonomie der Migration*. In: Peripherie, 97/98, pp. 35-64.

Kasparek, Bernd (2016): *Routes, Corridors, and Spaces of Exception: Governing Migration and Europe*. In: Near Futures Online, 1(1).

Kasparek, Bernd; Matheis, Christian (2016): *Complementing Schengen: The Dublin System and the European Border and Migration Regime*. In: Bauder, Harald; Matheis, Christian (Eds.), Migration Policy and Practice: Interventions and Solutions (pp. 59-78). New York: Palgrave Macmillan.

Kasparek, Bernd; Schmidt-Sembdner, Matthias (2019): *Renationalization and Spaces of Migration: the European Border Regime after 2015*. In: Mitchell, Katharyne; Jones, Reece; Fluri, Jennifer L. (Eds.), Handbook on Critical Geographies of Migration (pp. 206-218). Cheltenham: Edward Elgar Publishing.

Kasparek, Bernd; Schmidt, Matthias (2016): *Residenzpflicht*. In: Widersprüche, 33(127), pp. 43-48.

Kasparek, Bernd; Speer, Marc (2013): *At the Nexus of Academia and Activism: Bordermonitoring.eu*. In: Postcolonial Studies, 16(3), pp. 259-268. doi:10.1080/13688790.2013.850044

— (2015): Of Hope. Hungary and the Long Summer of Migration. Retrieved from http://bordermonitoring.eu/ungarn/2015/09/of-hope-en/

King, Natasha (2016): *No Borders: The Politics of Immigration Control and Resistance*. London: Zed Books.
Kirchhoff, Maren (2020): *Differential Solidarity: Protests against Deportations as Structured Contestations over Citizenship*. In: Citizenship Studies, 24(4), pp. 568-586. doi:10.1080/13621025.2020.1755178
Kirsch, Thomas G. (2016): *Undoing Apartheid Legacies? Volunteering as Repentance and Politics by Other Means*. In: Brown, Hannah; Prince, Ruth (Eds.), Volunteer Economies. The Politics and Ethics of Voluntary Labour in Africa (pp. 201-221). Oxford: James Currey.
— (2017): *The Domestication of Partisan Volunteering. Volunteers, Activism and Anti-Politics in Zambia*. Unpublished Workshop Paper.
Kleres, Jochen (2018): *Emotions in the Crisis: Mobilising for Refugees in Germany and Sweden*. In: della Porta, Donnatella (Ed.), Solidarity Mobilizations in the 'Refugee Crisis' (pp. 209-241). Cham: Springer.
Koch, Verena (2007): *Kann das Ehrenamt den Sozialstaat retten? Möglichkeiten und Grenzen des diakonischen Ehrenamtes als eine Praxisform des Sozialstaats - eine kritische Reflexion*. Hamburg: Diplomica Verlag.
Kolb, Kenneth (2014): *Moral Wages. The Emotional Dilemmas of Victim Advocacy and Counseling*. Oakland: University of California Press.
Komter, Aafke E. (2005): *Social Solidarity and the Gift*. New York: Cambridge University Press.
Komter, Aafke E.; Leer, Mirjam van (2012): *Hospitality as a Gift Relationship: Political Refugees as Guests in the Private Sphere*. In: Hospitality & Society, 2(1), pp. 7-23. doi:10.1386/hosp.2.1.7_1
Koutsouba, Maria (1999): *'Outsider' in an 'Inside' World, or Dance Ethnography at Home*. In: Buckland, Theresa J. (Ed.), Dance in the Field: Theory, Methods and Issues in Dance Ethnography (pp. 186-195). London: Palgrave Macmillan.
Krimphove, Petra (2005): *Bürgerschaftliches Engagement und Sozialstaat: Ein Vergleich zwischen Deutschland und den USA*. Retrieved from http://csn.uni-muenster.de/Uni-Site%20Plus/zimmer/krimphove_buerg%20engagement%20deut%20usa.pdf
Kristeva, Julia (1982): *Powers of Horror: An Essay on Abjection*. New York: Columbia University Press.
Kukovetz, Brigitte; Sprung, Annette (2019): *Questioning Power Relations. Learning Processes through Solidarity with Refugees*. In: Finnegan, Fergal; Grummell, Bernie (Eds.), Power and Possibility. Adult Education in a Diverse and Complex World (pp. 131-142). Leiden/Boston: Brill Sense.

Laclau, Ernesto (1996): *Emancipation(s)*. London/New York: Verso Books.

Lagroye, Jacques (1996): *La production de la solidarité*. Rapport du groupe de travail sur la solidarité du centre de recherches politiques de la Sorbonne. Paris.

Landry, Olivia (2015): *'Wir sind alle Oranienplatz'! Space for Refugees and Social Justice in Berlin*. In: Seminar: A Journal of Germanic Studies, 51(4), pp. 398-413. doi:10.3138/seminar.2015.51.4.398

Laziridis, Gabriella (2015): *International Migration into Europe: From Subjects to Abjects*. Basingstoke: Palgrave Macmillan.

Lebuhn, Henrik (2013): *Local Border Practices and Urban Citizenship in Europe: Exploring Urban Borderlands*. In: City, 17(1), pp. 37-51. doi:10.1080/13604813.2012.734072

Lefebvre, Henri (1996): *Writings on Cities*. Oxford: Blackwell Publishers.

Lemke, Thomas (2001): *'The Birth of Bio-Politics': Michel Foucault's Lecture at the Collège de France on Neo-Liberal Governmentality*. In: Economy and Society, 30(2), pp. 190-207. doi:10.1080/03085140120042271

— (2002): *Foucault, Governmentality, and Critique*. In: Rethinking Marxism, 14(3), pp. 49-64. doi:10.1080/089356902101242288

Lessenich, Stephan (2011): *Constructing the Socialized Self: Mobilization and Control in the 'Active Society'*. In: Bröckling, Ulrich; Krasmann, Susanne; Lemke, Thomas (Eds.), Governmentality - Current Issues and Future Challenges (pp. 304-320). New York/London: Routledge.

Liebersohn, Harry (2011): *The Return of the Gift: European History of a Global Idea*. Cambridge: Cambridge University Press.

Lipsky, Michael (2010 [1980]): *Street-Level Bureaucracy: Dilemmas of the Individual in Public Services* (30th Ann. ed.). New York: Russell Sage Foundation.

Madison, D. Soyini (2008): *Critical Ethnography: Method, Ethics, and Performance*. Thousand Oaks: Sage Publications

Maestri, Gaja; Monforte, Pierre (2020): *Who Deserves Compassion? The Moral and Emotional Dilemmas of Volunteering in the 'Refugee Crisis'*. In: Sociology, pp. 1-16. doi:10.1177/0038038520928199

Malinowski, Bronislaw (2014 [1922]): *Argonauts of the Western Pacific: An Account of Native Enterprise and Adventure in the Archipelagoes of Melanesian New Guinea* (Revised ed.). Abingdon: Routledge.

Malkki, Liisa (1992): *National Geographic: The Rooting of Peoples and the Territorialization of National Identity Among Scholars and Refugees*. In: Cultural Anthropology, 7(1), pp. 24-44. doi:10.1525/can.1992.7.1.02a00030

— (1995): *Refugees and Exile: From 'Refugee Studies' to the National Order of Things*. In: Annual Review of Anthropology, 24, pp. 495-523. doi:10.1146/annurev.an.24.100195.002431

— (1996): *Speechless Emissaries: Refugees, Humanitarianism, and Dehistoricization*. In: Cultural Anthropology, 11(3), pp. 377-404. doi:10.1525/can.1996.11.3.02a00050

— (2015): *The Need to Help: The Domestic Arts of International Humanitarianism*. Durham: Duke University Press.

Mallard, Grégoire (2011): *The Gift Revisited: Marcel Mauss on War, Debt, and the Politics of Reparations*. In: Sociological Theory, 29(4), pp. 225-247. doi:10.1111/j.1467-9558.2011.01398.x

Marcus, George E. (1998): *Ethnography through Thick and Thin*. Princeton: Princeton University Press.

Marshall, Thomas H. (1950): *Citizenship and Social Class, and Other Essays*. New York: Cambridge University Press.

Martin, Deborah G.; Hanson, Susan; Fontaine, Danielle (2007): *What Counts as Activism?: The Role of Individuals in Creating Change*. In: Women's Studies Quarterly, 35(3/4), pp. 78-94.

Matejskova, Tatiana; Antonsich, Marco (2015): *Governing through Diversity - Migration Societies in Post-Multiculturalist Times*. Basingstoke: Palgrave Macmillan.

Mauss, Marcel (1990 [1925]): *The Gift: The Form and Reason for Exchange in Archaic Societies*. London: Routledge.

Mayer, Margit (2017): *Cities as Sites of Refuge and Resistance*. In: European Urban and Regional Studies, 25(3), pp. 232-249. doi:10.1177/0969776417729963

Mayo, Marjorie (2017): *Changing Communities: Stories of Migration, Displacement and Social Cohesion*. Bristol: Bristol University Press.

McGee, Darragh; Pelham, Juliette (2018): *Politics at Play: Locating Human Rights, Refugees and Grassroots Humanitarianism in the Calais Jungle*. In: Leisure Studies, 37(1), pp. 22-35. doi:10.1080/02614367.2017.1406979

McNevin, Anne (2011): *Contesting Citizenship: Irregular Migrants and New Frontiers of the Political*. New York: Columbia University Press.

Mecheril, Paul (2003): *Prekäre Verhältnisse: Über natio-ethno-kulturelle (Mehrfach-)Zugehörigkeit*. Münster: Waxmann.

Mezzadra, Sandro (2011): *The Gaze of Autonomy: Capitalism, Migration and Social Struggles*. In: Squire, Vicki (Ed.), The Contested Politics of Mobility: Borderzones and Irregularity (pp. 121-142). London: Routledge.

— (2018): *In the Wake of the Greek Spring and the Summer of Migration*. In: South Atlantic Quarterly, 117(4), pp. 925-933. doi:10.1215/00382876-7166092

Millner, Naomi (2011): *From 'Refugee' to 'Migrant' in Calais Solidarity Activism: Restaging Undocumented Migration for a Future Politics of Asylum*. In: Political Geography, 30(6), pp. 320-328. doi:10.1016/j.polgeo.2011.07.005

Minca, Claudio (2017): *Agamben and Geography: Sovereignty, Biopolitics and Spaces of Exception*. London: I.B. Tauris.

Mitchell, Timothy (1991): *The Limits of the State: Beyond Statist Approaches and Their Critics*. In: The American Political Science Review, 85(1), pp. 77-96.

Monforte, Pierre (2020): *From 'Fortress Europe' to 'Refugees Welcome'*. In: Flesher Fominaya, Cristina; Feenstra, Ramón A. (Eds.), Routledge Handbook of Contemporary European Social Movements: Protest in Turbulent Times (pp. 46-58). Abingdon, New York: Routledge.

Monteith, William (2017): *Showing 'Heart' through Ethnography: Ethical Entanglements in a Ugandan Marketplace*. In: City, 21(2), pp. 178-189. doi:10.1080/13604813.2017.1353341

Montesinos Coleman, Lara (2015): *Ethnography, Commitment, and Critique: Departing from Activist Scholarship*. In: International Political Sociology, 9(3), pp. 263-280. doi:10.1111/ips.12096

Moulin, Carolina (2012): *Ungrateful Subjects? Refugee Protests and the Logic of Gratitude*. In: Nyers, Peter; Rygiel, Kim (Eds.), Citizenship, Migrant Activism and the Politics of Movement (pp. 66-84). Abingdon: Routledge.

Moulin, Carolina; Nyers, Peter (2007): *'We Live in a Country of UNHCR' - Refugee Protests and Global Political Society*. In: International Political Sociology, 1(4), pp. 356-372. doi:10.1111/j.1749-5687.2007.00026.x

Mountz, Alison (2011): *The Enforcement Archipelago: Detention, Haunting, and Asylum on Islands*. In: Politcal Geography, 30(3), pp. 118-128. doi:10.1016/j.polgeo.2011.01.005

Mountz, Alison; Hiemstra, Nancy (2013): *Chaos and Crisis: Dissecting the Spatiotemporal Logics of Contemporary Migrations and State Practices*. In: Annals of the Association of American Geographers, 104(2), pp. 382-390. doi:10.1080/00045608.2013.857547

Muehlebach, Andrea (2012): *The Moral Neoliberal: Welfare and Citizenship in Italy*. Chicago: University of Chicago Press.

— (2013): *The Catholicization of Neoliberalism: On Love and Welfare in Lombardy, Italy*. In: American Anthropologist, 115(3), pp. 452-465. doi:10.1111/aman.12028

Nader, Laura (1972): *Up the Anthropologist: Perspectives Gained from Studying Up.* In: Hymes, Dell (Ed.), Reinventing Anthropology (pp. 284-311). New York: Vintage Books.

Nencel, Lorraine (2014): *Situating Reflexivity: Voices, Positionalities and Representations in Feminist Ethnographic Texts.* In: Women's Studies International Forum, 43, pp. 75-83. doi:10.1016/j.wsif.2013.07.018

Nettelbladt, Gala; Boano, Camillo (2019): *Infrastructures of Reception: The Spatial Politics of Refuge in Mannheim, Germany.* In: Political Geography, 71, pp. 78-90. doi:10.1016/j.polgeo.2019.02.007

Neumann, Daniela (2016): *Das Ehrenamt nutzen. Zur Entstehung einer staatlichen Engagementpolitik in Deutschland.* Bielefeld: transcript Verlag.

Ntarangwi, Mwenda (2010): *Reversed Gaze: An African Ethnography of American Anthropology.* Urbana: University of Illinois Press.

Nyers, Peter (2006a): *Rethinking Refugees: Beyond States of Emergency.* New York: Routledge.

— (2006b): *Taking Rights, Mediating Wrongs: Disagreements over the Political Agency of Non-Status Migrants.* In: Huysmans, Jef; Dobson, Andrew; Prokhovnik, Raia (Eds.), The Politics of Protection. Sites of Insecurity and Political Agency (pp. 48-67). London: Routledge.

— (2010a): *Abject Cosmopolitanism: The Politics of Protection in the Anti-Deportation Movement.* In: De Genova, Nicholas; Peutz, Nathalie (Eds.), The Deportation Regime. Sovereignty, Space and the Freedom of Movement (pp. 413-442). Durham: Duke University Press.

— (2010b): *No One is Illegal Between City and Nation.* In: Studies in Social Justice, 4(2), pp. 127-143. doi:10.26522/ssj.v4i2.998

— (2011): *Forms of Irregular Citizenship.* In: Squire, Vicki (Ed.), The Contested Politics of Mobility: Borderzones and Irregularity (pp. 184-198). London: Routledge.

Nyers, Peter; Rygiel, Kim (2012): *Introduction: Citizenship, Migrant Activism and the Politics of Movement.* In: Nyers, Peter; Rygiel, Kim (Eds.), Citizenship, Migrant Activism and the Politics of Movement (pp. 1-19). Abingdon: Routlegde.

O'Gorman, Kevin (2006): *Jacques Derrida's Philosophy of Hospitality.* In: The Hospitality Review, 8(4), pp. 50-57.

Oikonomakis, Leonidas (2018): *Solidarity in Transition: The Case of Greece.* In: della Porta, Donatella (Ed.), Solidarity Mobilizations in the 'Refugee Crisis': Contentious Moves (pp. 65-98). Cham: Palgrave Macmillan.

Ong, Aihwa (1999): *Flexible Citizenship: The Cultural Logics of Transnationality*. Durham: Duke University Press.
— (2005): *(Re)Articulations of Citizenship*. In: Political Science and Politics, 38(4), pp. 697-699. doi:10.1017/S1049096505050377
— (2006): *Mutations in Citizenship*. In: Theory, Culture & Society, 23(2/3), pp. 499-505. doi:10.1177/0263276406064831
Oosterlynck, Stijn; Loopmans, Maarten; Schuermans, Nick; Vandenabeele, Joke; Zemni, Sami (2016): *Putting Flesh to the Bone: Looking for Solidarity in Diversity, Here and Now*. In: Ethnic and Racial Studies, 39(5), pp. 764-782. doi:10.1080/01419870.2015.1080380
Ophir, Adi (2010): *The Politics of Catastrophization: Emergency and Exception*. In: Fassin, Didier; Pandolfi, Mariella (Eds.), Contemporary States of Emergency: The Politics of Military and Humanitarian Interventions (pp. 40-61). New York: Zone Books.
Otto, Karl A. (1977): *Vom Ostermarsch zur APO: Geschichte der außerparlamentarischen Opposition in der Bundesrepublik 1960 - 1970*. Frankfurt am Main: Campus Verlag.
Pailey, Robtel Neajai (2018): *Between Rootedness and Rootlessness: How Sedentarist and Nomadic Metaphysics Simultaneously Challenge and Reinforce (Dual) Citizenship Claims for Liberia*. In: Migration Studies, 6(3), pp. 400-419. doi:10.1093/migration/mnx056
Pain, Rachel; Francis, Peter (2003): *Reflections on Participatory Research*. In: Area, 35(1), pp. 46-54. doi:10.1111/1475-4762.00109
Papadopoulos, Dimitris; Stephenson, Niamh; Tsianos, Vassilis (2008): *Escape Routes: Control and Subversion in the Twenty-First Century*. London: Pluto Press.
Papadopoulos, Dimitris; Tsianos, Vassilis (2013): *After Citizenship: Autonomy of Migration, Organisational Ontology and Mobile Commons*. In: Citizenship Studies, 17(2), pp. 178-196. doi:10.1080/13621025.2013.780736
Papastergiadis, Nikos (2000): *The Turbulence of Migration: Globalization, Deterritorialization and Hybridity*. Cambridge: Polity Press.
— (2006): *The Invasion Complex: The Abject Other and Spaces of Violence*. In: Geografiska Annaler. Series B, Human Geography, 88(4), pp. 429-442. doi:10.1111/j.0435-3684.2006.00231.x
Paragi, Beáta (2017): *Contemporary Gifts: Solidarity, Compassion, Equality, Sacrifice, and Reciprocity from an NGO Perspective*. In: Current Anthropology, 58(3), pp. 317-339. doi:10.1086/692086

Parsanoglou, Dimitris (2020): *Volunteering for Refugees and the Repositioning of State Sovereignty and Civil Society: the Case of Greece*. In: Citizenship Studies, 24(4), pp. 457-473. doi:10.1080/13621025.2020.1755158

Pfaff-Czarnecka, Joanna; Toffin, Gerard (2011): *The Politics of Belonging in the Himalayas. Local Attachments and Boundary Dynamics*. New Delhi: Sage Publications.

Picozza, Fiorenza (2017): *Dublin on the Move. Transit and Mobility across Europe's Geographies of Asylum*. In: Movements. Journal for Critical Migration and Border Regime Studies, 3(1), pp. 71-88.

Povrzanović Frykman, Maja; Mäkelä, Fanny (2020): *Post-2015 Refugees Welcome Initiatives in Sweden: Cosmopolitan Underpinnings*. In: Hemer, Oscar; Povrzanović Frykman, Maja; Ristilammi, Per-Markku (Eds.), Conviviality at the Crossroads: The Poetics and Politics of Everyday Encounters (pp. 165-188). Cham: Palgrave Macmillan.

Pries, Ludger (2019): *Introduction: Civil Society and Volunteering in the so-called Refugee Crisis of 2015 - Ambiguities and Structural Tensions*. In: Feischmidt, Margit; Pries, Ludger; Cantat, Celine (Eds.), Refugee Protection and Civil Society in Europe (pp. 1-23). Cham: Palgrave Macmillan.

Purcell, Mark (2002): *Excavating Lefebvre: The Right to the City and its Urban Politics of the Inhabitant*. In: GeoJournal, 58, pp. 99-108. doi:10.1023/B:GEJO.0000010829.62237.8f

Rajaram, Prem Kumar (2002): *Humanitarianism and Representations of the Refugee*. In: Journal of Refugee Studies, 15(3), pp. 247-264. doi:10.1163/9789004413320_012

Rakopoulos, Theodoros (2016): *Solidarity: The Egalitarian Tensions of a Bridge-Concept*. In: Social Anthropology, 24(2), pp. 142-151. doi:10.1111/1469-8676.12298

Ramsay, Georgina (2017): *Impossible Refuge: The Control and Constraint of Refugee Futures*. London: Routledge.

Rancière, Jacques (1998): *Disagreement: Politics and Philosophy*. Minneapolis: University of Minnesota Press.

— (2001): *Ten Theses on Politics*. In: Theory & Event, 5(3). doi:10.1353/tae.2001.0028

— (2009): *Dissensus: On Politics and Aesthetics*. London: Continuum International Publishing.

Ratfisch, Philipp (2015): *Zwischen nützlichen und bedrohlichen Subjekten. Figuren der Migration im europäischen 'Migrationsmanagement' am Beispiel des Stock-*

holmer Programms. In: Movements. Journal für kritische Migrations- und Grenzregimeforschung, 1(1), pp. 1-21.

Rea, Andrea; Martiniello, Marco; Mazzola, Alessandro; Meuleman, Bart (2019): Introduction. *The Refugee Reception Crisis in Europe. Polarized Opinions and Mobilizations.* In: Rea, Andrea; Martiniello, Marco; Mazzola, Alessandro; Meuleman, Bart (Eds.), The Refugee Reception Crisis in Europe. Polarized Opinions and Mobilizations. (pp. 11-30). Bruxelles: Éditions de l'Université de Bruxelles.

Reason, Peter; Bradbury, Hilary (2008): *The Sage Handbook of Action Research: Participative Inquiry and Practice* (2. ed.). Los Angeles: Sage Publications.

Redfield, Peter (2011): *The Impossible Problem of Neutrality.* In: Bornstein, Erica; Redfield, Peter (Eds.), Forces of Compassion: Humanitarianism between Ethics and Politics (pp. 53-70). Santa Fe: School for Advanced Research Press.

Reshaur, Ken (1992): *Concepts of Solidarity in the Political Theory of Hannah Arendt.* In: Canadian Journal of Political Science, 25(4), pp. 723-736. doi:doi.org/10.1017/S0008423900004479

Ridgley, Jennifer (2008): *Cities of Refuge: Immigration Enforcement, Police, and the Insurgent Genealogies of Citizenship in U.S. Sanctuary Cities.* In: Urban Geography, 29(1), pp. 53-77. doi:10.2747/0272-3638.29.1.53

— (2011): *Refuge, Refusal, and Acts of Holy Contagion: The City as a Sanctuary for Soldiers Resisting the Vietnam War.* In: ACME, 10(2), pp. 189-214.

Rigby, Joe; Schlembach, Raphael (2013): *Impossible Protest: Noborders in Calais.* In: Citizenship Studies, 17(2), pp. 157-172. doi:10.1080/13621025.2013.780731

Riley, Dylan (2011): *Hegemony, Democracy, and Passive Revolution in Gramsci's Prison Notebooks.* In: California Italian Studies, 2(2).

Rose, Gillian (1997): *Situating Knowledges: Personality, Reflexivities and other Tactics.* In: Progress in Human Geography, 21(3), pp. 305-320. doi:10.1191/030913297673302122

Rose, Nikolas (1996): *Governing 'Advanced' Liberal Democracies.* In: Barry, Andrew; Osborne, Thomas; Rose, Nikolas (Eds.), Foucault and Political Reason: Liberalism, Neo-Liberalism, and Rationalities of Government (pp. 37-64). Chicago: The University of Chicago Press.

Rosenberger, Sieglinde; Winkler, Jakob (2014): *Com/passionate Protests: Fighting the Deportation of Asylum Seekers.* In: Mobilization: An International Quarterly, 19(2), pp. 165-184. doi:10.17813/maiq.19.2.h464488477p76grm

Rotter, Rebecca (2016): *Waiting in the Asylum Determination Process: Just an Empty Interlude?* In: Time & Society, 25(1), pp. 80-101. doi:10.1177/0961463X15613654

Rozakou, Katerina (2016): *Socialities of Solidarity: Revisiting the Gift Taboo in Times of Crises.* In: Social Anthropology, 24(2), pp. 185-199. doi:10.1111/1469-8676.12305

Rygiel, Kim (2011): *Bordering Solidarities: Migrant Activism and the Politics of Movement and Camps at Calais.* In: Citizenship Studies, 15(1), pp. 1-19. doi:10.1080/13621025.2011.534911

Sandri, Elisa (2018): *'Volunteer Humanitarianism': Volunteers and Humanitarian Aid in the Jungle Refugee Camp of Calais.* In: Journal of Ethnic and Migration Studies, 44(1), pp. 65-80. doi:10.1080/1369183X.2017.1352467

Santer, Kiri; Wriedt, Vera (2017): *(De-)Constructing Borders. Contestations in and around the Balkan Corridor in 2015/16.* In: Movements. Journal for Critical Migration and Border Regime Studies, 3(1), pp. 141-150.

Sasse, Laura; Scholl, Franziska; Vey, Judith; Walk, Heike (2014): *Ein Kampf gegen Windmühlen? Die Flüchtlingsbewegung zwischen Residenzpflicht, Protestcamp und RechtspopulistInnen.* In: Forschungsjournal Soziale Bewegungen, 27(1), pp. 104-107. doi:10.1515/fjsb-2014-0114

Sassen, Saskia (2003): *The Repositioning of Citizenship: Emergent Subjects and Spaces for Politics.* In: The New Centennial Review, 3(2), pp. 41-66. doi:10.1353/ncr.2003.0028

Scheel, Stephan (2013): *Studying Embodied Encounters: Autonomy of Migration beyond its Romanticization.* In: Postcolonial Studies, 16(3), pp. 279-288. doi:10.1080/13688790.2013.850046

Scheel, Stephan; Ratfisch, Philipp (2014): *Refugee Protection Meets Migration Management: UNHCR as a Global Police of Populations.* In: Journal of Ethnic and Migration Studies, 40(6), pp. 924-941. doi:10.1080/1369183X.2013.855074

Scheper-Hughes, Nancy (1995): *The Primacy of the Ethical: Propositions for a Militant Anthropology.* In: Current Anthropology, 36(3), pp. 409-440. doi:10.1086/204378

Scherr, Albert (2013): *Solidarität im postmodernen Kapitalismus.* In: Billmann, Lucie; Held, Josef (Eds.), Solidarität in der Krise: Gesellschaftliche, soziale und individuelle Voraussetzungen solidarischer Praxis (pp. 263-270). Wiesbaden: Springer.

Schindel, Estela (2016): *Bare Life at the European Borders. Entanglements of Technology, Society and Nature*. In: Journal of Borderlands Studies, 31(2), pp. 219-234. doi:10.1080/08865655.2016.1174604

Schmid, Josef (1990): *Parlament und Bewegung. Baden-Württembergs Grüne und die Anti-AKW-Bewegung seit Tschernobyl*. Hamburg: Umwelt-und-Politik-Verlag.

Schmid, Verena; Evers, Adalbert; Mildenberger, Georg (2019): *More or Less Political: Findings on a Central Feature of Local Engagement for Refugees in Germany*. In: Social Inclusion, 7(2), pp. 165-175. doi:10.17645/si.v7i2.1939

Schmitt-Beck, Rüdiger (1990): *Die Friedensbewegung in der Bundesrepublik Deutschland: Ursachen und Bedingungen der Mobilisierung einer neuen sozialen Bewegung*. Wiesbaden: Springer Fachmedien.

Schuhmacher, Nils (2015): *Die Antifa im Umbruch: Neuformierungen und aktuelle Diskurse über Konzepte politischer Intervention*. In: Forschungsjournal Soziale Bewegungen, 28(2), pp. 5-16. doi:10.1515/fjsb-2015-0203

Schwiertz, Helge (2016): *Transformations of the Undocumented Youth Movement and Radical Egalitarian Citizenship*. In: Citizenship Studies, 20(5), pp. 610-628. doi:10.1080/13621025.2016.1182680

Schwiertz, Helge; Schwenken, Helen (2020): *Introduction: Inclusive Solidarity and Citizenship along Migratory Routes in Europe and the Americas*. In: Citizenship Studies, 24(4), pp. 405-423. doi:10.1080/13621025.2020.1755155

Scott-Smith, Tom (2016): *Humanitarian Dilemmas in a Mobile World*. In: Refugee Survey Quarterly, 35(2), pp. 1-21. doi:10.1093/rsq/hdw001

Sennett, Richard (1976): *The Fall of Public Man*. New York: Knopf.

Shachar, Ayelet (2009): *The Birthright Lottery: Citizenship and Global Inequality*. Cambridge: Harvard University Press.

Shore, Cris; Wright, Susan (1997): *Policy: A New Field of Anthropology*. In: Shore, Cris; Wright, Susan (Eds.), Anthropology of Policy: Critical Perspectives on Governance and Power (pp. 3-42). Abingdon: Routledge.

Siapera, Eugenia (2019): *Refugee Solidarity in Europe: Shifting the Discourse*. In: European Journal of Cultural Studies, 22(2), pp. 245-266. doi:10.1177/1367549418823068

Sidaway, James D. (1992): *In Other Worlds: On the Politics of Research by 'First World' Geographers in the 'Third World'*. In: Area, 24(4), pp. 403-408.

Sinatti, Giulia (2019): *Humanitarianism as Politics: Civil Support Initiatives for Migrants in Milan's Hub*. In: Social Inclusion, 7(2), pp. 139-148. doi:10.17645/si.v7i2.1968

Sirriyeh, Ala (2018): *The Politics of Compassion: Immigration and Asylum Policy*. Bristol: Bristol University Press.

Soguk, Nevzat (1999): *States and Strangers: Refugees and Displacements of Statecraft*. Minneapolis: University of Minnesota Press.

Soysal, Yasemin Nuhoğlu (1994): *Limits of Citizenship: Migrants and Postnational Membership in Europe*. Chicago: University of Chicago Press.

— (2012): *Post-National Citizenship: Rights and Obligations of Individuality*. In: Amenta, Edwin; Nash, Kate; Scott, Alan (Eds.), The Wiley-Blackwell Companion to Political Sociology (pp. 383-393). Malden: Wiley-Blackwell.

Squire, Vicki (2009): *The Exclusionary Politics of Asylum*. Basingstoke: Palgrave Macmillan.

— (2011a): *The Contested Politics of Mobility: Borderzones and Irregularity*. London: Routledge.

— (2011b): *From Community Cohesion to Mobile Solidarities: The City of Sanctuary Network and the Strangers into Citizens Campaign*. In: Political Studies, 59(2), pp. 290-307. doi:10.1111/j.1467-9248.2010.00865.x

— (2018): *Mobile Solidarities and Precariousness at City Plaza: Beyond Vulnerable and Disposable Lives*. In: Studies in Social Justice, 12, pp. 111-132. doi:10.26522/ssj.v12i1.1592

Squire, Vicki; Darling, Jonathan (2013): *The 'Minor' Politics of Rightful Presence: Justice and Relationality in City of Sanctuary*. In: International Political Sociology, 7(1), pp. 59-74. doi:10.1111/ips.12009

Staeheli, Lynn A.; Ehrkamp, Patricia; Leitner, Helga; Nagel, Caroline R. (2012): *Dreaming the Ordinary: Daily Life and the Complex Geographies of Citizenship*. In: Progress in Human Geography, 36(5), pp. 628-644. doi:10.1177/0309132511435001

Steinhilper, Elias (2017): *Politisiert in der Migration, vernetzt in der Stadt. Transnationaler politischer Protest von Geflüchteten in Berlin*. In: Forschungsjournal Soziale Bewegungen, 30(3), pp. 77-87. doi:10.1515/fjsb-2017-0062

Stierl, Maurice (2017): *A Fleet of Mediterranean Border Humanitarians*. In: Antipode, 50(3), pp. 704-724. doi:10.1111/anti.12320

Stock, Inka (2019): *Buddy Schemes between Refugees and Volunteers in Germany: Transformative Potential in an unequal Relationship?* In: Social Inclusion, 7(2), pp. 128-138. doi:10.17645/si.v7i2.2041

Sutter, Ove (2019): *Narratives of 'Welcome Culture': The Cultural Politics of Voluntary Aid for Refugees*. In: Narrative Culture, 6(1), pp. 19-43. doi:10.13110/narrcult.6.1.0019

Tazzioli, Martina (2018): *The Temporal Borders of Asylum. Temporality of Control in the EU Border Regime*. In: Political Geography, 64, pp. 13-22. doi:10.1016/j.polgeo.2018.02.002

Theodossopoulos, Dimitrios (2016): *Philanthropy or Solidarity? Ethical Dilemmas about Humanitarianism in Crisis-Afflicted Greece*. In: Social Anthropology, 24(2), pp. 167-184. doi:10.1111/1469-8676.12304

Thobani, Sitara (2015): *Living History, Performing Coloniality: Towards a Postcolonial Ethnography*. In: Anthropology in Action, 22(3), pp. 43-51. doi:10.3167/aia.2015.220306

Ticktin, Miriam (2006): *Where Ethics and Politics Meet: The Violence of Humanitarianism in France*. In: American Ethnologist, 33(1), pp. 33-49.

— (2011): *Casualties of Care: Immigration and the Politics of Humanitarianism in France*. Berkeley: University of California Press.

— (2014): *Transnational Humanitarianism*. In: Annual Review of Anthropology, 43, pp. 273-289. doi:10.1146/annurev-anthro-102313-030403

— (2016): *Thinking Beyond Humanitarian Borders*. In: Social Research: An International Quarterly, 83(2), pp. 255-271.

Togral Koca, Burcu (2019): *Local Bordering Practices, Refugees, and Civil Society: The Case of Berlin*. In: Geographical Review, 109(4), pp. 544-561. doi:10.1111/gere.12351

Topak, Özgün E. (2016): *Migrant Protest in Times of Crisis: Politics, Ethics and the Sacred from Below*. In: Citizenship Studies, 21(1), pp. 1-21. doi:10.1080/13621025.2016.1191428

Torpey, John (2000): *The Invention of the Passport: Surveillance, Citizenship and the State*. Cambridge: Cambridge University Press.

Turinsky, Theresia; Nowicka, Magdalena (2019): *Volunteer, Citizen, Human: Volunteer Work Between Cosmopolitan Ideal and Institutional Routine*. In: Feischmidt, Margit; Pries, Ludger; Cantat, Celine (Eds.), Refugee Protection and Civil Society in Europe (pp. 243-268). Cham: Springer International Publishing.

Turnbull, Sarah (2016): *'Stuck in the Middle': Waiting and Uncertainty in Immigration Detention*. In: Time & Society, 25(1), pp. 61-79. doi:10.1177/0961463X15604518

Tyler, Imogen (2013): *Revolting Subjects: Social Abjection and Resistance in Neoliberal Britain*. London: Zed Books.

Tyler, Imogen; Marciniak, Katarzyna (2013): *Immigrant Protest: An Introduction*. In: Citizenship Studies, 17(2), pp. 143-156. doi:10.1080/13621025.2013.780728

Urry, John (2007): *Mobilities*. Cambridge: Polity Press.
Vandevoordt, Robin (2016): *Between Humanitarian Assistance and Migration Management: On Civil Actors' Role in Voluntary Return from Belgium*. In: Journal of Ethnic and Migration Studies, 43(11), pp. 1-16. doi:10.1080/1369183X.2016.1245609
— (2019): *Subversive Humanitarianism: Rethinking Refugee Solidarity through Grass-Roots Initiatives*. In: Refugee Survey Quarterly, 38(3), pp. 245-265. doi:10.1093/rsq/hdz008
— (2020): *Resisting Bare Life: Civil Solidarity and the Hunt for Illegalized Migrants*. In: International Migration, pp. 1-16. doi:10.1111/imig.12715
Vandevoordt, Robin; Fleischmann, Larissa (2020): *Impossible Futures? The Ambivalent Temporalities of Grassroots Humanitarian Action*. In: Critical Sociology. doi:10.1177/0896920520932655
Vandevoordt, Robin; Verschraegen, Gert (2019): *Subversive Humanitarianism and Its Challenges: Notes on the Political Ambiguities of Civil Refugee Support*. In: Feischmidt, Margit; Pries, Ludger; Cantat, Celine (Eds.), Refugee Protection and Civil Society in Europe (pp. 101-128). Cham: Palgrave Macmillan.
Varsanyi, Monica W. (2006): *Interrogating 'Urban Citizenship' vis-à-vis Undocumented Migration*. In: Citizenship Studies, 10(2), pp. 229-249. doi:10.1080/13621020600633168
Vaughan-Williams, Nick (2009): *The Generalised Bio-Political Border? Re-Conceptualising the Limits of Sovereign Power*. In: Review of International Studies, 35(4), pp. 729-749. doi:10.1017/S0260210509990155
Virchow, Fabian (2016): *PEGIDA: Understanding the Emergence and Essence of Nativist Protest in Dresden*. In: Journal of Intercultural Studies, 37(6), pp. 541-555. doi:10.1080/07256868.2016.1235026
Vorländer, Hans; Herold, Maik; Schäller, Steven (2016): *PEGIDA: Entwicklung, Zusammensetzung und Deutung einer Empörungsbewegung*. Wiesbaden: Springer VS.
Walters, William (1997): *The 'Active Society': New Designs for Social Policy*. In: Policy and Politics, 25(3), pp. 221-234. doi:10.1332/030557397782453264
— (2006): *No Border: Games With(out) Frontiers*. In: Social Justice, 33(1), pp. 21-39.
— (2008): *Acts of Demonstration: Mapping the Territory of (Non-)Citizenship*. In: Isin, Engin; Nielsen, Greg (Eds.), Acts of Citizenship (pp. 182-206). New York: Zed Books.
— (2011): *Foucault and Frontiers: Notes on the Birth of the Humanitarian Border*. In: Bröckling, Ulrich; Krasmann, Susanne; Lemke, Thomas (Eds.), Govern-

mentality: Current Issues and Future Challenges (pp. 138-164). New York: Routledge.

Welander, Marta (2019): The Politics of Exhaustion and the British Sea Crossings Spectacle. *Border Criminologies*. Retrieved from https://www.law.ox.ac.uk/research-subject-groups/centre-criminology/centreborder-criminologies/blog/2019/01/politics

Wilcke, Holger; Lambert, Laura (2015): *Die Politik des O-Platzes. (Un-)Sichtbare Kämpfe einer Geflüchtetenbewegung.* In: Movements. Journal für kritische Migrations- und Grenzregimeforschung, 1(2), pp. 1-14.

Williams, Jill M. (2016): *The Safety/Security Nexus and the Humanitarianisation of Border Enforcement.* In: Geographical Journal, 182(1), pp. 27-37. doi:10.1111/geoj.12119

Williams, Raymond (1981): *Keywords: A Vocabulary of Culture and Society*. London: Fontana.

Wimmer, Andreas; Glick Schiller, Nina (2002): *Methodological Nationalism and the Study of Migration*. In: European Journal of Sociology, 43(2), pp. 217-240. doi:10.1017/S000397560200108X

Wright, Susan; Reinhold, Sue (2011): *'Studying through': A Strategy for Studying Political Transformation. or Sex, Lies and British Politics*. In: Wright, Susan; Shore, Cris; Peró, Davide (Eds.), Policy Worlds: Anthropology and the Analysis of Contemporary Power (pp. 86-104). Oxford: Berghahn Books.

Wyller, Trygve (2019): *'Something More': The Citizenship Performativity of Religiously Founded Refugee Projects*. In: Feischmidt, Margit; Pries, Ludger; Cantat, Celine (Eds.), Refugee Protection and Civil Society in Europe (pp. 269-290). Cham: Palgrave Macmillan.

Ybema, Sierk; Kamsteeg, Frans (2009): *Making the Familiar Strange: A Case for Disengaged Organizational Ethnography*. In: Ybema, Sierk; Yanow, Dvora; Wels, Harry; Kamsteeg, Frans (Eds.), Organizational Ethnography: Studying the Complexities of Everyday Life (1. publ. ed., pp. 101-119). Los Angeles: Sage Publications.

Youkhana, Eva (2015): *A Conceptual Shift in Studies of Belonging and the Politics of Belonging*. In: Social Inclusion, 3(4), pp. 10-24. doi:10.17645/si.v3i4.150

Yurdakul, Gökçe; Römhild, Regina; Schwanhäußer, Anja; Zur Nieden, Birgit; Ajayi, Folashade M.; Kneffel, Charlotte; Liftin, Marnie; Tran, Hieu Hanh Hiang; Lakić, Aleksandra (2018): *Witnessing the Transition: Moments in the Long Summer of Migration*. Berlin: Humboldt-Universität zu Berlin.

Yuval-Davis, Nira (2006): *Belonging and the Politics of Belonging*. In: Patterns of Prejudice, 40(3), pp. 197-214. doi:10.1080/00313220600769331

— (2011): *The Politics of Belonging: Intersectional Contestations*. Los Angeles: Sage Publications.

Zamponi, Lorenzo (2017): *Practices of Solidarity: Direct Social Action, Politicisation and Refugee Solidarity Activism in Italy*. In: Mondi Migranti, 5(3), pp. 97-117. doi:10.3280/MM2017-003005

Zoll, Rainer (2000): *Was ist Solidarität heute?* Frankfurt am Main: Suhrkamp.

Zuparic-Iljic, Drago; Valenta, Marko (2019): *Opportunistic Humanitarianism and Securitization Discomfort along the Balkan Corridor: The Croatian Experience*. In: Feischmidt, Margit; Pries, Ludger; Cantat, Celine (Eds.), Refugee Protection and Civil Society in Europe (pp. 129-160). Cham: Palgrave Macmillan.

Acknowledgements

The book at hand is the outcome of six years of exchange, dialogue and discussion. This process would not have been possible without the invaluable input and support by many who contributed to the research and writing stages in manifold ways. Above all, I am indebted to my research participants and interlocutors for their trust and openness during my fieldwork. Many willingly opened their homes and doors for me, took time to share their most personal stories and let me partake in their experiences, hopes and challenges. This book lives from your insights and I cannot thank you enough. My fullest respect goes to all those who dedicated their time and energy to the support of refugees and asylum seekers in the course of 2015 and who continue to do so until today. Beyond that, I owe my deepest gratitude to my supervisor Thomas G. Kirsch for his never ceasing support, his wise words and his constructive criticisms throughout this project. Thank you for letting me see things through your sharp anthropological eye. I would also like to express my gratitude to my co-supervisor Eva Youkhana and my third referee Judith Beyer for their support and their helpful comments on an earlier version. Thank you Kirsten Mahlke for taking time as a head examiner and for sharing ideas on earlier drafts. I would like to acknowledge the invaluable discussions and input from the Colloquium of the Social and Cultural Anthropology Research Group at the University of Konstanz. Thank you to all fellow anthropologists for reading and discussing earlier drafts. I am particularly indebted to Anna Hüncke who became not only an inspiring colleague but also a warm friend over the years. The fieldwork for this project was made possible with the financial support by the Centre of Excellence "Cultural Foundations of Social Integration" at the University of Konstanz, in which I found a most inspiring interdisciplinary research environment. My special thanks go to colleagues and friends at the doctoral program "Europe in the Globalized World" for their enriching debates and warm hearts on and off work, in particular to Corinna Di Stefano, Philipp Schäfer, Wolfgang Egner, Sarah Schwab, Ferdinand Kiesel. Thank you to the head professors of the program and to Estela Schindel and Tilmann Heil for supporting and believing in my project from the very beginning. My gratitude also goes to Iain Reynolds who did an excellent job in English copy-editing an earlier manuscript; thank you for your helpful remarks and modifications despite the tough timetable. I would also like to acknowledge Caroline Bonnes, Marius Bayer, Maike Krannich and Markus Herz, without whom my time in Konstanz would not have been the same. In the newer chapter of my life in Halle, I owe my deepest gratitude and respect to Jonathan Everts, who is the most supportive, understanding and cordial supervisor one could imagine in the transition phase to becoming a Postdoc. Thank you for your open doors and helpful advice in all matters. I would also like to thank my colleagues in the Human Geography Research Group at the Martin Luther University in Halle, in particular Christine Wenzl, Florian Ringel, Michael Wollrath, for always caring and for their help in proofreading chapters of this book. Last but not least, I owe much to my mother Rita and my father Klaus; I thank you for everything and dedicate this book to you.

Social and Cultural Studies

Ashley J. Bohrer
Marxism and Intersectionality
Race, Gender, Class and Sexuality
under Contemporary Capitalism

2019, 280 p., pb.
29,99 € (DE), 978-3-8376-4160-8
E-Book: 26,99 € (DE), ISBN 978-3-8394-4160-2

Hilkje Charlotte Hänel
What is Rape?
Social Theory and Conceptual Analysis

2018, 282 p., hardcover
99,99 € (DE), 978-3-8376-4434-0
E-Book: 99,99 € (DE), ISBN 978-3-8394-4434-4

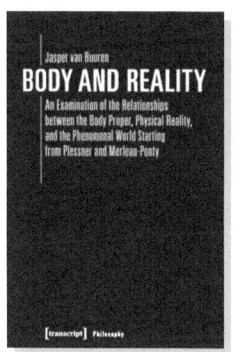

Jasper van Buuren
Body and Reality
An Examination of the Relationships
between the Body Proper, Physical Reality,
and the Phenomenal World Starting from Plessner
and Merleau-Ponty

2018, 312 p., pb., ill.
39,99 € (DE), 978-3-8376-4163-9
E-Book: 39,99 € (DE), ISBN 978-3-8394-4163-3

**All print, e-book and open access versions of the titles in our list
are available in our online shop www.transcript-verlag.de/en!**

Social and Cultural Studies

Sabine Klotz, Heiner Bielefeldt,
Martina Schmidhuber, Andreas Frewer (eds.)
Healthcare as a Human Rights Issue
Normative Profile, Conflicts and Implementation

2017, 426 p., pb., ill.
39,99 € (DE), 978-3-8376-4054-0
E-Book: available as free open access publication
E-Book: ISBN 978-3-8394-4054-4

Michael Bray
Powers of the Mind
Mental and Manual Labor
in the Contemporary Political Crisis

2019, 208 p., hardcover
99,99 € (DE), 978-3-8376-4147-9
E-Book: 99,99 € (DE), ISBN 978-3-8394-4147-3

Iain MacKenzie
Resistance and the Politics of Truth
Foucault, Deleuze, Badiou

2018, 148 p., pb.
29,99 € (DE), 978-3-8376-3907-0
E-Book: 26,99 € (DE), ISBN 978-3-8394-3907-4
EPUB: 26,99 € (DE), ISBN 978-3-7328-3907-0

**All print, e-book and open access versions of the titles in our list
are available in our online shop www.transcript-verlag.de/en!**

Social and Cultural Studies

Ashley J. Bohrer
Marxism and Intersectionality
Race, Gender, Class and Sexuality
under Contemporary Capitalism

2019, 280 p., pb.
29,99 € (DE), 978-3-8376-4160-8
E-Book: 26,99 € (DE), ISBN 978-3-8394-4160-2

Hilkje Charlotte Hänel
What is Rape?
Social Theory and Conceptual Analysis

2018, 282 p., hardcover
99,99 € (DE), 978-3-8376-4434-0
E-Book: 99,99 € (DE), ISBN 978-3-8394-4434-4

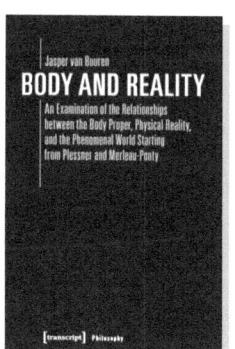

Jasper van Buuren
Body and Reality
An Examination of the Relationships
between the Body Proper, Physical Reality,
and the Phenomenal World Starting from Plessner
and Merleau-Ponty

2018, 312 p., pb., ill.
39,99 € (DE), 978-3-8376-4163-9
E-Book: 39,99 € (DE), ISBN 978-3-8394-4163-3

**All print, e-book and open access versions of the titles in our list
are available in our online shop www.transcript-verlag.de/en!**

Social and Cultural Studies

Sabine Klotz, Heiner Bielefeldt,
Martina Schmidhuber, Andreas Frewer (eds.)
Healthcare as a Human Rights Issue
Normative Profile, Conflicts and Implementation

2017, 426 p., pb., ill.
39,99 € (DE), 978-3-8376-4054-0
E-Book: available as free open access publication
E-Book: ISBN 978-3-8394-4054-4

Michael Bray
Powers of the Mind
Mental and Manual Labor
in the Contemporary Political Crisis

2019, 208 p., hardcover
99,99 € (DE), 978-3-8376-4147-9
E-Book: 99,99 € (DE), ISBN 978-3-8394-4147-3

Iain MacKenzie
Resistance and the Politics of Truth
Foucault, Deleuze, Badiou

2018, 148 p., pb.
29,99 € (DE), 978-3-8376-3907-0
E-Book: 26,99 € (DE), ISBN 978-3-8394-3907-4
EPUB: 26,99 € (DE), ISBN 978-3-7328-3907-0

**All print, e-book and open access versions of the titles in our list
are available in our online shop www.transcript-verlag.de/en!**